MICHAEL BARRY'S
FOOD & DRINK
Cookbook

Michael Barry has been broadcasting about food since 1975. He began with an eleven-year stint on Capital Radio's *Michael Aspel Show*, has appeared on HTV and TV-am, and in 1984 joined BBC 2's *Food and Drink* series. Michael Barry writes regularly for several national magazines and newspapers, including *BBC Good Food*, and is a consultant to a number of companies in the food industry.

MICHAEL BARRY'S

FOOD & DRINK
Cookbook

250 OF YOUR FAVOURITE RECIPES

BBC BOOKS

Published by BBC Books,
a division of BBC Enterprises Limited,
Woodlands, 80 Wood Lane, London W12 0TT

First published in hardback 1991
First published in paperback 1992

ISBN 0 563 36455 6

Illustrations by Angela McAllister
Photographs by James Murphy
Styling by Jane McLeish
Home Economist: Allyson Birch

Set in Bembo by Butler & Tanner Ltd, Frome and London
Printed and bound in Great Britain by Butler & Tanner Ltd, Frome and London
Colour separations by Technik Ltd, Berkhamsted
Cover printed by Lawrence Allen Ltd, Weston-super-Mare

Contents

Please note that the oven temperatures given in the recipes are for conventional ovens only. Those of you using fan ovens may need to adjust temperatures accordingly.

For Jennie, the essential ingredient from the first stirrings to the last full stop.

INTRODUCTION

S teak in cream sauce, Low-fat Christmas pudding, Salmon *en croûte* . . . For me, the last decade seems punctuated by special recipes, and also by issues: salmonella, healthy eating, omega-three oils. It's all part of the enormous privilege and excitement of working for, and helping to present, *Food and Drink*, Britain's leading food and cookery television programme.

This book is the pick of my recipes from the series so far – my pick and yours. We have 'garlanded' the ones you told us were your all-time favourites, so if you want a dish that is almost guaranteed to be a hit with your family or friends, look for one of these dozen or so recipes. The other dishes have also been pretty popular. Some are everyday ones with a little twist. Some are more elaborate. What I hope you will find is that they are all *crafty*.

Craftiness is my speciality. I love eating and I really enjoy cooking, but I have never understood why preparing food has to be hard work. So many of us have to cook every day it seemed like a good idea to make it as much fun as possible. And so 'Crafty Cooking' was born. It's real cooking, but with all my tried and true labour-saving devices, short cuts and, above all, crafty techniques. They save effort or make a difficult dish easy – and the final result tastes *good*. If it doesn't taste good and look great, it's not crafty! Although some of the recipes may be a little unexpected, either in their methods or approach, do trust me and try them. Some crafty techniques are not exactly time-honoured, but they do work, and they save time.

A word about ingredients. As will be pretty clear from a glance at the recipes, I'm a fresh food fan. I believe that fresh food cooked the crafty way is convenience food. However, some processed foods are invaluable. Tomatoes in Britain never seem to have the real, red sweetness you find in the south of Europe, even when they are imported. So tinned Italian-style tomatoes or tomato purée are essential at times. Dried herbs and their modern cousins, freeze-dried herbs, are not only a great stand-by, but I often use them for the intensity of flavour they provide. I also buy puff pastry (the vegetarian kind) as it takes an age to make from scratch. I'm not at all obsessive about organic foods either, or free-range produce; I just have a suspicion they not only taste better, but probably are better for us and the planet. And so, the last criterion of Crafty Cooking is that good food should be good for you, too.

No book about the food on *Food and Drink* would be complete without a word of thanks to all the people, Jane and Suzy and Alison in particular, who have helped so much, and in praise of my friends and colleagues Jilly Goolden and Chris Kelly, and our friend and producer Peter Bazalgette. Always supportive, always acute, always striving for excellence, they have been a constant inspiration, help and tasting-panel. For what more could one ask?

SOUPS

*F*rom my very first days on *Food and Drink* soup has played an important role in the programme. To start with, it is the one substance that fits the title perfectly: it is both food and drink. What's more, my first foray into filming for the programme was a hunt for wild mushrooms, somewhere to the east of the M3. It was successful and we returned triumphantly to the London Hilton where, during an English Food Festival, the mushrooms were turned into Wild mushroom soup (see p.12) and Wild mushroom salad (see p.158).

The soup, in a way my first *Food and Drink* recipe, was a revelation because of the intensity of flavour the wild mushrooms brought to it. (I later learned that you can get the same intensity with dried mushrooms if you can't find wild ones.) It was also a reminder of just how wonderfully a good soup can convey the essence of its ingredients to the palate. And, of course, a soup is the best way of stretching expensive ingredients.

Not that all the ingredients have to be expensive. Perhaps the most popular soup we have ever done on the programme was the result of reading the list of ingredients on a tinned one. After we'd worked our way through the E numbers and the various kinds of gum that appeared to be needed to stabilise the soup, I suggested a rather simpler solution: butter, potatoes, leeks and carrots with water. You'll find the details on page 14 where it's called French vegetable soup.

In parts of France, *la soupe* is synonymous with lunch. Indeed, in rural areas, the term is still used to denote this meal. But the *Food and Drink* soups are by no means all from France. There is a Pumpkin soup which has its origins in the bright, spicy cooking of South America. Chowders come from North America, Gazpacho from Spain and Cullen Skink from Scotland. Citronelle soup, with its lovely sharp flavour of lemon grass, is from south-east Asia. The range is considerable and so, too, is the purpose of the soups. Some, like the chowders, are meant to be meals in their own right; eaten with good chunky bread, with fruit and cheese to follow, they are certainly filling. Others, like the Carrot and apple or Tomato and orange soups are intended to whet the appetite for what's to come, with their smoother textures and light, bright flavours. There are cold soups – Gazpacho and Vichyssoise – as well as winter warmers like the restoring Les Halles Onion soup. Soups, then, for all seasons, all tastes and all budgets and, to begin with, some ideas for stock: chicken and vegetable. There is a school of thought, originally I think propounded by the much-lamented Jane Grigson, that it is better to use water for simple vegetable soups because it doesn't compete with the flavour of the vegetables. Try some of these soups both ways and, as always, be the best judge.

Chicken Stock

This wonderful broth (excellent on its own) is also the basis of many other dishes. Can you compare it to a stock cube? Don't bother: there is no comparison. To make really great chicken stock, however, you have to start with a chicken — or at least quite a lot of one. Certainly the giblets, but not the liver which will make the stock cloudy. The carcass is the real essential and (if you ever see them) wing tips or even carefully washed feet. You can use the stock in soups, casseroles or with a few noodles or mushroom slices (plus seasoning) on its own.

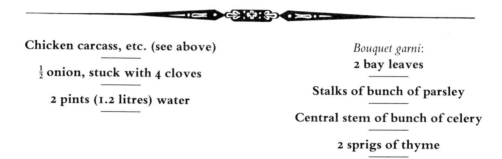

Chicken carcass, etc. (see above)

½ onion, stuck with 4 cloves

2 pints (1.2 litres) water

Bouquet garni:

2 bay leaves

Stalks of bunch of parsley

Central stem of bunch of celery

2 sprigs of thyme

Simmer all the ingredients in the water for 45 minutes. Strain, remove the meat if you want to use it and keep the stock. Don't boil it and don't cook it longer — all you get is more 'bone' stock.

To remove the fat, chill the stock: the fat will float to the surface in a layer and is easy to spoon off.

Vegetable Stock

To make an equally intense Vegetable stock which, like the Chicken stock, can be used either as a soup base or for casseroles or risottos, you will need:

8 oz (225 g) onions	Freshly ground black pepper
8 oz (225 g) carrots	$\frac{1}{2}$ teaspoon celery salt
2 stalks celery (including leaves)	1 tablespoon tomato purée (optional)
2 oz (50 g) open mushrooms	*Bouquet garni:*
1 clove garlic	1 bay leaf
2 tablespoons oil (preferably olive)	1 sprig of thyme
1 teaspoon sugar	Stalks of $\frac{1}{2}$ bunch of parsley
2 pints (1.2 litres) water	

Peel the onions but keep the clean skins. Peel the carrots, trim the celery, wash the mushrooms. Chop the onions, carrots, celery, mushrooms and garlic finely, but keep the onions separate. Put the oil in a large, heavy saucepan and add the onions. Cook over a medium heat until they begin to brown. Add the sugar and stir continuously until the onions begin to caramelise, that is, turn medium toffee brown. Do not let them burn! Add the other vegetables and the garlic and stir for 2 minutes. Add the water and the *bouquet garni*, pepper and celery salt and the onion skins. Cover and simmer for 50 minutes.

Strain the stock through a fine sieve and return to the pan. Check for seasoning. You can now add the tomato purée if you want a thicker and richer stock.

Wild Mushroom Soup

This is the soup we cooked after my first filming foray into the woods. It's intended to be made with wild mushrooms of almost any sort. Be careful collecting them — it is important to ensure that they are not poisonous. There are a number of good field guides on the subject with pictures and drawings to identify safe and not-so-safe mushrooms, and most areas have societies, often based on universities or polytechnics, which organise mushroom-gathering courses in the early autumn. A list of local courses is available from Dr D.W. Minter, The Foray Secretary, Commonwealth Mycological Institute, Ferry Lane, Kew, Surrey, TW9 3AF.

If you can't be bothered to foray for yourself use, as I suggest, 12 oz (350 g) cultivated mushrooms with just 1 oz (25 g) dried mushrooms which will provide an extraordinary, intense flavour in their own right. If you are using dried mushrooms, soak them for 15 minutes in boiling water and use the water as part of the liquid for the soup. Once they have been soaked, treat the dried mushrooms like fresh ones.

This soup is good served with Croûtons (see p. 20).

SERVES 4

1 lb (450 g) wild mushrooms, or 12 oz (350 g) cultivated mushrooms and 1 oz (25 g) dried mushrooms, soaked

2 oz (50 g) butter

1 onion, chopped

1½ pints (900 ml) chicken stock

2 slices white bread, crusts removed

Salt and freshly ground black pepper

5 fl oz (150 ml) single cream

Wash, trim and slice the mushrooms but don't peel them. Melt the butter in a saucepan and cook the onion and mushrooms over a medium heat for 5 minutes. Add the chicken stock and simmer, covered, for 20 minutes. Crumble the bread into the soup. Add seasoning and liquidise or purée the soup until it is smooth. Add the cream and re-heat gently.

Minestrone

We tend to think of minestrone as a tomato-based vegetable and pasta soup. Not so. It is a rich broth and the vegetables it contains are only those in season. Traditionally, minestrone may not contain any tomatoes – the only essentials are dried white or pale-green beans and some pasta. The vegetables may be the leeks, carrots and cabbage of autumn and winter; broad beans, mushrooms and cauliflower in the spring; or pumpkin, tomatoes, courgettes and peppers in high summer. The soup can even be served cold. Here's a basic recipe that uses some tomato but no tomato purée. You can add or subtract vegetables according to availability. Serve the Minestrone with plenty of crusty bread.

SERVES 4

8 oz (225 g) dried cannellini or haricot beans, or 1 lb (450 g) tinned beans, drained

2 pints (1.2 litres) beef stock or water

2 medium onions, chopped

8 oz (225 g) celery, trimmed and chopped

8 oz (225 g) carrots, diced

8 oz (225 g) turnips, diced

5 fl oz (150 ml) olive oil

2 oz (50 g) vermicelli or other small pasta

Good pinch of dried oregano

Good pinch of dried thyme

Good pinch of dried basil

Salt and freshly ground black pepper

8 oz (225 g) tomatoes, roughly chopped

4 oz (100 g) green cabbage, shredded

4–8 oz (100–225 g) mushrooms, chopped

Freshly grated Parmesan cheese

Soak the beans overnight if you are using dried ones, and then drain. Add the beans to the stock or water in a large saucepan. Boil for at least 20 minutes, then simmer for about 2 hours. Sauté the onions, celery, carrots and turnips in the olive oil for 3–4 minutes, until softened. Add these and the vermicelli to the beans, season with the herbs, salt and pepper and simmer until tender. Add the tomatoes, cabbage and mushrooms (adding more water if necessary), and simmer for a further 5 minutes.

Sprinkle with the freshly grated Parmesan cheese.

French Vegetable Soup

A classic potage aux légumes *as featured in countless French bistros and homes. The formula is simple but perfect – fresh ingredients mixed in the right proportions, cooked in the classic way and served without delay – and it results in one of the great soups of all time. You can use the same principle for a number of different vegetables, but do use fresh and not already cooked ones. And never mix more than two vivid flavours together or you may find they cancel each other out. (Parsnip and walnut go well together, as do Jerusalem artichoke and spring onion.) Serve with wholemeal bread.*

SERVES 4

1 oz (25 g) butter	Salt and freshly ground black pepper
8 oz (225 g) leeks, washed and chopped	1¾ pints (1 litre) water or vegetable stock
8 oz (225 g) potatoes, chopped	Chopped parsley
8 oz (225 g) carrots, chopped	

Melt the butter in a pan and add the leeks, potatoes and carrots. Stir for 2–3 minutes until all the vegetables are well coated in butter. Season, add the water or stock and simmer for 20 minutes.

Pour the contents into a food processor or liquidiser and mix until blended but still reasonably textured. (This soup can be eaten without liquidising.)

Sprinkle with chopped parsley.

Tomato and Orange Soup

A modern soup with a rich yet sharp taste, this makes use of one of the new products that the latest technology has given us: passata – a light purée of Italian tomatoes, sieved and pasteurised with nothing added but a pinch of salt. Additive-free, it provides the rich tomato flavour and colour that are so often missing in English tomatoes, because of our climate – and our preference for shape rather than taste. Passata is available all year round in supermarkets and grocers – you can buy it in the bottle or tetra pack. I always think it's better to buy it in the tetra pack as it's the same product but cheaper.*

If you'd like to make a Cream of tomato soup leave the orange out and, just before serving, stir in 2 tablespoons double cream or, if you want a low-fat version, Greek yoghurt. Don't boil after adding the cream or yoghurt.

SERVES 4

1 tablespoon olive oil

1 onion, finely chopped

Juice and grated rind of an orange

1¾ pints (1 litre) passata

10 fl oz (275 ml) water

Salt and freshly ground black pepper

Cubed tomato and/or orange slices, to garnish

Heat the oil in a deep saucepan and add the onion. Cook until the onion is translucent and then add the orange rind and juice and stir thoroughly. Add the passata and water and bring to the boil. Simmer for not more than 5 minutes. Season to taste, and garnish with the cubed tomato or the orange slices.

This makes a delicious thick soup but, if you prefer, you can add more water to thin it down.

Chicken Noodle Soup

*C*hicken noodle soup is one of those dishes that has been ridiculed by over-use. It's one of our earliest packet soups and has been produced and served in a variety of less than wonderful ways for as long as I can remember. But, in its original form, which comes from China, it's a very delicate, extremely pretty and quite delicious soup. The method I've given here is crafty but pretty authentic. You can, if you like, substitute for the home-made chicken stock, a good-quality chicken stock cube or two to provide the necessary strength. It's a good start to a Chinese meal but also, like its debased brethren, a nice light start to a substantial English meal.

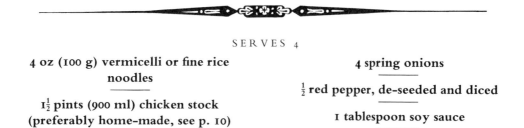

SERVES 4

4 oz (100 g) vermicelli or fine rice noodles

1½ pints (900 ml) chicken stock (preferably home-made, see p. 10)

4 spring onions

½ red pepper, de-seeded and diced

1 tablespoon soy sauce

Boil the noodles in the stock for 3 minutes. Trim and chop the spring onions, green and all, and add to the soup with the pepper. Mix in the soy sauce and continue to cook for 5 minutes.

Serve hot.

New England Cod Chowder

Chowders are a very ancient form of cooking. The name is supposed to derive from the chaudron or cauldrons that French settlers first brought to what we now know as Canada and New England, to cook whatever they could glean from the sea or land. So there are many different versions in the north-east of North America. You will find a couple here. This is a crafty, but pretty authentic, version from around Boston. Sweetcorn, green peppers, tomatoes and shrimps are all tasty additions, but then it isn't New England Cod Chowder!

SERVES 4

$1\frac{1}{2}$ lb (750 g) potatoes, in 1 in (2.5 cm) cubes

8 oz (225 g) onions, in 1 in (2.5 cm) cubes

10 fl oz (300 ml) water

$1\frac{1}{2}$ lb (750 g) chunky cod fillet, skinned and cubed

1 pint (600 ml) milk

1 teaspoon cornflour

Salt and freshly ground black pepper

8 water biscuits, or Ritz crackers, to garnish

In a large saucepan, cook the potato and onion cubes in the water until almost tender. Add the fish and all but 5 fl oz (150 ml) of the milk. Simmer for 5 minutes. Mix the cornflour and remaining milk in a bowl, season lightly and add to the chowder. Simmer till it thickens. Serve with the biscuits or crackers crumbled over the top.

Corn Chowder

Corn, or maize, like clams and cod, was a staple food in the diet of the early American settlers and this vegetarian version of a chowder grew up alongside the fishy kinds. Like them, it can be a meal in its own right. The only problem is getting the right corn, as the only kind we can buy here, off the cob, is either frozen or tinned. My own preference is for frozen – it seems to have a slightly better texture and in this soup it's eaten whole – but tinned is fine. Make sure you drain the tinned variety thoroughly and rinse it through before using it for the soup; the brine it's kept in is very strong-tasting.

SERVES 4

1 lb (450 g) potatoes, diced

10 oz (275 g) Spanish onions, diced

1 tablespoon vegetable oil

Salt and freshly ground black pepper

10 fl oz (300 ml) milk

1 pint (600 ml) water

1 bay leaf

Pinch of dried thyme

Pinch of dried oregano

12 oz (350 g) frozen sweetcorn and peppers, defrosted, or use frozen or tinned sweetcorn and add ½ each de-seeded and chopped green and red pepper

Chopped parsley

Water biscuits, to garnish

Gently sweat the diced potatoes and onions in a saucepan with the oil over a low heat for about 5 minutes, without browning them. Add a good pinch of salt and pepper, and the milk, water and herbs. Bring to the boil and simmer for 10–15 minutes until the potatoes are soft. Add the sweetcorn and peppers and heat through for another 3–4 minutes. Sprinkle with the chopped parsley, and serve with water biscuits crumbled over the top.

Apple and Stilton Soup

*T*his is a soup that I developed for a big family party a September or two ago. It's perfect for that time of year because English apples, with their marvellous flavours and sharp sweetness, are at a peak, and Stiltons are coming to their best. It's a soup with enough body to compensate for the chills of an early autumn, but sophisticated enough to serve at a smart party.

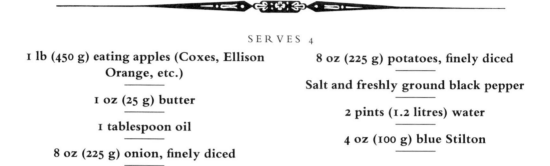

SERVES 4

1 lb (450 g) eating apples (Coxes, Ellison Orange, etc.)

1 oz (25 g) butter

1 tablespoon oil

8 oz (225 g) onion, finely diced

8 oz (225 g) potatoes, finely diced

Salt and freshly ground black pepper

2 pints (1.2 litres) water

4 oz (100 g) blue Stilton

Core but do not peel the apples, and cut into walnut-sized pieces. Melt the butter in the oil and fry the onion and potatoes in it over a medium heat for 3–4 minutes. Season generously and add the apple chunks and water. Bring to the boil and simmer for 15 minutes until fruit and vegetables are soft. Put into a food processor or liquidiser and blend until fine. Add 2 oz (50 g) of the Stilton and blend again. Re-heat the mixture.

Serve in bowls with the remaining cheese, crumbled with a fork, sprinkled on top.

Pumpkin Soup (Fonda del Sol)

*This is a wonderful autumn soup: rich, golden and warming – and named after 'the heart of the sun' in its native South America. You can make it any time you buy pumpkin, but it's particularly fun if you buy one around Hallowe'en and, having scraped the flesh out for the soup, use the shell as a serving tureen before turning it into a lantern. (Be careful not to make the shell too thin!) To prepare the pumpkin, discard all the seeds and the soft pulp around them, then peel off the hard rind and chop the remaining flesh.
Croûtons are great with this (see p. 20).*

SERVES 4

1 tablespoon oil (preferably peanut)

1 clove garlic, chopped

1½ lb (750 g) prepared pumpkin (see above)

8 oz (225 g) tomatoes, chopped

8 oz (225 g) onions, chopped

3–4 teaspoons tomato purée

Salt and freshly ground black pepper

2 pints (1.2 litres) water or vegetable stock

Heat the oil in a saucepan and add the garlic. Then add the pumpkin, tomatoes and onions. Mix in the tomato purée and stir the ingredients over a low heat for 3–4 minutes. Season generously. Add the water or stock carefully: the consistency should be like single cream.

Simmer for 30 minutes with the lid on and then purée in a food processor or liquidiser. Re-heat and serve in a hollowed-out pumpkin or a tureen.

Carrot and Apple Soup

*C*arrot and apple soup, delicious in its own right, has also emerged because of the tremendous benefit the ingredients are supposed to give to your health. As you might expect of a soup containing carrot, it is full of beta-carotene, the basic ingredient of Vitamin A, which is said to be especially good at preventing many serious diseases. The other delicious flavour it contains is apple – and, surprise, surprise, it seems that an apple or two a day does help keep the doctor away! The croûtons add fibre and crunch to the soup.

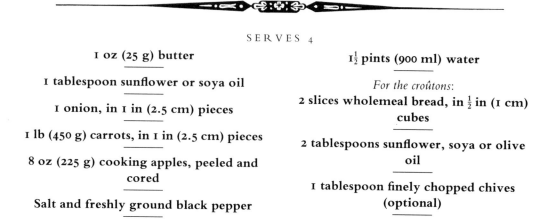

SERVES 4

1 oz (25 g) butter

1 tablespoon sunflower or soya oil

1 onion, in 1 in (2.5 cm) pieces

1 lb (450 g) carrots, in 1 in (2.5 cm) pieces

8 oz (225 g) cooking apples, peeled and cored

Salt and freshly ground black pepper

$1\frac{1}{2}$ pints (900 ml) water

For the croûtons:

2 slices wholemeal bread, in $\frac{1}{2}$ in (1 cm) cubes

2 tablespoons sunflower, soya or olive oil

1 tablespoon finely chopped chives (optional)

Melt the butter in the oil in a large saucepan. Add the onion, carrots and apples and stir for 5 minutes over a medium heat. Season generously and add the water. Bring to the boil then simmer for 15 minutes. Transfer to a food processor and blend.

To make the **croûtons**, fry the bread in the oil until pale brown. At the last minute you can sprinkle them with chives if you wish.

Onion Soup

This is the soup that Parisian roisterers are legendarily supposed to have drunk as dawn came up over the famous Les Halles market in the centre of the city. But, like Covent Garden market, in London, traffic jams and commercial necessity have moved the stalls to an out-of-town location and Les Halles has become a developers' paradise. Unfortunately, my roistering-in-Paris days were a bit too late to taste the authentic soup on its home ground. When I got there they were just starting to pull Les Halles down, but I checked the soup out from other sources whose roistering was authenticated and this is the crafty version. It needs serving on a chill evening (or a cool morning). You can prepare the soup in advance and add the bread and cheese at the last minute – just flash it under a grill.

SERVES 4

2 tablespoons oil

4 oz (100 g) butter, or, properly, beef dripping

2 lb (1 kg) large onions, thinly sliced

1 dessertspoon sugar

1 clove garlic, chopped

Salt and freshly ground black pepper

2 pints (1.2 litres) beef stock (not Oxo-flavour) or vegetable stock

4 rounds French bread

4 oz (100 g) Gruyère cheese, grated

Put the oil and butter or dripping into a large thick pan. Add the onions and cook over a medium heat for about 10 minutes, stirring gently, until they are coloured a rich brown. Do not let them burn. Add the sugar and allow that to mix with the onions and caramelise, stirring continuously for about 3–4 minutes. Add the garlic and season generously. Add the stock, bring to the boil, then simmer for at least 30 minutes. A low oven (gas mark 2, 300°F, 150°C) if you've got it on for other reasons, is ideal for this. Simmering should be uncovered to allow the liquid to reduce a little.

Ladle into bowls and top with the French bread. You can first toast the bread in the oven for 10 minutes to dry out. Top the bread in turn with a generous spoonful of grated Gruyère and put the bowls under a grill or into a hot oven (gas mark 7, 425°F, 220°C) until the cheese bubbles and melts.

Serve immediately. Remind your guests that hot Gruyère cools down very slowly.

Cullen Skink Soup

Despite its extraordinary name, this is a Scottish soup of great distinction and long pedigree. It's based on smoked haddock, and you will need to make a careful choice between the kind of haddock that has no colouring in it (apart from that naturally produced by the smoke) and the bright golden kind. My vote is clearly for the one in which the colour is natural. Indeed, all over Scotland, it's the only kind of smoked haddock you can buy. This is quite important, because otherwise the soup tends towards an orange colour which isn't as attractive as it might be. The other ingredients are the simple kind you'd expect to find in a Scottish winter: potatoes and onions. The combination, however, is remarkably sophisticated and can be served either in chunks for a hearty meal-type soup or blended in a food processor for a substantial, but more delicate, first course. This soup is particularly nice with oat bread, or scoffa if you can get it.

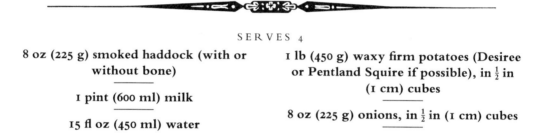

SERVES 4

8 oz (225 g) smoked haddock (with or without bone)

1 pint (600 ml) milk

15 fl oz (450 ml) water

1 lb (450 g) waxy firm potatoes (Desiree or Pentland Squire if possible), in $\frac{1}{2}$ in (1 cm) cubes

8 oz (225 g) onions, in $\frac{1}{2}$ in (1 cm) cubes

2 tablespoons chopped parsley

Cut the fish into moderate-sized pieces, put in a large pan with the milk and water, bring to the boil and simmer very gently for about 15 minutes until the fish comes off the bone or flakes easily. Decant it from the saucepan, straining it to separate the fish from the liquid. In the same saucepan, put the potatoes and onions. Return the fish liquid to the saucepan, bring to the boil and simmer, covered, for 10 minutes. Separate the fish pieces from the bones and skin, add them to the saucepan and allow to heat through. At this point you can, if you wish, liquidise the soup for a smooth and creamy version.

Either way, serve into bowls and top with a generous teaspoonful of finely chopped parsley.

Provençal Fish Soup

While we have very few traditions for fish soup in Britain, Cullen Skink being an honourable exception, all over the world there are many different kinds. This is the version from the south of France. It's not a bouillabaisse, because that requires special fish available only on the Mediterranean coast, but it has that kind of flavour and style – the zest of summer mixed with the flair of Provence. You can vary the kinds of fish you use but, if possible, try and get a reasonable mixture to provide the richness of flavour. This soup is usually served with a spoonful of rouille (overleaf) stirred into it, topped with a sprinkling of garlic and herb croûtons (overleaf) and a spoonful of grated Gruyère or an equivalent cheese. Gouda is probably the best cheap alternative.

SERVES 4

1½ lb (750 g) fish, including at least 3 kinds, if possible red mullet or gurnard, conger eel or cod, monkfish or sole

2 pints (1.2 litres) water

4 tablespoons olive oil

8 oz (225 g) onions, finely chopped

2 cloves garlic, finely chopped

1 x 14 oz (400 g) tin Italian tomatoes

Pinch of saffron powder

1 bay leaf

2 oz (50 g) long-grain rice

1 lb (450 g) mussels, in the shell, cleaned (see p. 63)

1 oz (25 g) chopped fennel leaf or parsley

Put the fish, which can at this stage contain heads, bones, etc., but should be cleaned and scaled if necessary, into a saucepan. Cover with the water, bring to the boil and simmer, covered, for 10 minutes. Decant from the saucepan, and strain to separate the fish from the liquid. Put the olive oil into the empty saucepan. Add the onions and garlic and fry over a medium heat for 3 minutes. Add the tomatoes, saffron, bay leaf, rice and the liquid from the fish.

Bring to the boil and simmer, covered, for 25 minutes. Add the mussels and simmer for 5 minutes. Remove the fish flesh from the bones and debris, cut into small cubes and return to the soup. Check for seasoning and add a little more water if the soup has thickened too much.

To serve, ladle into bowls making sure everyone gets a share of the fish and rice. Top each bowl with the fennel leaf or parsley.

Rouille

Rouille is classically made from a bread and oil mixture, and the craftiest way to produce a substitute is to take 4 tablespoons mayonnaise (not salad dressing!) and add $\frac{1}{2}$ a crushed clove of garlic and 6 drops of Tabasco sauce.

Garlic and Herb Croûtons

4 slices white or brown bread, $\frac{1}{2}$ in (1 cm) thick

4 tablespoons cooking oil (sunflower is best)

$\frac{1}{2}$ teaspoon garlic salt

1 teaspoon mixed dried herbs (basil, thyme, chives)

Cut the crusts off the bread. Slice the bread into $\frac{1}{2}$ in (1 cm) fingers, then across into $\frac{1}{2}$ in (1 cm) cubes. Heat the oil in a frying-pan big enough to take the cubes in a single layer. Add the cubes and turn every 30 seconds for 2–3 minutes over a medium heat. When they are golden, take out and drain on kitchen paper. While still hot, sprinkle with the garlic salt and mixed herbs.

The croûtons will stay crisp for 12 hours, but are best hot.

Citronelle Soup

Citronelle *is the French name for what we now know as 'lemon grass'. It's a south-east Asian herb that looks like dried spring onions and is widely available in ethnic shops and many supermarkets. If you don't see it in a supermarket, ask for it, because it can be obtained by their vegetable and produce buyer. A couple of stalks crushed into a sauce and simmered produce the most wonderful vivid citrus flavour, much used in Indonesian, Thai and Malaysian cooking. It also makes the basis for a lovely, lemony clear soup that you can serve as part of an exotic meal or as a refreshing start to something more conventional. You can use lemon juice as a substitute for lemon grass, but the flavours just aren't so intense or accurate.*

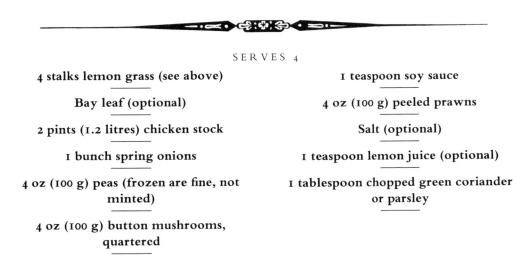

SERVES 4

4 stalks lemon grass (see above)

Bay leaf (optional)

2 pints (1.2 litres) chicken stock

1 bunch spring onions

4 oz (100 g) peas (frozen are fine, not minted)

4 oz (100 g) button mushrooms, quartered

1 teaspoon soy sauce

4 oz (100 g) peeled prawns

Salt (optional)

1 teaspoon lemon juice (optional)

1 tablespoon chopped green coriander or parsley

Crush the lemon grass stalks with a rolling pin or kitchen mallet. Put into the stock, with a bay leaf if you like, and simmer for 35 minutes. All the flavour should come out of the herb and into the stock. Discard the lemon grass. Clean and cut the spring onion, white and green sections, into $\frac{1}{4}$ in (5 mm) dice. Add the spring onions, peas, mushrooms and soy sauce to the stock. Simmer for 5 minutes. Add the prawns and allow to heat through (unless they are raw, in which case they also need 5 minutes cooking). Check for seasoning, it may need a little salt or lemon juice if your lemon grass was not at full strength.

Serve in delicate Chinese bowls, sprinkled with the green coriander or parsley.

COLD SOUPS

Vichysoisse

There is a rumour, which many French deny, that Vichyssoise was invented in America by a French chef so tired of waiting for his American employer to come to table that he allowed the Leek and potato soup he had prepared to go cold. In a panic, when the employer finally turned up, the chef stirred some cream into the cold confection, and served it to what turned out to be great acclaim. It's a nice story and, in so far as cold soups don't have much history in France, it may well be true. Whether it is or not, the soup is certainly delicious and, surprisingly enough, very pleasant eaten in cold weather before a hearty meal, as well as in high summer. Modern variants substitute watercress for leek. This provides a brighter colour but not such a subtle taste. On a healthy note, you can substitute fromage frais for the double cream, although it does give the soup a slightly sharper flavour.

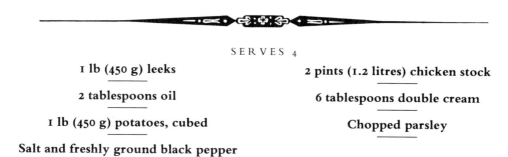

SERVES 4

1 lb (450 g) leeks	2 pints (1.2 litres) chicken stock
2 tablespoons oil	6 tablespoons double cream
1 lb (450 g) potatoes, cubed	Chopped parsley
Salt and freshly ground black pepper	

Trim the leeks, keeping as much of the green part as you can. Split them and wash in lots of cold water to get rid of any sand or grit, then cut them into 1 in (2.5 cm) sections. Heat the oil in a saucepan and fry the potatoes and leeks in it gently for about 5 minutes, not allowing them to take colour. Season generously, add the chicken stock, bring to the boil and simmer until the vegetables are thoroughly soft. Liquidise or process in a food processor until completely blended. You may need to scrape the sides down with a spatula to make sure of this. Return to the saucepan, add the cream, stir and pour in a bowl to cool.

The soup can be put in the refrigerator to chill once it's below blood heat (that means you can put your finger in without screaming).

To serve, stir thoroughly to re-mix the soup and sprinkle with chopped parsley.

Gazpacho

This is the famous cold soup from the south of Spain. It has, as does so much Spanish cooking, a strong Arab style to it though most of the ingredients are the result of the Spanish conquest of the New World where tomatoes and peppers were first developed. It is very much a summer soup to be eaten when the weather is warm enough to remind you of southern Spain. It's also quite pungent so be sure, if you're including the full measure of garlic, that you eat it with really good friends.

SERVES 4

1 large Spanish onion	1 pint (600 ml) tomato juice (tinned or tetra pack)
1 cucumber	4 tablespoons olive oil
4 spring onions	2 tablespoons wine vinegar
2 cloves garlic	Approximately 10 fl oz (300 ml) water
1 green pepper, de-seeded	8 oz (225 g) ice cubes
1 red pepper, de-seeded	2 slices brown bread
8 ripe tomatoes	

Peel and cut the onion into chunks. Split the cucumber and trim the spring onions and crush the garlic. Cut a quarter of the green and the red pepper and 2 of the spring onions and 2 in (5 cm) of the cucumber into fine dice. Mix in a bowl and reserve as a garnish.

Cut the tomatoes, and the rest of the cucumber, spring onions and peppers into suitable sized chunks and put into a food processor or liquidiser with the Spanish onion and garlic. Add the tomato juice and process to a coarse purée. Some of the vegetables should still be in recognisable, if small, chunks. Put the mixture into a bowl, stir in the olive oil and wine vinegar, and dilute with water until it is the consistency of whipping cream before it's whipped. Add half the ice cubes and allow to chill.

Cut the brown bread into $\frac{1}{2}$ in (1 cm) cubes and bake in an oven pre-heated to gas mark 3, 325°F (160°C) for 10–15 minutes until dried out but not browned.

To serve, spoon a serving of the soup into individual bowls and add 2–3 ice cubes. Serve the chopped reserved vegetables and the brown bread croûtons for diners to add for themselves.

STARTERS

'Starters' is a modern term for a modern idea. It's really a direct result of the concept of a three-course meal, something our ancestors, when they could afford it, would have regarded as barely a warm-up to a proper five- or seven-course repast. The modern taste, though, is to replace many of the early courses with one appetising dish or a combination of two or three. In fact, some restaurants have made quite a reputation by serving a selection of starters instead of a main course. I suspect this may be quite profitable: starter dishes tend to be quite small. There is no question, though, that they offer some of the most interesting and exciting choices in cooking. They also provide the opportunity to experiment with more exotic ingredients.

My selection from the many starters we've shown on *Food and Drink* includes a section on pizza. In Naples, it's often eaten as a fast-food, portable breakfast, available from street stalls in the early morning. For us, it often constitutes a whole meal. However, a pizza cut into slices like a pie makes a terrific starter in its own right. The ones in this chapter are also perfectly suitable for a light, or indeed quite a heavy, lunch, depending on whether you consume one between two, or one per person. They also have the great advantage of being authentic as to flavour and ingredients. No pineapple pizzas here!

The other dishes I've chosen display the versatility of starters. There are pâtés – carnivorous, vegetarian and fishy – fruit, fish and eggs.

What's more, they don't have to be served in solitary splendour. A selection of Coriander mushrooms, Rainbow stuffed eggs and Crisp fried aubergine slices served with Avocado dip and crisp and grainy breads makes a terrific and modern *hors d'oeuvre* for a large party, with guests helping themselves to a variety of dishes. Whatever your choice of combinations, or pleasure in individual recipes, crafty starters are a great way to say '*bon appetit*'.

Mushrooms Baked with Cream

This old country recipe is very simple, quite scrumptious and can be done only with big mushrooms. Wild 'horse' mushrooms are the best, but if you find cultivated ones over 4 in (10 cm) across they will do very well. A rich dish, it's ideal for a rustic starter, or for a high tea with other country goodies. Serve with wholemeal bread to soak up the lovely juices and cream.

PRE-HEAT THE OVEN TO GAS MARK 7, 425°F (220°C)

For each person:

1 large open mushroom

2 tablespoons double cream

1 oz (25 g) butter

Salt and freshly ground black pepper

1 teaspoon chopped parsley

Remove the stalks from the mushroom caps. Wipe and trim the caps but do not peel them. Butter a baking dish large enough to hold all the mushrooms flat and put them in, black side up. Spoon the cream on to each mushroom, with a knob of butter and generous seasoning. Bake in the oven for 15 minutes.

Sprinkle with the parsley.

Coriander Mushrooms

*T*his is mushrooms à la grecque *with a little added spiciness. The idea originally came from Elizabeth David, the creative instigator of so much that's become good in modern British food. It makes a delicious starter on its own, and a good foil for other dishes in a mixed hors-d'oeuvre. It keeps well in the refrigerator; indeed, it may well improve with 24 hours for the flavours to blend.*

SERVES 4

5 fl oz (150 ml) water

5 fl oz (150 ml) olive oil

2½ fl oz (65 ml) lemon juice (fresh or bottled)

1 lb (450 g) small closed mushrooms, washed and trimmed

1 clove garlic, chopped

1 tablespoon chopped celery leaf or parsley

Salt and freshly ground black pepper

1 teaspoon ground coriander

Bring the water, oil and lemon juice to the boil and add the mushrooms and garlic. Simmer for 5 minutes. Add the celery leaf or parsley and season. Pour into a basin and leave to cool. Drain the mushrooms and place in a serving dish, reserving the liquid. Sprinkle the coriander over the mushrooms and moisten them with 4 tablespoons of the liquid.

Serve well-chilled.

Crisp Fried Aubergines

Aubergines cooked like this have a world-wide pedigree – I've eaten them in Japan, south-east Asia, the West Indies and the Mediterranean. The only variations seem to be the oil in which they're cooked, and whether they're shallow- or deep-fried. I'm recommending shallow-frying and olive oil for health reasons, but they're very good deep-fried in a standard frying oil in a chip pan. These aubergines are particularly good as part of a mixed hors-d'oeuvres or, in rather substantial quantities, can be served with a tomato sauce flavoured with basil as a vegetarian main course. The trick is to drain them thoroughly after salting and to cook them as quickly as possible in really hot oil.

SERVES 4

1 lb (450 g) aubergines	**8 tablespoons olive oil**
4 tablespoons cooking salt	**4 tablespoons seasoned flour**

Cut the aubergines lengthwise into $\frac{1}{4}$ in (5 mm) slices. Salt thoroughly with the cooking salt and drain in a colander for 30 minutes. Rinse and pat dry. Heat the oil in a thick frying-pan till almost smoking. Dip the aubergine slices in the seasoned flour and cook a few at a time until browned – about $1\frac{1}{2}$ minutes a side. Drain on kitchen paper and serve as quickly as possible.

Pears and Stilton

The combination of pear, walnuts and Stilton is more usual at the end of a meal, but I think it makes a spectacular starter.
This recipe uses an apple cutter that divides apples or pears into 12 sections while cutting out the core. It was available in most kitchen shops until I demonstrated it on television – then most of them seemed to disappear overnight!
Fromage frais, by the way, is a French-style cottage cheese made from fermented skimmed milk. It's deliciously creamy and low in fat. A number of different varieties are available from supermarkets and dairies. The main differences are between the French version, which comes in both zero and 8 per cent fat versions, and the German version, known as 'quark'. This contains 12 per cent fat and is slightly drier and grainier than fromage frais. There is a view that it's best to use fromage frais for uncooked dishes and quark for cooking. Either will do very well for this recipe.

SERVES 4

4 oz (100 g) Stilton cheese

4 oz (100 g) fromage frais or quark

2 oz (50 g) walnuts, shelled

4 ripe Comice pears

Lemon juice

Cream the cheese and fromage frais or quark together until smooth. Chop all but 4 walnut halves and add to the cheese mixture. Divide the mixture into 4 and place in the middle of 4 saucers. Peel the pears and segment into 12 pieces each. To stop them browning, dip them into water to which some lemon juice has been added. Press the pear sections into the cheese, re-creating the shape of the pear, and top each with a walnut half. Serve within 30 minutes.

Rainbow Stuffed Eggs

*P*retty, *and pretty simple to do! I've suggested three flavour/colour combinations, but you can ring the changes to suit your own tastes and what's available in the garden or larder. Do fill the eggs carefully: the simpler the dish, the more appearance matters. The method for hard-boiling the eggs is worth noting too. It avoids grey yolks and dark rings, which is always worthwhile, even when the eggs are just for a picnic.*

SERVES 4

6 eggs (free-range if possible)
6 tablespoons real mayonnaise

1 teaspoon tomato purée
½ teaspoon dried basil
Salt and freshly ground black pepper

4 anchovy fillets, chopped
1 tablespoon finely chopped parsley

1 tablespoon mango chutney
½ teaspoon curry powder
Salt and freshly ground black pepper

Put the eggs in cold water, bring to the boil and simmer for 10 minutes. Run under cold water, crack the shells, and peel when cool. Halve each egg lengthways and remove yolks.

Divide yolks into 3 bowls and mix 2 tablespoons of mayonnaise into each. Then add one of the flavour/colour combinations to each bowl: tomato for red; parsley and anchovies for green; curry and mango chutney for yellow. Mix thoroughly and then fill 4 egg halves with each colour, moulding the mixture up to a peak. Serve each person one half-egg of each colour.

Mushroom Pâté

*M*ushrooms make a lovely pâté. Its texture and colour are very similar to some of the finer liver pâtés, but it has two splendid advantages. First, it's much better for you because it's lower in saturated fat and, second, it's lighter to eat so makes a less heavy start to a meal than some of the very solid meat pâtés. Eat it with hot, buttered wholemeal toast or the Scandinavian-style rye-crisp rolls that are like large, deliciously textured rusks. I like to serve it with thinly sliced pickled gherkins for a contrast in texture and flavour.

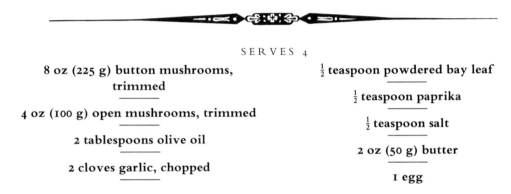

SERVES 4

8 oz (225 g) button mushrooms, trimmed

4 oz (100 g) open mushrooms, trimmed

2 tablespoons olive oil

2 cloves garlic, chopped

$\frac{1}{2}$ teaspoon powdered bay leaf

$\frac{1}{2}$ teaspoon paprika

$\frac{1}{2}$ teaspoon salt

2 oz (50 g) butter

1 egg

Wash the mushrooms in a colander for 30 seconds to 1 minute, using extremely hot water. Do not peel them. Cut into moderate-sized pieces. Heat the olive oil in a frying-pan, add the mushrooms and garlic and fry over a medium heat until the mushrooms give off liquid. Increase the heat and boil the liquid away until the mushrooms are quite, but not absolutely, dry. Put them into a food processor or liquidiser with the powdered bay leaf, paprika and salt. Add the butter to the frying-pan and scramble the egg in it to take up all the remaining liquid and mushroom debris. When the egg is set, add it to the mushrooms and herbs in the processor and purée until the mixture is very fine-grained. Pack into individual ramekins or into a single soufflé dish and chill for at least 4 hours before serving.

You can seal the pâté with melted butter and keep it in the refrigerator for up to 3 days covered with foil or cling film.

Smoked Salmon Scramble

This is one of my favourite treats. It's a chance to use a luxury ingredient in an extremely economical way. It requires 2 oz (50 g) smoked salmon but it's not necessary to use the beautifully and elegantly cut expensive slices: the off-cuts, which are often sold for the same price per lb (450 g) as a $\frac{1}{4}$ lb (110 g) of the grander version, will do perfectly well. This dish makes a nice starter popped into pretty little pots – and an absolutely scrumptious high tea or Sunday night supper piled on to granary toast.

If you serve this in ramekins, be sure to provide plenty of thin wholemeal toast.

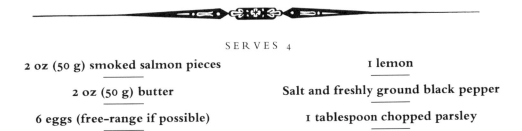

SERVES 4

2 oz (50 g) smoked salmon pieces	**1 lemon**
2 oz (50 g) butter	**Salt and freshly ground black pepper**
6 eggs (free-range if possible)	**1 tablespoon chopped parsley**

Cut the smoked salmon into the smallest ribbons you can – they should be at least as thin as matchsticks and about 1 in (2.5 cm) long. Melt the butter in a non-stick pan. Break and lightly beat the eggs, and scramble them for about $1\frac{1}{2}$ minutes until they are still soft but starting to form curds. Add half the salmon pieces and the juice of half the lemon. Continue to scramble for only about another 30 seconds until the eggs start to set. They will continue to cook out of the pan. Season, being careful with the salt – the salmon has a little bit in it already. Pile the egg and salmon mixture into individual ramekins or on to toast. Sprinkle with the remaining pieces of smoked salmon and a little parsley, and serve the rest of the lemon cut into 4 for diners to squeeze over their eggs if they fancy a little more sharpness

Smoked Mackerel Pâté

S moked mackerel has become the most popular smoked fish eaten in England. There was a time when kippers had this honour, but with the over-fishing of herrings people began to discover how well mackerel took to the smoking process. In fact, there are two kinds of smoked mackerel: hot- and cold-smoked. Hot-smoked are normally used for pâtés. It is possible to eat the cold-smoked variety (which is treated in the same way as kippers and smoked salmon) raw — just as kippers and smoked salmon can be eaten raw — but it doesn't make a very good pâté.

This recipe uses hot-smoked mackerel and is very simple, particularly if you have a blender or food processor. You can also make it by hand with very little effort. Just make sure that you soak the slices of white bread long enough for them to break up and crumble easily.

You can serve this as a starter, but it's also great for a picnic. Keep it in its pot so that it can be scooped out with a spoon, and dolloped on to crusty French bread.

SERVES 4–6

1 thick slice white bread, crust removed

Approximately 4 tablespoons milk

2 large fillets hot-smoked mackerel, skinned

Juice of $\frac{1}{2}$ lemon

2 oz (50 g) butter, melted

1 teaspoon chopped fresh dill, or 1 heaped teaspoon dried dill or parsley

2 tablespoons natural yoghurt or fromage frais

Soak the bread in the milk until it's saturated. Put the mackerel into a blender or food processor and mix until it's a smooth paste, then add all the other ingredients and mix for 10 seconds. Scrape the mixture down and mix for a further 5 seconds. Pile the pâté high in individual ramekins, or put in a soufflé dish and smooth over the surface.

Serve with wholemeal toast or hot French bread.

Note: If you want to keep the pâté for more than 2 days, cover with a thin layer of melted butter and store in the refrigerator tightly covered with foil; it will last up to 1 week.

Kedgeree

There is much argument about the origins of this dish. It's certain that it reached Britain in the nineteenth century from India, where it was a popular dish on tiffin tables, but its exact nature is disputed. An Indian dish called Khichri, also made with rice, but with lentils instead of smoked haddock, is probably its ancestor.

Even the kedgeree we eat in Britain comes in a variety of guises. I've found this one the craftiest. Not only is it a delicious breakfast dish for the truly hungry, it is also a marvellous weekend brunch centrepiece, as you can easily make it in large quantities.

We recently introduced a group of Louisiana senators to this recipe, at an exchange of brunch ideas in New Orleans. If one fact emerged from the film, it was that politicians all over the world aren't stopped from talking even when their mouths are full.

Served in small quantities, particularly in attractive little dishes, this makes a terrific starter, especially if the main course is fairly light. It may not be entirely authentic, but it's great served with mango chutney.

SERVES 4

8 oz (225 g) smoked haddock and/or cod

10 fl oz (300 ml) milk

8 oz (225 g) long-grain rice

2 oz (50 g) butter

1 small onion, chopped

1 teaspoon mild (or home-made) curry powder

To garnish:

4 hard-boiled eggs, quartered

$1\frac{1}{2}$ in (4 cm) piece cucumber, very thinly sliced

Poach the fish in the milk for about 10 minutes or until it flakes easily. Drain, reserving the milk. Flake the fish, discarding skin and bones. Measure the rice in a cup, then put it in a saucepan and add the milk the fish was cooked in, and enough water to make double the quantity of liquid to rice. Cook, covered, over a moderate heat until all the liquid is absorbed and the rice is tender, about 12 minutes.

In a separate saucepan, melt the butter and very gently fry the onion with the curry powder for 5 minutes. Add the rice and flaked fish and gently stir until thoroughly mixed together. Take care not to break up the fish too much.

Turn into a serving dish and garnish with the hard-boiled eggs and cucumber.

Morning-After Eggs

One of the return compliments from Louisana was this version of Huevos rancheros or Ranch eggs as an idea for brunch. In New Orleans, where this recipe originates, they say it was what was served to young bucks after a night on the town, to restore their energies before they returned to their wives. No comment on their efficacy, but they are delicious! Serve in long canoe-shaped pastry cases for authenticity, or ramekins if you are feeling really crafty (or morning afterish).

SERVES 4

1 red pepper, de-seeded, thinly sliced

1 onion, sliced

1 clove garlic, chopped

2 tablespoons oil

1 x 14 oz (400 g) tin Italian tomatoes, drained, or 8 oz (225 g) really ripe tomatoes, chopped

1 teaspoon chilli sauce (Tabasco sauce or equivalent)

Salt and freshly ground black pepper

8 soft-boiled eggs, shelled (5 minutes each in boiling water)

Fry the pepper, onion and garlic in the oil over a medium heat until soft. Add the tomatoes with a little of their juice and the chilli sauce. Stir and simmer, uncovered, for 20 minutes. Season with salt and pepper.

Serve the eggs on the sauce, with a little sauce spooned over each one.

Chicken Liver Pâté

*C*hicken liver pâté is one of my all-time favourite starters. I've used a number of different recipes over the years, but always come back to this one which has a combination of richness and simplicity that always appeals. I've been cooking it for more than 25 years and only recently has a problem emerged: the salmonella issue which has so bedevilled poultry and eggs for the last couple of years. The rights and wrongs of the issue aren't the point here. The problem is that when the dish is properly made, the liver should still be a little pink after it's been cooked, to give the centre of the pâté a delicate, rosy colour. If you aren't sure about the provenance of chicken livers these days, you may want to cook them a little more thoroughly to be on the safe side.

Whatever you decide to do, the pâté is particularly good eaten with hot crusty French bread: put it in an oven pre-heated to gas mark 4, 350°F (180°C) for 5 minutes before hand-breaking it into chunks. Add a little French grain mustard and the gherkins they call cornichons *to turn a starter into a feast.*

SERVES 4

1 tablespoon oil	Salt and freshly ground black pepper
8 oz (225 g) chicken livers	2 fl oz (50 ml) apple juice
1 clove garlic, chopped	3 oz (75 g) butter, melted
$\frac{1}{2}$ teaspoon dried thyme	2 bay leaves, for decoration
$\frac{1}{2}$ teaspoon dried marjoram	

Heat the oil in a frying-pan, add the chicken livers and fry over a high heat until cooked: 3 minutes for pink, 5 minutes for brown. Add the garlic, thyme, marjoram and seasoning and cook for a further $\frac{1}{2}$ minute. Tip into a blender or food processor and add the apple juice and $\frac{3}{4}$ of the melted butter then process until smooth. Turn out into a $\frac{1}{2}$ pint (300 ml) dish.

Pour the rest of the melted butter over and decorate with the bay leaves. Chill in the refrigerator and eat within 5 days.

Gravad Lax

This is the Scandinavian way with raw salmon that rivals our smoking techniques — and has the unique advantage that it can be made at home. Gravad Lax needs fresh dill, a marvellous herb for fish, that also goes well with new potatoes. It is much used in Scandinavian cooking but was not readily available here. However, with the arrival of a wide range of fresh herbs, including dill, in most supermarket chains, it has suddenly become possible to make Gravad Lax very easily.

There is another option. I used to say that dried dill wouldn't do, but that was before I discovered the new freeze-dried herbs that have only just come on the market. Freeze-dried dill, rehydrated carefully in a little water with a drop of lemon juice, makes an adequate if not perfect substitute for the fresh herb.

This is a dish for high days and holidays and is, I think, particularly nice at Christmas time when it will keep in the refrigerator for a week or more, to be sliced and eaten as and when needed as a refreshing change from the heavier meals of the festival. Serve with lots of brown bread and butter.

SERVES 4–6

1 lb (450 g) salmon fillet; ask your fishmonger to fillet and skin the tail piece of a salmon weighing about 1–1½ lb (450–750 g)

1 tablespoon salt

2 tablespoons brown sugar

2 oz (50 g) fresh dill, finely chopped, or 1 oz (25 g) freeze-dried dill, rehydrated

Juice of 1 lemon

Fromage frais

Rub the salmon fillets with the salt and sugar and leave to marinate for an hour in a shallow bowl. Take one fillet and, placing it cut side up, spread the dill across the whole surface. Cover with the other salmon fillet, cut side down, to make a 'sandwich'. Add the lemon juice to the liquids which came off the salmon while it was marinating in the salt and sugar. Pour these over the fillet sandwich and leave to marinate in the refrigerator, in a dish covered with cling film. Make sure the film does not touch the salmon. After a day, turn the sandwich over so that the marinade has a chance to reach the other side. Do this 3 times over a total of 4 days.

To serve, take half of the salmon sandwich, put it on a cutting-board and cut it across the grain into thin slices. Cut downwards at an angle of about 80° — it must be cut into short oblong slices, not long, thin pieces like smoked salmon.

Gravad Lax is traditionally served with a mustard and dill sauce, but I think it's nicest with a little 8 per cent fromage frais with a spoonful of the dill-laden marinade stirred in. Put 3 or 4 slices on to a plate, in an elegant arrangement, and serve the sauce separately in a bowl.

The remaining piece of salmon will keep under the cling film for another 4–5 days in a cool part of the refrigerator.

Avocado Dip

This is a simple version of a Mexican dish called guacamole. *The avocado pear was first developed in Mexico, where it is mashed up, mixed with other ingredients and served as a relish and as a sauce to go with much of their food. As with so much Mexican cooking, it can be a spicy experience. I leave the authentic chilli out to get a refreshing (and totally vegetarian) pâté. It's particularly nice eaten with something crisp: tortilla chips, Italian-type breadsticks, or even toast. It's very easy to make, but the best method is undoubtedly in a food processor.*

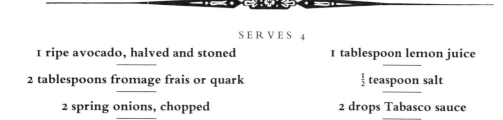

SERVES 4

1 ripe avocado, halved and stoned	**1 tablespoon lemon juice**
2 tablespoons fromage frais or quark	**$\frac{1}{2}$ teaspoon salt**
2 spring onions, chopped	**2 drops Tabasco sauce**

Scoop the flesh from the halved avocado into a blender or food processor. Add all the other ingredients and purée in 3 or 4 3-second bursts. Check for seasoning and balance and pack the mixture into an attractive dish. You can put the stone back in the middle and cover the dish with cling film if you will be eating the dip more than 30 minutes after making it. However, it won't keep for more than about 3 hours without starting to go very brown.

PASTA

If you think the Neapolitans take their pizza seriously, you need to consider the lengths to which one of Italy's premier pasta companies has gone. The Voiello company hired one of the world's top industrial designers, Signor Giuggiaro, whose skills have been used to design Fiats and Ferraris, to produce a new designer pasta. It made one of the most extraordinary films we've ever shown on *Food and Drink* with the early prototypes of the pasta being sold on the Italian black market at ridiculous prices. What finally emerged was a pasta called 'Marille', which can best be described as two parallel tubes with a wing on one side – slightly reminiscent, I fear, of an early Chevrolet. I think, when we tasted it, most of us found it a little heavy. Pasta comes in many different shapes and textures, designed to accompany specific types of sauces. British tinned-food manufacturers – true to form – have taken this variety one stage further and produced bizarre versions such as space-invader-shaped pasta, aimed at children's imaginations and their mothers' purses. They may look different, but they all taste curiously alike. Our advice is to stick to traditional pastas. The pasta shapes, and the sauces which best complement them, are as follows:

Fusilli spirals are good for creamy sauces which stick in their complex folds and curlicues.

Tagliatelle are white, yellow or green flat noodles. The colour depends on whether they are plain or egg- or spinach-flavoured. They are often eaten with rich sauces for which they are an excellent base. Cheese, especially Parmesan, is often added for its flavour and slightly granular texture.

Conghile, or snail shells, are little pasta pockets, good for holding sauces with chunky ingredients.

Spaghetti is often eaten with very simple flavourings in Italy: olive oil, garlic and Parmesan cheese – or just butter and cheese.

The recipes below are for dried pasta which you can buy in packets from any grocer or supermarket. Allow up to 3 oz (75 g) per person for a starter, and 4 oz (100 g) if the pasta is served as a main course.

Fresh pasta is becoming more widely available. It cooks much more quickly than dried pasta – about 3 minutes in boiling water – but is more expensive and doesn't keep that long.

Here are some suggestions, including a sauce for Marille, in the unlikely event of your acquiring some. If not, it's great with spaghetti.

Carbonara

This rich but simple recipe is good with fusilli as the spirals have a sufficiently large surface area to 'cook' the eggs. The crisp, fried salami and cheese add an interesting contrast of textures. This makes enough to accompany 12 oz (350 g) uncooked pasta.

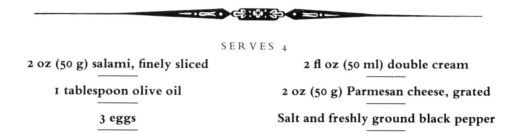

SERVES 4

2 oz (50 g) salami, finely sliced

1 tablespoon olive oil

3 eggs

2 fl oz (50 ml) double cream

2 oz (50 g) Parmesan cheese, grated

Salt and freshly ground black pepper

Cut the salami into matchsticks and fry in hot oil until crisp; 2 minutes should do it. Beat the eggs with the cream. Cook the pasta spirals until just tender. Drain and return the pasta to the pan. Add the egg and cream mixture and stir off the heat until the eggs have thickened (like scrambled eggs). Mix in the salami and Parmesan and season generously.

Serve piping hot.

Gorgonzola alla Crème

This is also a rich but simple sauce – perfect for the flat green noodles called 'tagliatelle verdi', which get their colouring from spinach. The sauce is a speciality of Sicily and the quantities given make enough to accompany 12 oz (350 g) uncooked pasta.

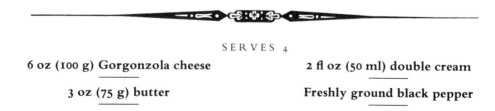

SERVES 4

6 oz (100 g) Gorgonzola cheese

3 oz (75 g) butter

2 fl oz (50 ml) double cream

Freshly ground black pepper

Cream the cheese and butter together (a food processor or blender does this very well). Shape into a roll and chill in the refrigerator. Cook the pasta. Slice the roll into ½ in (1 cm) sections. Heat the cream gently in a saucepan but don't allow to boil. Add the cheese and butter sections and stir over a low heat until melted. When the sauce is smooth, but not boiling, toss the tagliatelle in it. Serve with plenty of black pepper.

Zucchini and Snails

Not an Italian take-over of a French left-over, but the recipe uses snail-like conghile. This is a vegetarian sauce that's great for summer eating. In small quantities it makes a good starter. The amounts given make enough sauce to accompany 12 oz (350 g) uncooked pasta.

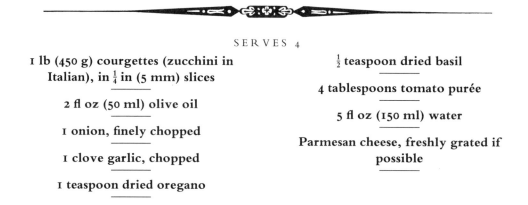

SERVES 4

1 lb (450 g) courgettes (zucchini in Italian), in $\frac{1}{4}$ in (5 mm) slices

2 fl oz (50 ml) olive oil

1 onion, finely chopped

1 clove garlic, chopped

1 teaspoon dried oregano

$\frac{1}{2}$ teaspoon dried basil

4 tablespoons tomato purée

5 fl oz (150 ml) water

Parmesan cheese, freshly grated if possible

Cook the conghile according to the instructions on the packet. Heat the oil in a frying-pan that's deep enough to hold all the sauce ingredients. Add the courgettes and onion and fry briskly for 2 minutes. Add all the other ingredients and stir until well mixed. Simmer part-covered for 3 minutes and pour over the cooked shells.

Serve with the Parmesan cheese.

Ragù alla Bolognese

*T*his is the authentic Bolognese sauce. It is very rich and creamy, and makes enough to accompany 12 oz (350 g) uncooked pasta. Use Marille if you can get it – or spaghetti. Freeze-dried herbs, if you use them, will add lightness and colour.

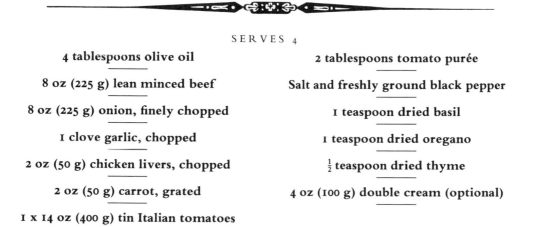

SERVES 4

4 tablespoons olive oil	2 tablespoons tomato purée
8 oz (225 g) lean minced beef	Salt and freshly ground black pepper
8 oz (225 g) onion, finely chopped	1 teaspoon dried basil
1 clove garlic, chopped	1 teaspoon dried oregano
2 oz (50 g) chicken livers, chopped	$\frac{1}{2}$ teaspoon dried thyme
2 oz (50 g) carrot, grated	4 oz (100 g) double cream (optional)
1 x 14 oz (400 g) tin Italian tomatoes	

Heat the oil in a heavy-based saucepan. Add the beef and sauté in the hot oil until brown. Add the onion, garlic, chicken livers and carrot and sauté for 1 minute more before adding the tomatoes and tomato purée. Season the mixture and simmer, part-covered, for 45 minutes, adding a little water when necessary to keep the sauce moist. Add the herbs 5 minutes before serving.

In Bologna, where the sauce comes from, they often add double cream – lovely but very naughty!

PIZZA

There has been a pizza explosion in the last few years or so. Few towns are now without a pizza parlour competing with Chinese and Indian take-aways: the varieties – fresh or frozen – to be found in supermarkets make the mind boggle. Hawaiian pizzas complete with pineapple cubes have arrived, and motor-cyclists deliver boxed deep-dish versions to our doors. But such travesties have not escaped the notice of the Italians. In Naples, the home of the pizza, a society for the protection of the genuine article has been formed. It insists on pure ingredients, classic toppings and swift cooking in the traditional beehive-shaped brick oven fired by beechwood. To test whether the Italians were being over-sensitive, or the British malnourished, we asked six expatriate Neapolitans to test a range of British shop-bought pizzas. Their reactions were unanimous: all were bad, most were dreadful, and the bigger the supermarket the worse the pizza. They were outraged by the thick, doughy bases and skimpy, unauthentic ingredients. Strangely enough, the only shop-bought pizza they could stomach was the French-bread version; they thought the base crispy and light, and the toppings generous. But they all agreed that anyone could do better at home, even without a beehive-oven and a beechwood fire. What follows is a crafty way of making proper pizza. Approved, by the way, by the Italian hardliners. Do try it. It is a far nicer dough than the one made with baking powder, and takes very little longer to prepare.

Quick Pizza Dough

Vitamin C is the crafty quick ingredient here. It's available in powdered form from any chemist. Don't be tempted to use more than I suggest or to substitute dried yeast. Try spreading the dough with your hands rather than a rolling pin: it's easier, and more authentic.

Traditionally, pizza dough takes 12 hours to rise. This version takes just 15 minutes and produces pizzas that are crisp, savoury and subtle. Do heat the oven properly and try pre-heating the baking sheet or a ceramic tile before putting the pizza on top.

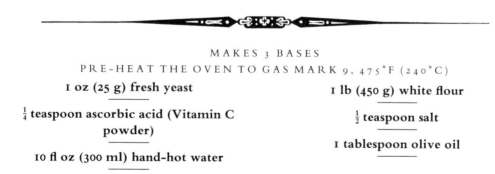

MAKES 3 BASES
PRE-HEAT THE OVEN TO GAS MARK 9, 475°F (240°C)

1 oz (25 g) fresh yeast

$\frac{1}{4}$ teaspoon ascorbic acid (Vitamin C powder)

10 fl oz (300 ml) hand-hot water

1 lb (450 g) white flour

$\frac{1}{2}$ teaspoon salt

1 tablespoon olive oil

Mix the yeast and the Vitamin C in enough water to make a paste. Add to the flour, then mix with salt and olive oil and the rest of the water in a warmed bowl. Knead until smooth. Leave in a warm place to rise for 15 minutes. Knead again, then divide the dough into 3 balls and spread each ball into an 8 in (20 cm) pizza base. Add one of the toppings below and bake for 15 minutes, putting the pizzas on a pre-heated ceramic tile or baking sheet in the oven. Eat hot!

I am giving suggestions for four traditional toppings but, notwithstanding the sensibilities of the Neapolitans, you can, of course, experiment with your own. The first suggestion, Margheurita, is the most-loved topping in Naples, where its more fanciful inhabitants claim that it was inspired by the colours of the Italian national flag: the green of the basil, the white of the Mozzarella and the red of the tomatoes. In all these recipes, fresh herbs are wonderful if you can get them (many delicatessens and supermarkets now stock them). If not, dried herbs are fine and often used by the Italians. There is now a third choice: freeze-dried herbs which combine the aroma and mild flavour of fresh herbs with the convenience of dried ones. If you are using fresh herbs, double the quantities given in the following recipes.

Margherita

For each pizza:
2 tablespoons chopped tinned Italian tomatoes

1 teaspoon tomato purée

2 oz (50 g) Mozzarella cheese, thinly sliced

1 teaspoon grated Parmesan cheese

1 teaspoon dried basil leaves

1 teaspoon dried oregano

Salt and freshly ground black pepper

1 teaspoon olive oil

Mix the chopped tomatoes and the tomato purée. Spread the mixture over the dough, leaving a $\frac{1}{2}$ in (1 cm) space around the edge. Sprinkle the Mozzarella over the tomatoes, then add the Parmesan cheese, herbs and seasoning. Lastly, trickle on the olive oil. Bake for 15 minutes (see Quick pizza dough, p. 44).

Mushroom

For each pizza:
2 oz (50 g) Mozzarella cheese, thinly sliced

2 oz (50 g) mushrooms, thinly sliced

1 clove garlic, chopped

Salt and freshly ground black pepper

1 teaspoon dried oregano

2 tablespoons olive oil

Spread the cheese and mushrooms over the dough, leaving a $\frac{1}{2}$ in (1 cm) space around the edge. Add the garlic, seasoning and oregano. Trickle on the olive oil. Bake in the oven for 15 minutes (see Quick pizza dough, p. 44).

Marinara

For each pizza:

2 tablespoons chopped tinned Italian tomatoes

1 tablespoon tomato purée

4 anchovy fillets

6 black olives

1 teaspoon capers

Salt and freshly ground black pepper

1 tablespoon olive oil, or anchovy oil (optional)

Mix the chopped tomatoes and the tomato purée. Spread the mixture over the dough, leaving a $\frac{1}{2}$ in (1 cm) space around the edge. Split the anchovy fillets and arrange them over the tomatoes like the spokes of a wheel. Then lay the olives and capers on top. Season lightly. Trickle on the oil (the oil from the anchovy tin is a good idea). Bake for 15 minutes (see Quick pizza dough, p. 44).

Double Mozzarella

For each pizza:

4 oz (100 g) Mozzarella cheese, half sliced, half coarsely grated

Salt and freshly ground black pepper

1 teaspoon dried basil

1 teaspoon dried oregano

1 tablespoon grated Parmesan cheese

2 tablespoons olive oil

Layer the sliced Mozzarella cheese over the dough. Season, then sprinkle with the herbs. Add the grated Mozzarella and Parmesan cheese. Trickle on the olive oil. Bake in the oven for 15 minutes (see Quick pizza dough, p. 44).

FISH

*T*he greatest of all the changes in our eating habits and tastes that have taken place in my 8 years on *Food and Drink* is our attitude to, and liking for, fish. At the beginning of the 1980s, fish shops were closing all over the country and it seemed that the only kind of fillet we could look forward to was a frozen one. But then things began to change. In particular there was growing concern over the amount of meat, especially red meat, that we ate. Fish started to become a fashionable alternative. At first this was a tentative development and, indeed, even now that the passion for fish is in full swing, I doubt if detailed statistics would be gasp-worthy. But developments like this build up a substantial momentum quite suddenly. What added to the cult for cod, the desire for John Dory, the trout that tickled our fancies, was the gradual emergence of research and information that suggested that fish wasn't just an alternative to meat. It seems it also has positive benefits to offer us in terms of health and well-being.

Now I haven't forgotten that fish is actually food not medicine, and that it is delicious in all sorts of ways in its own right. But the health issue is an important one and worth discussing before I get back to scrumptiousness on a plate. The main thrust of the argument is that certain chemical constituents in many fish oils (though in few other sources), known by their scientific code name 'omega-3', are particularly helpful in making our bodies less susceptible to heart and circulatory diseases and, indeed, possibly to a whole range of other debilitating or killing illnesses. Not surprisingly, a lot of this research is still controversial, but much of it is being carried out in Japan where the population has a higher consumption of fish per head than that of any country in the developed or developing world. It may be just a coincidence that Japanese men and women live longer than anybody else, but it does matter! There is more about this, with some of Japan's amazing fish recipes, in 'The Crafty Cook's Tour'. However, to return to a more culinary level, the fact is that fish has featured largely in *Food and Drink* cooking spots from the very beginning of the programme because of the flavour, lightness and versatility it brings to all sorts of dishes.

Even with our fairly limited consumption of fish, we eat a greater variety than we do of any other major source of protein. Our meat comes from two or three different animals, plus a little game. We primarily eat two or three kinds of cheese. We drink milk from only one animal. And even the vegetables that deliver bulk protein are a fairly narrow band of beans and peas. That's not the case with fish. If you're a fish-eater, just flat fish alone provide four or five well-known varieties on a regular basis: plaice, sole (Dover and lemon), halibut, turbot and, if you can get it, skate. Then there are shoal fish like herrings, mackerel and sprats, or white fish like cod and haddock, coley and hake. And I haven't touched on shellfish or the more exotic imports from places as far apart as the Seychelles and the Caribbean that find their way, amazingly, straight into our supermarkets.

That brings me to one of the other main changes: many larger supermarkets now have wet-fish counters that have rescued the skills of the fishmonger, not least by popular demand. If you do have a good practising fishmonger, though, cherish him – and encourage him by making as much use as you can of skills and services like filleting and skinning.

Another major change that's taken place over the last 8 years in the way we eat fish is the incredible growth in fish-farming. It's brought salmon, once an expensive delicacy, down to the same price as cod. Although there have been recent worries about the pest-control measures that are needed for such intensive rearing, many of the early problems with farmed salmon and trout – muddiness of flavour and poorness of texture – have been dealt with very successfully. Already there are reports that other, more ocean-going, fish have been successfully farmed and farming may well be the way much of our fish will come to us in the future.

But the traditional ways may still survive. Near where I live in Kent, more in-shore fishing boats are being built because of the recent success of ones from some of the small but traditional ports like Folkestone. It's a far cry from the great ocean-going trawlers that used to patrol the cod lanes from Iceland to Newfoundland in the days of my youth, but it's at least a resurgence, and in the right direction.

What, then, to do with the fish they catch? Well, I have a lot of ideas, many of them low on bones and smells and high on flavour, for different fish. Some are for old favourites like cod, haddock and herring; some for newly affordable salmon and trout; and quite a few for the shellfish that we never seem to lose our taste for – mussels and crab, shrimp and prawns. Some recipes are very traditional: Trout *amondine*, a classic dish. Or there's Skate in black butter, a traditional complement for the richly flavoured fish. There are also one or two new ideas of my own: Halibut in orange sauce, Monkfish kebabs and, not least, one of the great successes of all the *Food and Drink* recipes – Salmon *en croûte*. When we did this recipe on television shortly after Christmas it certainly looked attractive on camera, but it was only when two people told me they had Salmon *en croûte* at different dinner parties later in the week that I realised what an impact it had made. It is a grand dinner-party dish for special occasions, but not too expensive these days, and a wonderful way to persuade people who may not, in the first instance, put fish at the top of their priority list to give it a go, and be deliciously surprised.

Skate in Black Butter

*M**any of the fish we have little regard for these days are highly prized in other countries. One of these is ray, or skate. It tends to be one of the cheaper fish in our fish-and-chip shops and is hardly seen on menus otherwise. But it makes one of the classic dishes of northern France when served with a 'black butter' sauce.*

One of the advantages of skate is that it doesn't have conventional bones. Instead, long, thin tendons run through the wings. You can ignore and discard these, but the French regard them as a delicacy: they're very easy to crunch and don't have any nasty, splintery effects. They add what is described as 'extra texture' to the fish.

Be warned: the black butter sauce is not meant to be black at all; at most, it should be a pale hazelnut colour. The slight 'catching' of the butter gives it an appropriately nutty flavour. Serve very quickly straight out of the pan, on to hot plates. It doesn't like to be kept waiting and doesn't go very well with chips either. It's much better to serve a separate vegetable dish afterwards or, at most, boiled new potatoes with it. French bread to mop up the juices is, however, an excellent idea.

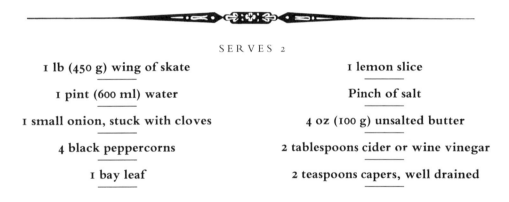

SERVES 2

1 lb (450 g) wing of skate	1 lemon slice
1 pint (600 ml) water	Pinch of salt
1 small onion, stuck with cloves	4 oz (100 g) unsalted butter
4 black peppercorns	2 tablespoons cider or wine vinegar
1 bay leaf	2 teaspoons capers, well drained

Put the skate in a large frying-pan into which it will fit flat. Pour over the water and add the onion, peppercorns, bay leaf, lemon slice and salt. Bring to the boil, turn down to a very low simmer, cover and cook for about 15 minutes, until the flesh on the top flakes easily. Drain carefully, place the fish on a hot plate and cover to keep it warm.

Discard the poaching liquid and flavourings. Melt the butter in the same pan and let it heat until it just starts to turn brown and gives off a slightly nutty aroma. Don't let it burn. Pour the butter over the fish and add the vinegar and capers to the unwashed pan. Boil for about 10 seconds and then pour over the fish and serve immediately.

The combination of the juicy fish, the slightly nutty butter and the sharpness of the vinegar and the capers is what gives this dish its legendary reputation.

Herrings in Oatmeal

After a ban of several years on most herring fishing, the fleets are out once more. That's the good news. The bad news is that many of us seem to have lost the habit of eating herrings. Let's get into it again: herrings are both cheap and nutritious. This recipe has always been a favourite for high tea in Scotland, where it was for many years the unofficial national fish dish. What is interesting is that, apart from their superb eating qualities, herrings are extra healthy because they're exactly the kind of fish that have the maximum amount of those 'omega-3' fish oils that are so good for us. The recipe, of course, combines the fish with oatmeal, the other 'wonder' ingredient of recent years in the fight against heart disease. Don't season the fish while you cook it, by the way, it will be seasoned already by the salt in the frying-pan. Serve with lemon wedges on warm plates with brown bread and butter.

SERVES 4

1 tablespoon salt	**4 tablespoons oatmeal or porridge oats**
4 herrings, cleaned	**Lemon wedges**

Heat a solid frying-pan with the salt sprinkled in. When the salt starts to change colour, carefully add the herrings. Let them cook for 3 minutes. Turn the herrings, then lower the heat and cook for another 5 minutes. Sprinkle the oatmeal on to the herrings. Turn the heat up high, and shake until the oatmeal starts to brown and the herrings are crispy. Serve with the lemon wedges.

Pickled Herrings

While we are on the subject of herrings, here's one of my favourite ways with them. Interestingly enough, although it's a British recipe, I was reminded how nice it is in a French restaurant. Food and Drink had been over to Paris to run the finals of one of our annual cookery competitions in the kitchens of a great hotel. The next night we went out looking for a small French local restaurant, the kind that everyone dreams of, and found one where a terrific first course was herrings done like this.

Pickled herrings are a British tradition we have just about forgotten – the harsh, astringent taste of rollmops is about all we have left of it. But this is subtle and delicate. Eaten with boiled new potatoes and good rye bread it makes a main course. Ask the Scandinavians, who still eat herrings like this.

SERVES 4

7 fl oz (200 ml) cider vinegar	6 peppercorns
5 fl oz (150 ml) boiled water	I teaspoon salt
I carrot, sliced	3 tablespoons sugar
½ onion, sliced	8 herring fillets (sold as such, or get your fishmonger working)
2 bay leaves	

Put all the ingredients except the herring into a saucepan and bring to the boil. Simmer for 10 minutes then cool.

Pour over the herring fillets and leave for at least 12 hours. This dish improves if left covered in the refrigerator for up to 1 week.

Trout Amondine

*W*ith fresh farm trout so widely available, I think they make a particularly attractive introduction to fish for people who are worried about the bones! Trout have only a few, which are very tidily arranged. If anyone is put off by the bones, it's a fair bet they will also be worried about the heads, so don't be affected by the old-fashioned belief that you're meant to serve trout with the heads on. If you, or your family or friends, think a reproachful stare from the plate is not conducive to a good appetite, cut the heads off before you coat the fish in the almonds.

The combination of trout and almonds is a classic: this version doubles the almonds. This is good with steamed cucumber pieces tossed in a little butter.

SERVES 4

4 oz (100 g) ground almonds	2 oz (50 g) butter
4 trout, cleaned	I oz (25 g) slivered almonds
2 tablespoons oil	2 tablespoons lemon juice

Put the ground almonds into a bag and shake each trout in it, coating thoroughly. Heat the oil in a large frying-pan and place the trout in it. Sauté them gently for 5 minutes a side, then remove and keep warm. Add the butter to the frying-pan turn up the heat and sauté the slivered almonds until they are just brown. Add the lemon juice and carefully pour over the trout. Serve at once on *hot* plates.

Sole Meunière

Now sole is a luxury, whether it's Dover or lemon, and there is little prospect at the moment of it being farmed. But this is still a wonderful dish to cook if you do happen to have deep pockets or a special occasion. If you're cooking for more than two people, you may need two frying-pans to make sure there's enough room to cook both fish at the same time lying flat. They don't improve with keeping when cooked this way. Ask your fishmonger if you want the sole filleted, as it's a fiddly job. If it's a Dover sole, ask him to skin it as well. Serve with boiled new potatoes.

SERVES 2

1 tablespoon oil

2 oz (50 g) butter

1 lb (450 g) Dover or lemon sole

2 tablespoons seasoned flour

Juice of ½ lemon

Salt and freshly ground black pepper

Parsley, to garnish

Heat the oil and half the butter in a frying-pan. Dip the sole in the flour and fry gently for 3 minutes each side if the fish is filleted, 5 minutes if it is on the bone. Transfer to warm plates. Wipe the frying-pan, then melt the rest of the butter till it stops sizzling – don't let it brown. Quickly add the lemon juice, and pour over the fish.

Season, and garnish with parsley.

Goujons of Sole

If you're trying to make the lovely firm texture and subtle flavour of sole go a little further, here is a recipe which traditionally requires deep-fat cooking. That's still the official way to do it, but I find that if you brown the goujons or strips of fish very quickly in a little shallow oil, you can put them in the oven at gas mark 4, 350°F (180°C) for 10–15 minutes and they'll cook quite crisply – but have a lower fat content, if that's a thought that consoles you.

SERVES 2

1 Dover or lemon sole, filleted and skinned

Juice of $\frac{1}{2}$ lemon

2 tablespoons seasoned flour

1 egg, beaten

8 oz (225 g) fresh white breadcrumbs

Oil for deep frying (or shallow frying)

Cut the fillets into $\frac{1}{3}$ in (8 mm) strips, diagonally across the grain. Soak these in the lemon juice for 5 minutes. Dip the strips in the flour, egg and breadcrumbs, in that order, and fry in the oil, pre-heated to just below smoking. Cook until golden, about 4 minutes.

Serve hot.

Haddock Duglère

*Y*ou *can buy skinned haddock fillets in all supermarkets these days, sometimes fresh and sometimes frozen. I prefer them fresh, but frozen fillets do very well in this dish with its pretty, creamy sauce. You can make the same dish with plaice fillets, which are best rolled up and secured with a toothpick before cooking. This makes for a really attractive presentation and plaice, being thin, cooks very quickly.*
Serve Haddock duglère with creamed potatoes.

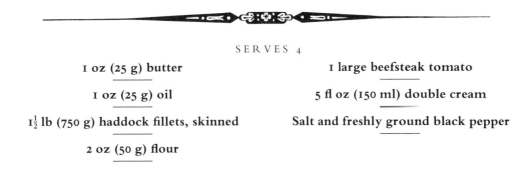

SERVES 4

1 oz (25 g) butter

1 oz (25 g) oil

1$\frac{1}{2}$ lb (750 g) haddock fillets, skinned

2 oz (50 g) flour

1 large beefsteak tomato

5 fl oz (150 ml) double cream

Salt and freshly ground black pepper

In a large non-stick pan melt the butter in the oil until it stops sizzling. Coat the fish in the flour, and fry gently in the pan for 4 minutes on each side. Skin the tomato by dipping it in boiling hot water for 30 seconds before removing the peel. Cut in half and scoop out the seeds. Cut the flesh into $\frac{1}{2}$ in (1 cm) strips and add to the pan. Cook gently for 1 minute. Lift the fish on to warm plates. Pour the cream into the pan and bring to the boil. Season and pour over the fish.

Haddock Mousse

*H*addock *is vastly under-rated south of the border. The Scots are rightly addicted to it. It has a firm texture and vivid flavour, ideal for that favourite nouvelle cuisine starter, a hot fish mousse sliced into elegant slivers.*
You can serve it hot or cold and, served in generous slices, it makes a good main course for those who, like me, think nouvelle cuisine is usually too little of a good thing. The tomato sauce, poured over or around it, as the 'nouvelles' like, is a fine addition.

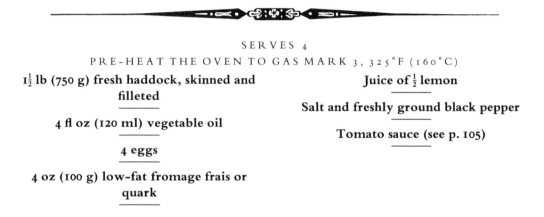

SERVES 4
PRE-HEAT THE OVEN TO GAS MARK 3, 325°F (160°C)

I½ lb (750 g) fresh haddock, skinned and filleted

4 fl oz (120 ml) vegetable oil

4 eggs

4 oz (100 g) low-fat fromage frais or quark

Juice of ½ lemon

Salt and freshly ground black pepper

Tomato sauce (see p. 105)

Cut the haddock into chunks. Put into a food processor or blender with the oil, eggs, fromage frais or quark, lemon juice and seasoning. Purée until smooth. Line a 2 lb (1 kg) loaf tin with greased paper and put the puréed mixture into this. Place the loaf tin in a bain-marie (a baking tin half-filled with water). Bake in the oven for 35–40 minutes, or until set. (The runnier the consistency of the fromage frais, the longer it will take to set: the low-fat varieties are generally runnier than the high-fat ones.) Remove from the oven and turn out of the loaf tin, removing the greased paper.

Cut into slices and serve with tomato sauce.

You can cook haddock mousse in individual ramekins or tea cups – reduce the baking time to just 20 minutes.

Cod in Mushroom Sauce

As fishing grounds have changed and cod has become more of a luxury and less of a staple, we've been given the chance to re-evaluate this lovely rich, creamy fish. It comes in smashing, big chunks, giving a generous feel on the plate and on the palate. I've partnered it with sour cream in this recipe. Sour cream is undervalued in Britain. Much lower in fat than double cream, it has a richness just tempered by the careful souring. Fresh cream which has gone off is not the same thing! This recipe, which combines cod steaks (fresh if possible) with sautéd mushrooms, is a great dish if you have an oven with a timer. Provided everything is cool when assembled, it can be left ready to cook for up to 4 hours. This is very good served with peas and lots of mashed potatoes.

SERVES 4

PRE-HEAT THE OVEN TO GAS MARK 6, 400°F (200°C)

Butter for greasing ovenproof dish

4 x 6 oz (175 g) de-boned cod steaks (fresh or frozen)

2 tablespoons oil

8 oz (225 g) button mushrooms, sliced

5 fl oz (150 ml) sour cream

Juice and grated rind of 1 lemon

Lightly butter an ovenproof dish and put in the cod steaks. Heat the oil in a frying-pan. Add the mushrooms and sauté them for 3 minutes over a medium heat. Allow to cool. Beat the sour cream, lemon juice and grated rind together. Stir in the mushrooms and pour the mixture over the cod steaks, making sure they are completely coated. Cover with foil. Bake for 25 minutes if using fresh fish, or 35 minutes if using frozen fish. Take the foil off for the last 5 minutes to allow the sauce to brown a little.

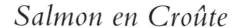

Salmon en Croûte

This is perhaps the most popular fish dish we've ever done on Food and Drink. *What is nice is that it comes out looking totally spectacular for remarkably little work. I always use ready-made puff pastry: a version made with vegetable fat that reduces the amount of saturated fat puff pastry used to contain is now widely available. This is not a dish for a quiet supper à deux. It's an impressive one for dinner parties or buffets. Ask your fishmonger to fillet a 2½ lb (1.25 kg) salmon and give you the bones and trimmings for one of the sauces. You don't have to serve two sauces, of course, that's just being flashy.*

SERVES 6–8

PRE-HEAT THE OVEN TO GAS MARK 6, 400°F (200°C)

12 oz (350 g) white fish (haddock, whiting or cod)

6 oz (175 g) fresh white breadcrumbs

Juice and grated rind of 1 lemon

1 tablespoon chopped chives

1 tablespoon chopped parsley

1 egg

4 tablespoons sunflower oil

Salt and freshly ground black pepper

1 lb (450 g) puff pastry

2 x 14 oz–1 lb (400 g–450 g) salmon fillets, skinned

Beaten egg

For the cucumber sauce:
½ large cucumber

4 oz (100 g) fromage frais

Salt and freshly ground black pepper

For the lemon cream sauce:
Fish trimmings

Juice of ½ lemon

1 bay leaf

4 peppercorns

4 tablespoons double cream

Salt

Put the white fish, breadcrumbs, lemon juice and rind, herbs, egg and oil into a food processor. Process until smooth. Season well. Roll out the pastry into a long oval shape 6 in (15 cm) longer than the salmon fillets and about 1½ times as wide. Place one fillet in the middle of the pastry, spread with the white-fish paste and sandwich with the other salmon fillet. Cut diagonal lines along each side of the puff pastry about ½ in (1 cm) apart, leaving 3 in (7.5 cm) at each end uncut. Lift the cut strips on either side of the salmon up and over the fish, crisscrossing them over each other. Secure the strips with beaten egg. Fold the flap of pastry at the top of the fish into a triangle to make the shape of a fish head, and cut a wedge from the bottom flap to make the shape of a tail.

Carefully lift the fish on to a greased baking sheet. Brush the pastry with beaten egg and bake for 35–40 minutes. To see if the fish is cooked, insert a skewer between the plaits; it should come out clean.

Serve plain or with either of the following sauces.

To make the **cucumber sauce**, grate the cucumber and sprinkle with salt; leave for 15 minutes for the excess water to drain from the cucumber. Rinse and pat dry with kitchen paper. Stir the cucumber into the fromage frais and season.

For the **lemon cream sauce**, boil the fish trimmings in a little water along with the lemon juice, bay leaf and peppercorns for 10 minutes. Strain the liquid into a clean pan and boil rapidly until the liquid has reduced to 5 fl oz (150 ml). Stir in the cream and season to taste with salt.

Herbed Salmon Steaks

*T*hough still a treat, salmon isn't the luxury item it has been for the last hundred years. Good and careful farming, especially in the cleaner waters of Scotland, has produced delicious and economical fish. This recipe, though simple, is still one of the all-time favourites for salmon. New potatoes and a cucumber salad – what more perfect for a sun-kissed evening?

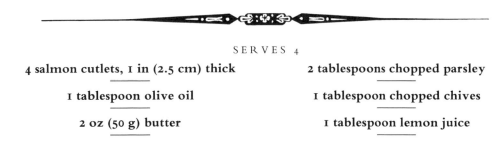

SERVES 4

4 salmon cutlets, 1 in (2.5 cm) thick	**2 tablespoons chopped parsley**
1 tablespoon olive oil	**1 tablespoon chopped chives**
2 oz (50 g) butter	**1 tablespoon lemon juice**

Brush the cutlets with the oil and grill under a very hot, pre-heated grill for 5 minutes on each side. Blend the butter, herbs and lemon juice together (a food processor does this easily). Divide the butter mixture into 4 and place one-quarter on each hot salmon cutlet. Serve quickly on warm plates.

Halibut in Orange Sauce

Halibut has fallen a little out of fashion. It's a great pity, for although it's not one of our cheaper choices, it really does have a lovely dense, solid flesh that lends itself to quite robust cooking styles. I'm very partial to it plain-grilled with lemon and a little butter and parsley, and, when I'm feeling flush, it's my favourite fish for grand fish and chips — but it's also delicious in this fruity sauce. Fruit and fish may seem an unusual combination, but halibut can not only take it, it thrives on it. Serve with a delicate rice pilau and a salad to follow.

SERVES 4

1 tablespoon olive oil

4 x 6 oz (175 g) halibut steaks

1 tablespoon good soy sauce

4 fl oz (120 ml) orange juice

Salt and freshly ground black pepper

Heat the oil until hot in a non-stick pan or well-seasoned frying-pan, and brown the halibut steaks on both sides. Turn the heat down, cover and cook for 4 minutes. Add the soy sauce and turn the heat up to sizzling. Turn over the fish and add the orange juice. Let it come to the boil and serve immediately, seasoning moderately on the plate. The sauce should be dark gold and syrupy.

Baked Mackerel

We've all become used to mackerel in its smoked form over the last few years, but the fresh fish seems to be rather ignored. I was reminded of this old-fashioned way of cooking it on a recent trip to southern Ireland. Much of the cooking that was traditional in mainland Britain years ago still continues there, without quite the resort to convenience foods that's more common here. This dish is light and delicious and you can cook the fish with or without their heads. It can be served hot, or as a cold salad or a very substantial first course.

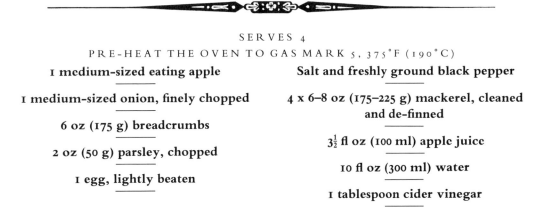

SERVES 4

PRE-HEAT THE OVEN TO GAS MARK 5, 375°F (190°C)

1 medium-sized eating apple

1 medium-sized onion, finely chopped

6 oz (175 g) breadcrumbs

2 oz (50 g) parsley, chopped

1 egg, lightly beaten

Salt and freshly ground black pepper

4 x 6–8 oz (175–225 g) mackerel, cleaned and de-finned

3½ fl oz (100 ml) apple juice

10 fl oz (300 ml) water

1 tablespoon cider vinegar

Core but don't peel the apple and chop finely. Mix with the onion, breadcrumbs, parsley and egg. Season generously and divide into 4. Stuff the mackerel cavities with the mixture, and put the fish in a baking dish into which they will all fit in one layer. Mix the apple juice, water and vinegar together and pour over the fish. Cover the dish with a piece of foil and bake for 30 minutes.

Fish Casserole

*T*he ancestors of this dish are found all around the Mediterranean. I've had versions in Italy, Turkey and Tunisia, and I'm sure it's pretty well universal. It uses the great Mediterranean summer vegetables – tomatoes, peppers, onions, garlic – to make a sauce that's the basis of what is really a very rich, fish stew. The fish you put into it vary depending upon where you're cooking it, but it's the sauce that gives the stew its pungency and flavour, and a variety of fish work equally well in it. Try and use at least three different kinds, including one kind of shellfish, to provide an interesting variety of texture as well as flavour. You can serve the stew in soup plates with rice, pasta, boiled new potatoes or, best of all I think, lots of crusty French or Greek-style bread. This version is for garlic-lovers; you can produce a slightly refined version using only half a clove of garlic.

SERVES 4–6

4 tablespoons olive oil

12 oz (350 g) onion, finely chopped

3 cloves garlic, finely chopped

1 lb (450 g) really ripe tomatoes, or 1 x 14 oz (400 g) tin Italian chopped tomatoes

8 fl oz (250 ml) passata

1 teaspoon each dried basil, fennel, thyme and oregano (if you're using fresh herbs, double the quantities)

1 red pepper, de-seeded and finely chopped

1 green pepper, de-seeded and finely chopped

8 oz (225 g) haddock fillet, skinned

8 oz (225 g) monkfish

$\frac{1}{2}$ teaspoon sugar

8 oz (225 g) large prawns, peeled

Salt and freshly ground black pepper

Heat the olive oil in a saucepan. Add the onion and garlic and fry over a medium heat until translucent. Add the tomatoes, passata and herbs. Add the peppers to the mixture. Simmer for 30–40 minutes with a lid on but not tightly sealed. Cut the haddock and monkfish into walnut-sized pieces and add to the sauce with the sugar. Simmer for 10 minutes and add the prawns. (If the prawns are raw, add them at the same time as the fish.)

Check for seasoning, and serve in bowls.

Multicoloured Fish Terrine

*T*his is a favourite dish in grand restaurants and at splendid dinner parties, but it's actually very easy to produce using my crafty method. However, it does need a food processor, otherwise fish mixtures must be forced through sieves – not a hobby for any but the most dedicated. Surprisingly, it's not an expensive dish. The main fish I suggest you use is whiting, one of the cheapest white fish available these days. The terrine will keep in its tin in the refrigerator for up to 3 days and, indeed, at least a day in the refrigerator improves it as it allows the flavours to blend. To serve, cut the terrine into $\frac{3}{4}$–*1 in (2–2.5 cm) slices and arrange them on attractive plates with a little curly leaf salad on one side, dressed with hazelnut- or walnut-oil dressing.*

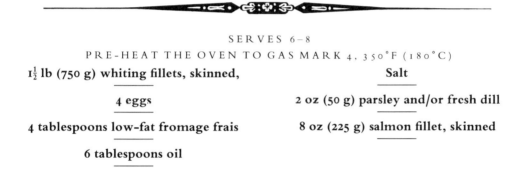

SERVES 6–8

PRE-HEAT THE OVEN TO GAS MARK 4, 350°F (180°C)

I$\frac{1}{2}$ lb (750 g) whiting fillets, skinned,

Salt

4 eggs

2 oz (50 g) parsley and/or fresh dill

4 tablespoons low-fat fromage frais

8 oz (225 g) salmon fillet, skinned

6 tablespoons oil

Cut the whiting up into postage-stamp-sized pieces and place in a food processor with 2 of the eggs, half the fromage frais and 4 tablespoons of the oil. Process in bursts of 5 seconds until the mixture is smooth. Season with salt but no pepper, and pack half the mixture into a greased 2 lb (1 kg) loaf tin lined with greaseproof paper. Add the dill or parsley to the remaining whiting mixture, and process again to produce a green-coloured mixture. Pour this in turn into the loaf tin. Rinse the processor. Cut the salmon into walnut-sized cubes and put it in the processor with the remaining oil, fromage frais and eggs. Process in 5-second bursts until the mixture is smooth, and pour it in turn into the loaf tin. Cover with butter paper and place in a baking dish into which you have put 1 in (2.5 cm) of hot or boiling water. Bake in the oven for 40–45 minutes. To check that it's done, put a skewer in. It should come out clean. If the skewer is smeared, the terrine needs another 5–10 minutes. Allow to cool and refrigerate in the tin.

To serve, slide a knife round the edges of the tin, tip out, remove the greaseproof paper and slice like a loaf to produce a marvellous 3-coloured effect.

Monkfish Kebabs

*M*onkfish used to be cheap in Britain: in fact, we used to export most of what we caught to the French who call it lotte *and think it's one of the best fish there is. They are quite right, of course: monkfish is a great delicacy and we have finally caught on to this, to the detriment of the price. It's firm and almost boneless, and when you buy it you should get solid fillets that need very little trimming. It's easy to prepare and will convert all but the most ardent fish-haters. This recipe uses the flavourings of the eastern Mediterranean for taste and the colours of South American peppers for decoration. It's a great combination. Use either flat-sided or wooden skewers: they make it much easier to turn the fish. Serve on a bed of long-grain rice.*

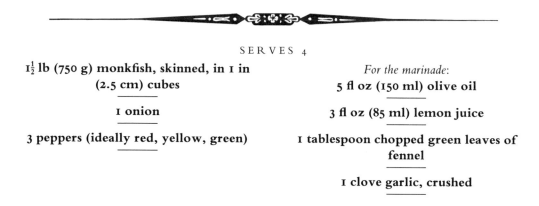

SERVES 4

1½ lb (750 g) monkfish, skinned, in 1 in (2.5 cm) cubes

1 onion

3 peppers (ideally red, yellow, green)

For the marinade:

5 fl oz (150 ml) olive oil

3 fl oz (85 ml) lemon juice

1 tablespoon chopped green leaves of fennel

1 clove garlic, crushed

Put the oil, lemon juice, fennel leaves and garlic into a large bowl and stir together. Place the cubed monkfish in the bowl and marinate for 2–6 hours.

Slice the onion and peppers into 1 in (2.5 cm) squares, and thread alternate slices of the vegetables and monkfish cubes on to flat skewers. Cook for 5 minutes on each side under a hot grill, brushing with the marinade.

SHELLFISH

Our shores grow some of the finest shellfish in the world, though pollution and carelessness have threatened many of our best sources. Mussels are still one of our cheapest delicacies, although the ones in the shops tend to come from Ireland or even Spain these days. The enterprising packers from these countries calculated that if they cleaned the shells most of the work (and the disincentive for the cook) would be done. Cleaned mussels come in $4\frac{1}{2}$ lb (2 kg) plastic bags.

Make sure the mussels are alive. They should be tightly shut when bought; discard any open ones that do not close when tapped sharply, and any with broken or cracked shells or loose hinges. If they haven't already been cleaned, thoroughly scrub the outside before cooking and remove the beard. Leave for 1–2 hours in a bucket of clean, salted water to clean them internally. Discard any mussel that floats to the top.

Moules Marinières

*T*he most famous of all mussel dishes comes from France and literally means 'sailors mussels'. A purist might actually call my recipe Moules à la crème, *but I've had Moules marinières with and without cream all around the French coast. This is my favourite way of doing mussels; the apple juice provides just a touch of sweetness in the sauce to match the natural sweetness of good fresh mussels.*

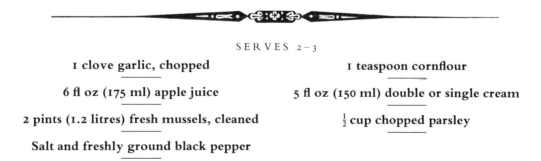

SERVES 2–3

1 clove garlic, chopped

6 fl oz (175 ml) apple juice

2 pints (1.2 litres) fresh mussels, cleaned

Salt and freshly ground black pepper

1 teaspoon cornflour

5 fl oz (150 ml) double or single cream

$\frac{1}{2}$ cup chopped parsley

Put the garlic, apple juice and cleaned mussels in a saucepan and season. Bring to the boil, cover with a lid and simmer for 5 minutes, shaking the saucepan frequently. The mussels will open when cooked – discard any that do not.

Mix the cornflour into the cream, add to the saucepan and stir. Bring back to the boil, shake again and cook for 1 minute more.

Spoon the mussels and sauce into bowls and sprinkle with the chopped parsley.

Bili Bi

This alternative recipe for mussels is a spicy transatlantic one. What its name means, I don't know. Serve with plenty of warm French bread.

SERVES 2–3

1 oz (25 g) butter

1 teaspoon curry powder

4 spring onions, cut into long matchsticks

1 carrot, cut into long matchsticks

2 pints (1.2 litres) fresh mussels, cleaned

10 fl oz (300 ml) water

5 fl oz (150 ml) double cream

Melt the butter in a large saucepan. Sprinkle in the curry powder and gently sauté for 2 minutes. Add the onions and the carrot. Cook for 2 minutes, then add the mussels and water. Bring to the boil, cover and cook over a high heat for 5 minutes. Discard any mussels that remain closed.

Transfer the mussels to a serving dish. Add the cream to the sauce in the pan and boil. Pour over the mussels.

Dressed Crab

Although lobsters have become prohibitively expensive, crab remains a cheap luxury. Perhaps this is because its shell is truly intimidating to all predators, mankind included. There is no quick way of cleaning crab, but the end results make all the effort worthwhile.

Crabs are usually bought ready-cooked in the shell. They vary in price enormously, depending on availability, but are generally cheaper in summer. Choose one that is heavy for its size with no sound of liquid inside when you shake it. Avoid crabs with cracked or broken shells.

Fishmongers often sell crab they have 'dressed' themselves, but you can prepare it yourself: twist off the legs and claws and slip a knife into the horizontal black line at the back of the shell. Twist the knife and the crab will open. Pull the top and bottom apart and remove the 'dead man's fingers' (the greyish-brown gills) lying on each side of the underbelly of the crab. Remove the mouth and the stomach sac behind it and discard. The rest is edible!

Serve with hot, buttered toast and a bowl of Crafty mayonnaise (see opposite).

1 x 2 lb (1 kg) crab, dressed (or see opposite)

Juice of $\frac{1}{2}$ lemon

2 tablespoons chopped parsley

2 tablespoons chopped chives

4 tablespoons soft brown breadcrumbs

1–2 tablespoons mayonnaise (see below)

1 teaspoon Dijon mustard

2 hard-boiled eggs, chopped

Take the brown meat from the main body of the crab and put into a bowl. Using a mallet or nutcracker, break open the claws and remove the white meat. More white meat can be found in the legs and central structure of the crab. (It does require some patience to pick all the flesh out, but is well worth it.) Put the white meat into a bowl and add to it the lemon juice and the parsley and chives. Put the brown meat in another bowl, and add the breadcrumbs, enough mayonnaise to moisten, and the mustard.

Mix the ingredients in both bowls thoroughly. Pile the brown meat in the centre of the cleaned crab shell and put a line of the white meat on either side. Decorate with the hard-boiled eggs.

Crafty Mayonnaise

This recipe produces light, creamy mayonnaise. This is partly because whole eggs, including the more delicate whites, are used, and partly because blenders or food processors beat in extra air. You can't make this recipe without a blender or processor, but with one it's effortless.

1 egg

$\frac{1}{2}$ teaspoon salt

$\frac{1}{2}$ teaspoon sugar

Juice of $\frac{1}{2}$ lemon

12 fl oz (350 ml) olive oil (or olive and/or peanut or sunflower oil)

Put the egg, salt, sugar and lemon juice into a food processor or blender. Add a quarter of the oil with the motor running and blend. Pour the remaining oil into the blender in a slow steady stream until the mayonnaise is light and creamy.

Potted Shrimps

When I first did this recipe on television, I was pulled up short by a number of Lancastrians outraged at the thought that I was making potted shrimps with what were in fact prawns: I was using the widely available frozen or chilled North Atlantic prawn. Properly made, potted shrimps, especially in Lancashire, are made with the tiny pink or brown Morecambe Bay shrimps. They are still available, occasionally, in places other than Morecambe Bay itself – the estuary of the Medway is one. But these tiny shrimps are difficult to find and very fiddly to clean, although the flavour and texture are wonderfully rewarding. Do use them if you can find them and feel up to cleaning them, but the ordinary commercial-style prawn also tastes very good done like this.
Serve with small rounds of wholemeal toast.

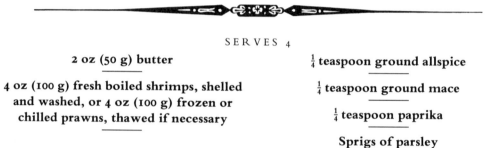

SERVES 4

2 oz (50 g) butter

4 oz (100 g) fresh boiled shrimps, shelled and washed, or 4 oz (100 g) frozen or chilled prawns, thawed if necessary

$\frac{1}{4}$ teaspoon ground allspice

$\frac{1}{4}$ teaspoon ground mace

$\frac{1}{4}$ teaspoon paprika

Sprigs of parsley

Melt the butter in a saucepan over a gentle heat. Add the shrimps or prawns and spices, and stir. Pour the mixture into small ramekin dishes, allow to cool, then refrigerate for 2–3 hours.

Decorate with sprigs of parsley.

Shrimp Gumbo

Gumbo is a style of cooking that comes from New Orleans. It's the Cajun answer to the daubes of France or the stir-fries of Canton: a rich, stew-like sauce thickened with either okra or a powdered version of the sassafras root. Gumbos can be made with a variety of ingredients, like chicken or spiced sausage, as well as shrimp, but my own favourite is this seafood version. You can use ordinary pink pre-cooked prawns to make this dish but it's absolutely outstanding if you can find raw prawns about the size of a little finger. They are usually headless, and are cooked in the sauce to enrich it, producing a much finer blend of flavours. Raw prawns are available from many supermarket fish counters as well as from regular fishmongers. I have even been known to use a mixture of both kinds; raw prawns are quite expensive, and one or two per diner with 6 oz (175 g) of conventional prawns to lift the sauce makes a good dish. Whatever sort you use, serve the gumbo piping hot with plenty of plain boiled rice.

SERVES 4

2 tablespoons oil	1 tablespoon tomato purée
2 onions, chopped	$\frac{1}{2}$ teaspoon dried thyme
4 celery sticks, sliced	$\frac{1}{2}$ teaspoon chilli powder
2 red peppers, de-seeded and sliced	Salt and freshly ground black pepper
2 green peppers, de-seeded and sliced	8 fl oz (250 ml) water
8 oz (225 g) okra, in 1 in (2.5 cm) pieces	1 lb (450 g) prawns, raw, headless and shelled, if possible
4 ripe tomatoes, skinned and chopped, or 1 x 7 oz (200 g) tin chopped Italian tomatoes	Fresh parsley, to garnish

Heat the oil in a large sauté pan. Fry the onions, celery, peppers and okra for about 10 minutes over a medium heat until soft. Add the tomatoes, tomato purée, thyme, chilli powder, seasoning and water. Bring to the boil and simmer for 30 minutes. Add the prawns for the last 7–10 minutes.

Check seasoning and garnish with parsley.

Prawn and Broccoli Gratin

This very simple dish can be made from store-cupboard and freezer ingredients if you use frozen broccoli. I like using fresh but the result, either way, is easy to achieve and surprisingly scrumptious. Don't leave out the nutmeg, it makes a considerable difference to the sauce, and one of the rather richer Continental cheeses like Gruyère or Gouda makes the nicest topping.

SERVES 4
PRE-HEAT THE OVEN TO GAS MARK 4, 350°F (180°C)

1 lb (450 g) broccoli florets

6 oz (175 g) cooked peeled prawns

$1\frac{1}{2}$ oz (40 g) flour

1 oz (25 g) butter

10 fl oz (300 ml) milk

$\frac{1}{4}$ teaspoon grated nutmeg

4 oz (100 g) cheese, grated (see above)

Salt and freshly ground black pepper

Trim the broccoli and blanch in boiling water for 1 minute. Drain, and place in a gratin dish. Sprinkle the cooked peeled prawns over the broccoli. Whisk the flour and butter into the milk. Heat gently until the sauce becomes smooth and shiny, whisking frequently. Add the nutmeg and most of the cheese and season generously. Pour the sauce over the broccoli, sprinkle the remaining cheese over the top and bake for 25 mintues.

Salad of Scallops and Asparagus

*T*his is an unashamedly luxurious dish, but one with a combination of such intense
flavours that a little goes a long way. Scallops are one of the most delicate and most
readily acceptable of shellfish – gleaming white and quite chewily textured. Classically
they are served in thick, and often cheesy, sauces but this salad, with the fish served
warm, is a revelation of texture and flavour.

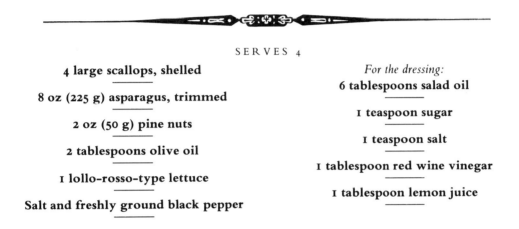

SERVES 4

4 large scallops, shelled

8 oz (225 g) asparagus, trimmed

2 oz (50 g) pine nuts

2 tablespoons olive oil

1 lollo-rosso-type lettuce

Salt and freshly ground black pepper

For the dressing:
6 tablespoons salad oil

1 teaspoon sugar

1 teaspoon salt

1 tablespoon red wine vinegar

1 tablespoon lemon juice

Remove the coral half-moons from the scallops and set them aside. Cut the
main bodies of the scallops across the grain into 3 slices. Steam the asparagus in
a colander over boiling water for 9 minutes. In a frying-pan, fry the pine nuts
in the olive oil for 2 minutes, making sure they don't burn but just brown.
Remove the nuts and reserve the oil in the frying-pan. Fill 4 elegant bowls with
the washed, drained lettuce torn into pieces about half the size of a postcard. Let
the asparagus cool a little then lay it on the lettuce and sprinkle with the nuts.
Mix the dressing ingredients together in a screw-top jar and shake vigorously.
Re-heat the oil you cooked the pine nuts in until it's very hot, and add the slices
of scallop. Cook for 1 minute on each side, add the coral half-moons, season
with a little salt and pepper, and cook 1 minute more.

Place the scallops on the lettuce and pour 2 tablespoons of dressing over each
bowl. Serve while still warm.

POULTRY AND GAME

*I*f I were to try and identify the kind of recipes that have been most popular on *Food and Drink* over the last 8 years, I think chicken ones would top the list. I'm not quite sure why that is, although obviously the fashion for lighter food and less red meat helps. Chicken, after all, has had its share of bad news with the salmonella scares of recent years. Though principally directed at eggs, they also obviously involved chickens.

But chicken has a lot going for it. Although we often complain that it doesn't 'taste/chew like it used to in the old days', the succulent and meaty birds available everywhere today have great palate appeal. What's more, in the last few years, the industry has been in the forefront of adapting to popular tastes. A decade ago the vast proportion of chickens were sold fully frozen. Now, with the exception of the very cheapest categories, most of them are chilled, which allows the meat to develop flavour and makes instant cooking easier. Portioning chicken, and pre-preparing it to make dishes like Chicken Kiev have been major features of the last few years. Today, you can buy chicken in any quantity, from nugget to large roaster, almost anywhere in the country. In addition, free-range and corn-fed chickens and poussins are now available – varieties that have been bred and fed to improve taste, texture and choice. Most of the pressure for this has come from us, the consumers, and it's nice to see part of the food-producing industry responding so promptly to public demand.

However, it's worth saying that reading the fine print is always important. There's free-range and free-range. The EEC lays down certain regulations, the Soil Association lays down others, and the matter is so complicated that there are now categories even among free-range birds, from those raised under the minimum EEC standards right the way through to 'farmyard fresh' chickens which have no space limitations or constraints placed on them beyond the walls of a real farmyard.

A year ago, Jilly Goolden and I did a major chicken-tasting test of 20 varieties under double-blind conditions. It was an extraordinary experience, in the dining-room of a very grand hotel just off Sloane Square in London's Chelsea. I don't think either of us could look a forkful of chicken in the face for nearly a month afterwards, but the test produced some very interesting results. Individual winners and losers aren't worth recalling as producers made adjustments in the light of our conclusions. Suffice it to say that some of the best-tasting chickens were those that had been best fed and best treated. So the kind of free-range life a chicken lives does seem to make a difference on the table. It certainly does affect the price, but it's worth remembering, if you're at all concerned about animal welfare, that it also makes a difference to the chickens.

Another reason for chicken's popularity is, of course, that it is a wonderful carrier of flavours. Whether grilled with garlic and lime, flavoured with curry spices, cooked with spinach and cream sauce, or with apples or saffron, it complements and carries flavours in a way that few main ingredients do. My recipes reflect all those tastes, and include one or two new favourites, especially for poussin, mini-chickens that have been popular for years in America but are new to Britain. There are also recipes for other poultry – turkey and duck – and a few ideas for game cookery. We haven't done many game recipes on *Food and Drink* but it's an area that may well prove to be more popular in the coming years. Game has many advantages to offer; it is usually naturally reared in the wild and is low in fat and very high in flavour. It also comes in an interesting variety, which may become more available as forms of game-farming develop and reduce the price of, for example, venison in the same way that the cost of salmon dropped when it was farmed. The particularly comforting aspect of game-farming is that, while the animals are looked after in a broad sense, they are not intensively cultivated but are merely kept under control on a wild range.

Last, but not least, there is a recipe for rabbit. In many other parts of the world, particularly across the Channel, rabbit is highly regarded, often as highly as chicken, and it certainly appears on most menus. There seems to be an emotional block against eating it in Britain. It's one I don't share, and I have named this particular recipe as an indication of where I place the blame for the problem. I think Beatrix Potter has a lot to answer for – although she wrote stories about Jemima Puddleduck as well as Peter Rabbit and I've noticed no emotional commitment to ducks when suitably cooked and presented. Maybe I'm on the wrong track after all. I hope that, with the recipes for duck from both Oxford and Peking, you'll test your level of enthusiasm for yourself.

CHICKEN

Normandy Chicken

*I*n Normandy, in northern France, there is a valley called the Auge, famous for its
apples and its cream. This recipe is a product of both.
*I've adapted it to include fresh apple juice. A recent tasting revealed how superior its
flavour is compared to juice made from concentrates. You can easily see which is which
in the shops – the concentrates are declared as such on the packet. You can actually taste
different apple varieties in the fresh juice: altogether a better product. This recipe is a
wonderful mixture of richness, sharpness and sweetness.*

SERVES 4
PRE-HEAT THE OVEN TO GAS MARK 4, 350°F (180°C)

1 tablespoon oil	**1 oz (25 g) butter**
1 chicken, in 4 joints, backbone removed	**2 Cox's apples, cored but not peeled**
½ Spanish onion, chopped	**1 teaspoon cornflour**
Salt and freshly ground black pepper	**5 fl oz (150 ml) double cream**
10 fl oz (300 ml) apple juice (fresh)	**Chopped parsley**

Heat the oil in a frying-pan and add the chicken joints and onion. Cook for 10
minutes over a medium heat until the chicken pieces are browned on both sides
and the onions are translucent. Transfer to a casserole and add seasoning. Pour
enough apple juice to come almost halfway up the chicken and place in the oven
for 25 minutes. Alternatively, the chicken can be simmered on top of the stove,
in the frying-pan, covered, for the same length of time.

Meanwhile, gently melt the butter in another frying-pan. Cut the apples into
12 segments each and fry over a high heat for 3–4 minutes until golden-brown.
Keep warm.

Add the cornflour to the cream and stir together. Blend the mixture into the
juices in the chicken pan, and heat gently until the liquid has thickened.

Place the fried apples on a serving dish and the chicken pieces next to them.
Pour the sauce over the chicken. Sprinkle with the parsley just before serving.

The Elastic Chicken

This is a silly name for a very good idea. A chicken, certainly a $3\frac{1}{2}$–$4\frac{1}{2}$ lb (1.5–2 kg) one, will do more than just provide one meal, especially if you use some of the old-fashioned techniques that extract more benefit from it. You need to cut the chicken up in a particular way to begin with, and I include detailed instructions for that. The technique produces nine portions as well as the giblets and carcass. You will need to use the carcass to make stock for a soup, and the bits that come off the cooked carcass to make at least one other dish that will feed four people generously. I have two sets of crafty recipes, each of which will give you the three dishes I have promised.

If that seems to be stretching it a little, it's the reason for the name 'elastic chicken'.

First, I'll explain how to cut or 'joint' the bird.

Before beginning the step-by-step cutting do make sure your chopping-board or work surface is large enough to give you plenty of room, and do use a really sharp knife. It should be 5–8 in (13–20 cm) long and have a good handle to give a safe grip. If you know how to sharpen it on a steel, do so, before you begin.

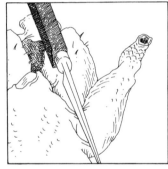 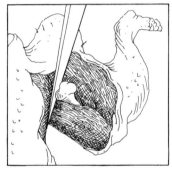 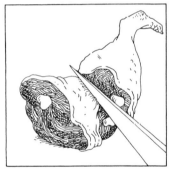

1 Cut all the trussing string off. Move the legs and wings to loosen them and remove giblets from inside the bird.

2 Pull the legs away from the sides and, cutting from the neck end as close to the body as possible, sever the skin between body and leg. Then separate the bone joint with the knife and the leg will come away from the body. Repeat on the other side.

3 Put legs skin-side down and separate drumstick and thigh by cutting firmly down the line of fat over the joint. If you follow the line carefully, you'll be amazed at how easy this is.

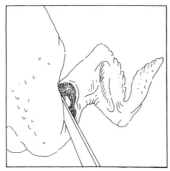 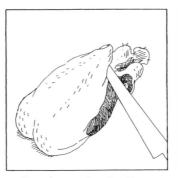 

4 Draw around the base of each wing with the knife, cutting to the bone. Twist the wing and separate the joint with the knife.

5 Cut down the fat line on the sides of the chicken breast starting at the tail end, separating the breast from the back.

6 Lay the breast flat and cut off a third at the pointed end.

7 Turn the breast over, split lengthways and you're ready!

(Practice helps. After two or three goes, you'll find it easy to cut along the fat lines and you'll be able to separate the joints with little effort.)

Here are two ways of using the pieces from the elastic chicken. The first consists of a French dish, a soup and some pancakes. The second set is an Italian dish, a Scottish soup and a Chinese stir-fry. Whichever you use, you'll feed four people very well three times over, from just one ordinary chicken.

THE FIRST SET

1 Chicken Provençal

A rich and sunny chicken casserole. It's often served with wide, flat noodles to take up the sauce, although rice is nice with it too. If you can't find passata, liquidised or sieved tinned tomatoes are an alternative.

SERVES 4

2 tablespoons olive oil

6 chicken joints (2 breasts, 2 thighs, 2 drumsticks)

1 onion, chopped

1 red pepper, de-seeded and chopped

1 clove garlic, crushed

17 fl oz (500 ml) passata or sieved, tinned tomatoes

1 teaspoon dried basil and oregano (mixed)

Salt and freshly ground black pepper

4 anchovy fillets

6 black olives

Heat the oil in a deep frying-pan. Add the chicken joints and fry over a medium heat until brown on both sides. Add the onion, pepper, garlic, passata or sieved tomatoes and herbs. Season to taste. Stir and cook over a medium heat for about 25 minutes until the chicken is tender and cooked through.

Serve garnished with the anchovy fillets and olives.

2 *Chicken and Sweetcorn Soup*

A simple Chinese-style soup that is a particular favourite with children. Use the wings and carcass to make a good stock for this. It makes a great start to an exotic meal or a good basis for a family supper with pancake rolls or hot French bread and cheese to follow.

SERVES 4

2 pints (1.2 litres) chicken stock (see p. 10)

1 x 14 oz (400 g) tin creamed sweetcorn

1 dessertspoon cornflour

1 tablespoon soy sauce

2 tablespoons cooked, chopped chicken meat (from carcass)

Salt and freshly ground black pepper

2 spring onions, finely chopped

Skim surface fat from cooled stock and discard. Mix together the sweetcorn and cornflour and put into a food processor or liquidiser with the stock and soy sauce. Liquidise for up to 1 minute, depending on preferred consistency. (If you haven't got a blender, pass the mixture through a sieve.) Add the chicken and seasoning and heat through, stirring.

Serve sprinkled with the spring onions.

3 Dijon Chicken Pancakes

You can make your own pancakes for this or buy the ready-made French ones available in packs of 10 in most supermarkets. They are a real convenience food!

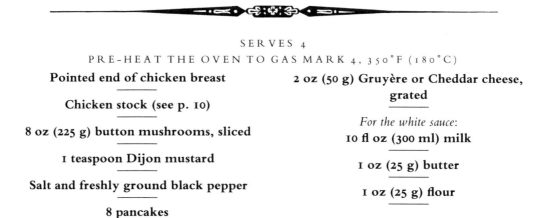

SERVES 4
PRE-HEAT THE OVEN TO GAS MARK 4, 350°F (180°C)

Pointed end of chicken breast

Chicken stock (see p. 10)

8 oz (225 g) button mushrooms, sliced

1 teaspoon Dijon mustard

Salt and freshly ground black pepper

8 pancakes

2 oz (50 g) Gruyère or Cheddar cheese, grated

For the white sauce:
10 fl oz (300 ml) milk

1 oz (25 g) butter

1 oz (25 g) flour

Cook the chicken in the stock made from the giblets and carcass and cut into hazelnut-sized pieces. Make the white sauce by putting the milk, butter and flour in a saucepan and whisking until thick over a medium heat. (This is a crafty method of making a basic béchamel sauce which I find a great time-saver.) Add the chicken, mushrooms, mustard and seasoning to the white sauce. Divide the mixture between the pancakes, piling it into the centre of each. Fold over 2 opposite sides of each pancake so that they meet in the middle. Then fold in the remaining sides to make a neat parcel. Arrange the pancake parcels in an ovenproof dish, fold-side down. Sprinkle with the cheese. Bake for about 20 minutes until the cheese is bubbling.

THE SECOND SET

1 Chicken Florentine

*This classic combination of spinach and cheese comes from Florence and traditionally accompanies fish or eggs, but I find it particularly good with chicken.
You can use frozen leaf spinach if you must, but there is no comparison with fresh leaves blanched in boiling water for 30 seconds before use.*

SERVES 4

PRE-HEAT THE OVEN TO GAS MARK 5, 375°F (190°C)

2 chicken breasts and 2 thighs	**$\frac{1}{2}$ teaspoon grated nutmeg**
10 fl oz (300 ml) water	**4 oz (100 g) Gruyère or Cheddar cheese, grated**
1 bay leaf	*For the white sauce:*
1 onion, peeled	**10 fl oz (300 ml) milk**
1 lb (450 g) leaf spinach, blanched	**1 oz (25 g) butter**
Knob of butter, melted	**1 oz (25 g) flour**

Poach the chicken pieces for 20 minutes in the water with the bay leaf and onion. While the chicken is poaching, make the white sauce by whisking the milk, butter and flour together in a saucepan over medium heat until thick. Cool and bone the chicken, leaving the flesh in large pieces. Toss the blanched spinach in the butter and line a fireproof dish with it. Lay the chicken on top in a single layer. Mix the nutmeg and 3 oz (75 g) of the cheese into the white sauce. Pour the sauce over the chicken, sprinkle with the rest of the cheese and bake for 15 minutes until the cheese sauce bubbles.

2   Cock-a-Leekie Soup

A Scottish soup of heartening flavour and some unusual ingredients. Have courage: the prunes, which can be stoned or unstoned, are traditional and the tastes do go wonderfully together. Serve with hot oat bread.

SERVES 4

Chicken carcass and wings	**8 oz (225 g) prunes**
1 lb (450 g) leeks, washed, in 1 in (2.5 cm) lengths	**Salt and freshly ground black pepper**

Poach the carcass and wings in water for 1 hour. Strain, pick the meat from the bones and return to the stock. Add the leeks, prunes and seasoning. Simmer for 30 minutes until the leeks are tender. Make sure there are chicken pieces and leeks in each serving.

3 Chinese Chicken and Peppers

*T*his is a stir-fry dish that would traditionally be made in a wok. Do use it if you've got one, if not a deep frying-pan does almost as well. Get it thoroughly hot at the beginning – the secret of stir-frying is fast cooking, to seal the food and steam it in its own juices. This should be served immediately on a bed of rice.

SERVES 4

Chicken meat from the drumsticks and separated breast joint (uncooked)

I tablespoon oil

I red pepper, de-seeded, in $\frac{1}{4}$ in (5 mm) strips

I green pepper, de-seeded, in $\frac{1}{4}$ in (5 mm) strips

I Spanish onion, in $\frac{1}{4}$ in (5 mm) strips

For the sauce:

2 teaspoons soy sauce

2 tablespoons water

I teaspoon brown sugar

I teaspoon cornflour

I teaspoon lemon juice

Cut the chicken meat into thin slices across the grain and fry for 2 minutes in the oil in the hot pan. Take the chicken out and set aside. Fry the peppers and onions for 2 minutes over a high heat, and return the chicken to the pan. Mix the sauce ingredients in a bowl until smooth, then add to the pan, stirring until the sauce thickens and turns shiny.

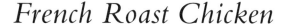

French Roast Chicken

*W*hen the French roast a chicken they do it rather differently from us. They don't stuff it with a thick bread-based stuffing and they don't cook it dry either. They put it on a wire rack, pour a little water underneath, and let the chicken make its own gravy. However, they do season it rather specially first. This is one of our favourite dishes for Sunday lunch or family occasions. An ordinary 3½ lb (1.5 kg) chicken will do four people.

You can allow a chicken cooked like this to cool and take it on a picnic or, best of all, serve it outdoors on a sunny summer's day with a big tossed salad and lots of crispy French bread, and cheese and grapes to follow. You could be miles away in the Dordogne!

FEEDS 4

PRE-HEAT THE OVEN TO GAS MARK 5, 375°F (190°C)

1 pint (600 ml) water	1 teaspoon paprika
1 x 3½ lb (1.5 kg) roasting chicken	1 teaspoon garlic salt
1 lemon	2 butter papers
1 teaspoon ground bay leaves	

Put a wire rack in your baking tin and pour the water into the tin. Put the chicken on the rack and squeeze half the lemon over it. Mix the ground bay leaves, paprika and garlic salt together and sprinkle over all the exposed surfaces of the chicken. Put the remaining half-lemon inside. Cover with the 2 butter papers, butter-side down. (I always save butter papers for purposes like this. They're better than greaseproof paper, cost nothing, and add a little buttery flavour.) Put into the oven and cook for 1 hour and 20 minutes. To check that the chicken is done, test the thick part of the leg with a skewer. When the juices are clear, it's done. If they're still pink, it needs cooking for a further 20 minutes and check again. Remember, if your chicken is larger than 3½ lb allow an extra 20 minutes per lb.

Remove from the oven and allow to stand 10 minutes before carving. Juices will have run out into the water and made a delicious light, clear gravy, while the steam from the water will have kept the chicken moist and delicious. You can remove the butter papers for the last 10 minutes of cooking if you want a particularly crisp and brown skin.

Chicken with Shrimp and Peanut Sauce

This dish has what seems at first to be an extraordinary combination of flavours, but they work very well together and produce an exotic, but quite mild, chicken dish which people who 'don't like their food messed about' eat with a certain amount of enjoyment. It comes from Brazil and is traditionally made with an oil called Dende which derived from West Africa and West African cooking. Thick, dark and red, it's used more as a flavouring than as a cooking medium. It was brought over by slaves when they were transported from West Africa to Brazil. Dende is available in this country, particularly in shops or markets specialising in West African ingredients where it's sometimes sold as 'palm oil'. If you're a traditionalist, it's an important ingredient in the dish for flavour, but I find that the chicken is interesting and delicious enough to manage very well without it. Serve with white rice. In Brazil it would also be served with cassava meal but I think we might find a crisp salad, perhaps dressed with a little lime juice, rather more to our taste.

SERVES 4

2 cloves garlic	**1 red pepper, de-seeded and finely chopped**
1 teaspoon salt	**2 tablespoons cooking oil**
4 tablespoons lemon juice	**Stock made from the carcass of the chicken cooked with 10 fl oz (300 ml) water for 20 minutes**
1 chicken, in 8 pieces	
1 large onion	
2 oz (50 g) dried shrimp	**A little Tabasco or pepper sauce (optional)**
2 oz (50 g) roasted peanuts	**4 tablespoons Dende oil (optional)**

Peel the garlic and crush it with the salt. Mix it with the lemon juice and marinate the chicken in this mixture for about 90 minutes. Finely chop the onion and dried shrimp with the peanuts – this is most easily done in a food processor in my experience. Mix the red pepper with the onion, shrimp and peanut mixture. Fry it in the oil for about 5 minutes over a medium heat in a pan which will take the chicken as well. Add the chicken pieces and allow them to take a little colour. Add the chicken stock and, if you like, a couple of shakes of the Tabasco or pepper sauce. Cover the pan and simmer gently for about 25 minutes until the chicken is cooked through. It would benefit from being turned over half-way through. If you have Dende oil and want to use it, add some now, though you might like to try it a spoonful at a time because the taste is quite strong.

Stir and cook for 1 minute longer and serve with white rice.

Chicken Pilau

While we're on the subject of chicken and rice, one of the classic food marriages, do try this one-pot mixture: Chicken pilau. It's a dish with strong traditions in many countries. Variations are cooked from Istanbul to the Burmese border, and perhaps beyond it to Malaysia. This version comes from the Afghan foothills. It's golden, savoury and a good party dish, especially if you sprinkle it with 2 oz (50 g) of crisp, salted almonds just before serving.

SERVES 4-6

1 chicken, in 9 joints (see p. 73)	8 oz (225 g) Basmati rice
1 tablespoon oil or clarified butter	15 fl oz (450 ml) chicken stock
1 large onion, chopped	Pinch of saffron powder
1 clove garlic, crushed	1 tablespoon hot water
2 bay leaves	Salt and freshly ground black pepper
1 or 2 cinnamon sticks	2 oz (50 g) salted almonds (optional)
2 cardamom pods	

In a saucepan, fry the chicken in the oil or clarified butter for 10 minutes over a medium heat until brown. Add the onion, garlic, bay leaves, cinnamon sticks, cardamom pods and rice and stir until the rice is translucent. Add the chicken stock steadily until the pan stops sizzling – you will need to use approximately twice the volume of stock to the rice. Season, stir well, and cover and simmer gently for 30 minutes. Dilute the saffron in the hot water and dribble it over the top of the dish. Replace the lid and cook for a further 10 minutes.

Remove the cinnamon sticks before serving, and sprinkle, if you wish, with salted almonds.

Stuffed Poussin

Poussin are what the Americans call spring chickens. They are small birds genetically, but even so are not allowed to grow to their full or maximum size. There is one big producer in Britain whose special stock develops good flavour and texture even when quite young, and who has developed a rearing method that is fairly humane, though it stops short of free-range by a reasonable distance. The result is that in most supermarkets you can find delicious $1\frac{1}{4}$–$1\frac{1}{2}$ lb (550–750 g) chickens that will feed two people (or one extremely hungry person). The style of the recipe comes from America where this kind of small, but succulent, bird has a long and popular history. It's a dish for special occasions, and a spectacular one at that. Mashed potatoes and lightly cooked broccoli are the traditional accompaniments in America.

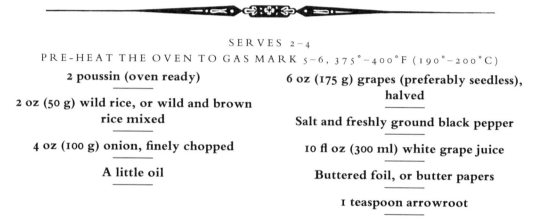

SERVES 2–4
PRE-HEAT THE OVEN TO GAS MARK 5–6, 375°–400°F (190°–200°C)

2 poussin (oven ready)	6 oz (175 g) grapes (preferably seedless), halved
2 oz (50 g) wild rice, or wild and brown rice mixed	Salt and freshly ground black pepper
4 oz (100 g) onion, finely chopped	10 fl oz (300 ml) white grape juice
A little oil	Buttered foil, or butter papers
	1 teaspoon arrowroot

Take the poussin out of their wrappings and wash thoroughly inside and out. Cook the rice according to the instructions on the packet that you buy it in – you will find it impossible to buy wild rice except in a packet with instructions. The dark-brown chewy-textured and aromatically flavoured wild rice from North America is still a gourmet item. Sauté the onion in a small quantity of oil. When it's translucent, add the wild rice and the grapes which you have seeded if necessary. Season generously and stuff the poussin with the mixture. If you have any left over, it can be baked in a small dish covered with a butter paper at the same time as you roast the chicken. Season the outside of the chicken with salt and pepper and place on a rack in a baking dish. Pour the grape juice into the dish under the rack, cover with foil or paper and roast for 40–45 minutes. Check to see that the birds are cooked right through – a skewer in the thick part of the thigh should produce clear, not pink, juices. If they are cooked, remove from the oven and allow to stand for 5 minutes while making the sauce.

You should have about a cup of liquid left in the bottom of the pan. If not, make up to this quantity with water. Blend the arrowroot with a little water in a cup and whisk into the chicken liquid. Put in a pan and bring to the boil. The sauce will clear and thicken at the same time. Cut the chickens in half with poultry shears or heavy scissors, or a very big, sharp knife.

Serve roasted side up on the stuffing, and coated with the sauce.

Chicken Simla

*T*his recipe is named after the hill station to which the British retreated when they *ruled India, in order to get away from the heat of the plains. Many of Rudyard Kipling's stories are written about Simla. I don't know whether he was ever served this dish as a young journalist there, but it certainly has all the hallmarks of Anglo-Indian cooking, using Indian spices and chutneys in a European way. It is a family favourite and you certainly should try it if you like a bit of spice but aren't convinced about a full-blown curry. It's best served with plain boiled rice and Anglo-Indian accompaniments like poppadoms, grated fresh coconut and yoghurt with mint leaves.*

SERVES 4

1 tablespoon good mild curry powder

2 tablespoons soft brown sugar (not demerara)

1 teaspoon garlic salt

4 chicken joints, approximately 8 oz (225 g) each

6 tablespoons mango chutney, with all the big bits chopped up

6 tablespoons water (traditionally some of the starchy water used to cook the rice)

Mix the curry powder, brown sugar and garlic salt together and rub the chicken pieces thoroughly with the mixture. Set aside for up to 1 hour if you can. Pre-heat your grill to as hot as it will go, line the grill pan with a piece of aluminium foil to help with the washing-up, and grill the chicken at 2 in (5 cm) from the heat for 10 minutes a side. Check to make sure it's done through by prodding the thick bit with a skewer – if the juices run clear it's cooked, if they're still pink it needs 1–2 minutes longer. The skin should brown and blister but not burn black. Put the chicken on a heated plate to keep warm and pour the juices from the grill pan into a small saucepan. Add the chutney and the water, then bring to the boil and stir. The sauce will be the thickness of single cream.

Serve the chicken pieces cut into smaller sections for serving, if you prefer, on a bed of rice. Pour over a little sauce, and hand round the rest in a sauce boat.

Spatchcock Chicken with Lime and Chilli

'Spatchcock' is an old English word for a chicken that has been split down the back and opened out like a butterfly before being grilled, or baked in a very hot oven. It's an attractive way of presenting a chicken, and produces lots of crispy skin covering a lot of succulent morsels of meat in a way that ordinary grilling doesn't seem able to achieve. The name 'spatchcock' is said to come from the fact that the chicken is cooked in a hurry: a 'despatch cock'. It's good grilled with perhaps a little garlic salt and lemon squeezed over it, but I recently discovered a marvellous combination of flavours for grilled chicken: lime and chilli. You can, if you're a garlic addict, add a little of that as well. This is a dish for eating with your fingers. I think it's nicest with a tossed green salad perhaps containing a few bitter leaves, and some flat pitta-style bread, preferably wholemeal, warmed in the oven.

SERVES 4

1 teaspoon chilli sauce or Tabasco sauce or equivalent	Juice of 2 limes
2 tablespoons oil	1 x 3½ lb (1.5 kg) roasting chicken, or, better, 2 x 1½ lb (750 g) poussins
1 teaspoon caster sugar	5 fl oz (150 ml) water
1 clove garlic, crushed, or 1 teaspoon bottled or jarred garlic purée	1 dessertspoon arrowroot or cornflour (optional)

Mix the chilli sauce or Tabasco, oil, sugar, crushed garlic or garlic purée and lime juice together to make a marinade. Split the chicken down the back with a cleaver or a big sharp knife (or get your butcher to do this for you) and spread out into a butterfly shape, pressing down with the side of the cleaver or bashing gently with the base of a heavy pan until the chicken lies pretty flat. Coat with the marinade on both sides and leave for at least 30 minutes and preferably 2 hours. Heat the grill to maximum heat or, if you prefer to do it in the top of a hot oven, heat the oven to gas mark 7, 425°F (220°C). Place the chicken on a rack in a grill pan (which you have lined with foil), pour the remaining marinade over it and pour the water into the pan, under (and not touching) the chicken. Grill (or bake) for 10 minutes a side. To see whether the chicken is done, stick a skewer into the thickest part of the thigh. If the juices are clear, it's ready. To make sure that the chicken doesn't burn before it's cooked through, you may have to lower it from the heat source, or turn the grill or oven down.

When the chicken is cooked, divide it into portions and serve on hot plates.

Pour the juices from the pan into a sauce boat and pass it separately. For a thicker sauce, blend the arrowroot or cornflour with a little water and whisk into the juices. Put in a pan and bring to the boil until the sauce clears and thickens.

Paella

This is another combination of chicken and rice, but one with rather a lot of additions. Paella, the most famous of all Spanish dishes, is a fabulous celebratory meal. It can also bring back memories of some of the better times spent on one of the many Costas. As the name implies, paella is of Arab origin, and dates from the days when Spain was ruled from the Andalusian palaces of Cordoba and Granada. Like its cousins, the pilaus and polos, it is a rice-based dish, but one that is adventurous in its mixing of flavours, meat and fish, spices and herbs. In Spain, it's eaten as a family dish, and it certainly seems best shared round a table, with time to enjoy it. It can be cooked, by the way, in any big open pan.

SERVES 6

1 chicken, in 9 joints (see p. 73)	**1 packet saffron powder**
4 tablespoons olive oil	**8 oz (225 g) French beans, in large dice**
8 oz (225 g) onions, finely chopped	**1 red pepper, de-seeded, in large dice**
1 clove garlic, finely chopped	**1 pint (600 ml) fresh mussels, washed and scraped (see p. 63)**
10 oz (275 g) long-grain rice	
1 teaspoon fresh thyme, or $\frac{1}{2}$ teaspoon dried thyme	**8 oz (225 g) prawns, peeled or unpeeled**
1 teaspoon fresh rosemary, or $\frac{1}{2}$ teaspoon dried rosemary	**8 oz (225 g) peas (frozen will do)**

Fry the chicken gently in the oil until it becomes golden, then add the onions and garlic. Measure the rice by volume, add it to the pan and then add twice the measure of water. Put in the thyme, rosemary and powdered saffron, and give the mixture a stir. Simmer for 25 minutes. You may find a lid or piece of foil helps though it's not traditional. Put the beans, pepper, mussels, prawns and peas to steam, uncovered, on top of the rice for 10 minutes.

Stir gently and serve the paella in the dish it was cooked in.

DUCK

Peking Duck

*P*eking roast duck is easy to find in this country, served with pancakes and traditional savoury plum and hoisin sauces. In China, the same duck would be used to make two further courses. If you do as they do, and add a dish of rice and a dish of vegetables, you will have three courses for four people from one bird. Peking duck uses the bird's crispy skin, but you can also eat the flesh this way – or make Stir-fried duck (see opposite).

SERVES 4
PRE-HEAT THE OVEN TO GAS MARK 6, 400°F (200°C)

1 x 4½–6 lb (2–2.75 kg) duck

1 tablespoon brown sugar

1 tablespoon water

12 Chinese pancakes (see opposite)

6 tablespoons hoisin sauce, or Chinese plum sauce, or plum jam mixed with 1 tablespoon soy sauce

1 cucumber, in very thin slivers

4 spring onions, in very thin slivers

Discard any visible fatty pieces on the duck, then place it in a large casserole and pour over a kettle of boiling water. Drain and leave to dry for at least 4 hours or overnight, but not in the refrigerator. This will crisp the skin when it roasts.

Put the duck on a wire rack over a roasting tin, and roast for 40 minutes. Dissolve the brown sugar in 1 tablespoon of water and brush over the duck, breast-side up. Roast for another 40 minutes. Remove from the oven and leave to rest for 10 minutes.

Heat the pancakes in the oven for 5 minutes. Skin the duck and cut the crispy skin into small pieces. Brush each pancake with your choice of sauce. Put a few slivers of cucumber and spring onion on top, cover with the crispy duck skin, and roll up the pancakes by folding in each side and turning them up at the bottom to stop the filling falling out.

Chinese Pancakes

MAKES 12

8 oz (225 g) plain flour	**4 fl oz (120 ml) water**
Large pinch of salt	**A little sesame or vegetable oil**

Sift the flour and salt into a mixing bowl, add the water and mix until they form a dough. Knead lightly on a floured surface and divide into 12 equal pieces. Roll out into circles the size of tea plates. Lightly brush the surface of 6 circles with the oil on one side. Cover each one carefully with another circle and roll out gently. Fry the pancakes in a dry frying-pan or griddle over a medium heat for 3–4 minutes, turning once, until firm but not too brown. Cool for a few minutes then peel the pancakes apart. They can be made in advance and stored in an airtight container until needed.

Stir-fried Duck

This is made with the flesh from the duck whose skin you ate as Peking duck.

SERVES 4

Meat from 1 x 4½–6 lb (2–2.75 kg) duck (see Peking duck, opposite)	**8 oz (225 g) bean sprouts**
1 tablespoon oil	**½ red pepper, de-seeded, in thin strips**
1 garlic clove, crushed	**½ green pepper, de-seeded, in thin strips**
Pinch of ground ginger	**1 tablespoon soy sauce**

Pull the duck meat from the bone and slice thinly. Heat the oil in a wok or frying-pan with the garlic and ginger. Add the duck and vegetables and stir-fry over a high heat for about 3 minutes. Add the soy sauce, stir and serve with rice.

In the great Peking restaurants where the duck is served as a speciality, the meal is finished with duck soup. Of course, the restaurants have the advantage that they're serving more than one duck, so your soup comes from the one that was served to an earlier diner. The soup takes 30 minutes or so to cook after the carcass is put in the water. As Peking duck with pancakes, followed by Stir-fried duck, takes a reasonable while to eat and is quite substantial, you may not mind waiting for your duck soup.

Duck Soup

SERVES 4–6

Duck carcass

1 teaspoon salt

½ Chinese leaf cabbage, in ½ in (1 cm) ribbon shreds

1 tablespoon good, light soy sauce

Put the duck carcass in a saucepan with water to cover, add the salt and bring to the boil. Simmer uncovered for 20–30 minutes. Add the cabbage to the soup. Simmer for a further 5 minutes. Serve without the bones, after the rich duck dishes, as a palate cleanser, with the soy sauce added to taste.

Marmalade Duck

As in many things, I'm obliged to Jane Grigson for this recipe, which I've adapted a little from her original. She used to make this with wild duck. The flavour combinations are classic – duck and orange are as solid a marriage as fish and chips – but it's not duck and orange in the classic manner.

SERVES 2
PRE-HEAT THE OVEN TO GAS MARK 6, 400°F (200°C)

1 oven-ready duck (wild is smaller)

1 orange

4 oz (100 g) marmalade (dark rather than jelly)

10 fl oz (300 ml) water

Cress, to garnish

Place the duck in the sink and pour a kettle of boiling water over it. Leave to dry for 4 hours, then put half the orange inside. Put it on a wire rack over a roasting pan and roast in the oven for 40 minutes. Take it out of the oven and pour away the fat from the pan. Coat the duck thoroughly with the marmalade. Pour the water into the pan, place the duck on the rack over the pan again and put it all back in the oven for 40 minutes. Remove the duck from the oven and leave to rest in a warm place for 10 minutes before carving. With the pan over a low heat, stir the juice of the remaining orange half into the water and marmalade juices to make the sauce. Decorate the duck with cress and serve.

RABBIT

Mr McGregor's Rabbit Stew

I'*ve named this recipe after the dish I'm sure Mr McGregor would have made if he'd ever managed to catch Peter Rabbit or Benjamin Bunny nibbling his lettuces. If you can put aside sentimental concern for a moment, it really is worth tasting. Rabbit used to be a great luxury when it was first brought to Britain in Norman times. Then rabbits became pests and myxomatosis followed. Now rabbit is available again, and ready to be turned into lovely rustic-flavoured dishes of some delicacy.*

Fresh farmed rabbit is delicious and good value. It has very little fat and tastes similar to chicken. If your butcher does not stock it, you can order it. Many supermarkets sell various cuts as well as frozen cubes. Wild rabbit is more difficult to obtain. Although it can be tougher than the farmed variety it is richer and more gamey in taste.

Serve with Brussels sprouts and new potatoes.

SERVES 6
PRE-HEAT THE OVEN TO GAS MARK 3, 325°F (160°C)

2 tablespoons oil	8 oz (225 g) celery, in 1 in (2.5 cm) pieces
1 oz (25 g) butter	15 fl oz (450 ml) good apple juice
A little flour	2 bay leaves
3 lb (1.5 kg) rabbit pieces	Parsley stalks
8 oz (225 g) onion, finely chopped	Marjoram
1 lb (450 g) leeks, washed, in 1 in (2.5 cm) pieces	Salt and freshly ground black pepper
1 lb (450 g) carrots, in 1 in (2.5 cm) pieces	6 small whole onions, peeled
	1 tablespoon made mustard

Heat the oil and butter in a flameproof casserole. Lightly flour the pieces of rabbit and brown in the fat over a medium heat. When golden add the onion and fry for a few minutes. Add the leeks, carrots and celery, stir well and fry for 5 minutes, then add the apple juice, bay leaves, parsley stalks, marjoram and season well. Place the whole onions on the top of the casserole, cover and cook in the oven for 1 hour. You can, if you prefer, cook the stew gently on top of the stove for the same length of time.

TURKEY

Turkey and Pumpkin Stew

This is from South America where pumpkins were first grown, somewhere on the borders of Argentina, Paraguay and Uruguay. As well as providing an ingredient in the stew, pumpkin can also be used as the cooking dish if you want to be really exotic. You don't have to be, of course. You can cook the stew in an ordinary casserole and serve it in the pumpkin, or just serve it in the casserole. If you do cook in the pumpkin, be very careful. Once the vegetable is cooked it's much softer and less rigid than when you put it into the oven and needs careful handling to make sure it doesn't leak or cause an accident.

The original recipe used veal rather than turkey and, if you like, you still can. Make sure though, that it's English veal with a bit of colour to it. As Food and Drink discovered, much of the veal sold in this country is from calves reared abroad in conditions that would be illegal here. If the calves were raised in England, or if the veal isn't pale and totally colourless, there is a reasonable chance that the animals were treated with proper care and kindness.

SERVES 8

PRE-HEAT THE OVEN TO GAS MARK 4, 350°F (180°C)

IF YOU WANT TO SERVE THE STEW IN THE PUMPKIN

2 tablespoons oil

2 lb (1 kg) turkey breast fillet, or stewing veal, in 1 in (2.5 cm) pieces

1 large onion, chopped

1 green pepper, de-seeded, in 1 in (2.5 cm) pieces

1 red pepper, de-seeded, in 1 in (2.5 cm) pieces

1 lb (450 g) potatoes, in 1 in (2.5 cm) pieces

1 lb (450 g) pumpkin flesh, in 1 in (2.5 cm) pieces, or 1 x 10 lb (4.5 g) whole pumpkin (if you want to cook or serve in the original container)

1 large tomato, chopped

4 oz (100 g) baby corns, in 1 in (2.5 cm) lengths

1 pint (600 ml) water

2 large firm pears, cored but not peeled, in 1 in (2.5 cm) pieces

10 dried apricots

3 oz (75 g) long-grain rice

1 tablespoon sugar

1 tablespoon chopped chives

Salt and freshly ground black pepper

90

If you're using the whole pumpkin, cut a lid off the top and reserve it. Scoop out all the seeds and cottonwool-like bits and scoop out the firm pumpkin flesh using a sharp knife and a strong spoon. Leave a 1 in (2.5 cm) wall all round. Reserve 1 lb (450 g) of the pumpkin flesh and use the rest to make Pumpkin pie (see p. 176) or Pumpkin soup (see p. 19).

In a large casserole, heat the oil and cook the turkey or veal pieces over a medium heat for 8 minutes until they go opaque. Add the onion, peppers, potatoes, pumpkin, tomato, corn and water and stew for 10 minutes over a moderate heat. You may need to add a little more water if it evaporates too much. Add the remaining ingredients, cover and simmer gently for 30 minutes. Season generously and, if you're using the whole pumpkin, bake it in the oven empty for 30 minutes with the lid beside it, but not on, while the stew is cooking. Pour the stew in and allow to cook on in the oven for another 20 minutes.

If you're not using the whole pumpkin, continue simmering on top of the stove for 20 minutes.

GAME

Pheasant Forestière

A marvellous dish for autumn, when pheasants come into season. Surprisingly enough, you can buy them in supermarkets as well as from more conventional game dealers these days, and many fishmongers also sell prepared pheasants. Buy one (or two) without bacon or larding wrapping; we're going to cut them up and there's no point in adding saturated fat to some of the healthiest meat available. Literally translated, the name of this dish means 'forester's pheasant' and it uses some of the other autumn ingredients that go so well with game. If you can find, or buy, wild mushrooms, do so. If not, use the chestnut mushrooms, or oyster mushrooms, that are coming more and more widely on to the market — their taste is richer than that of standard mushrooms, and goes very well with the flavour of pheasant. A cock pheasant, though slightly tougher than a hen, will feed four people, the hen by and large only three. For extra excitement, serve with a mixture of two-thirds mashed potato and one-third celeriac, the turnip-shaped celery-flavoured root. Boil the celeriac with the potato and mash them together. You don't need any other vegetables as there are plenty in the casserole itself.

SERVES 3–4

PRE-HEAT THE OVEN TO GAS MARK 4, 350°F (180°C)

1 pheasant, cleaned and prepared

1 oz (25 g) butter

1 tablespoon oil

1 large onion, finely chopped

4 sticks celery, in ½ in (1 cm) slices

8 oz (225 g) carrots, in 2 in (5 cm) long x ½ in (1 cm) wide batons

4 tablespoons red wine vinegar

Salt and freshly ground black pepper

10 fl oz (300 ml) red grape juice

Bouquet garni (2 sticks celery, 1 bay leaf, 1 sprig thyme, 4 parsley stalks tied together with thread)

8 oz (225 g) mushrooms (ceps or morrells if wild, chestnut or oyster if domestic), in walnut-sized pieces if large

10 pickling onions, peeled

1 dessertspoon arrowroot or potato flour

Chopped parsley

Joint the pheasant or get your game dealer or butcher to joint it for you. In an ovenproof casserole, heat the butter in the oil and brown the pheasant pieces over a high heat. Add the chopped onion, the celery and the carrots and turn in the juices. Pour in the wine vinegar, bring to the boil, and allow to almost boil away. Season generously with salt and pepper and add the grape juice and the bouquet garni. Bring back to the boil, cover and simmer for 25 minutes. Add the mushrooms and pickling onions and place in the oven for 20 minutes.

To serve, mix the arrowroot or potato flour (or cornflour at a pinch) into a little water to make a smooth paste and stir it into the casserole. Heat through until at boiling point when the sauce will thicken and clear.

Serve sprinkled with parsley, making sure each person gets a portion of baby onions and mushrooms and carrots as well as pheasant.

Venison in Ginger Sauce

*T*he ingredients in this dish may seem a little outlandish, but the combination of sweet and sour flavours is ideal with a rich-tasting meat like venison. The German dish on which this is based is called Sauerbraten, *and is usually made with a roll of beef like topside, so you can use that instead of venison. Serve with redcurrant jelly and mashed potatoes or noodles.*

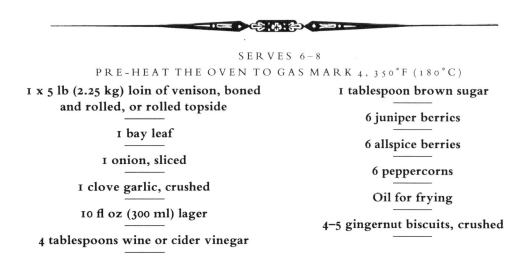

SERVES 6–8
PRE-HEAT THE OVEN TO GAS MARK 4, 350°F (180°C)

1 x 5 lb (2.25 kg) loin of venison, boned and rolled, or rolled topside

1 bay leaf

1 onion, sliced

1 clove garlic, crushed

10 fl oz (300 ml) lager

4 tablespoons wine or cider vinegar

1 tablespoon brown sugar

6 juniper berries

6 allspice berries

6 peppercorns

Oil for frying

4–5 gingernut biscuits, crushed

Put the meat into a non-metallic roasting pan. Make the marinade by putting the bay leaf, sliced onion, garlic, lager and vinegar into a saucepan with the brown sugar and bringing to the boil. Meanwhile, crush the juniper and allspice berries and peppercorns with a pestle and mortar. Put these into the hot marinade, stir, and pour over the meat while hot. Leave the meat to marinate for 1–2 days in a cool place, turning occasionally.

Take the meat out of the pan, strain the marinade and reserve. Sauté the joint in a little oil in a large frying-pan over a high heat for about 6 minutes until brown all over, then place it back in the roasting pan. Pour over the strained marinade, cover the pan with foil, and roast for 20 minutes per lb. Put to stand in a warm place. Mix the crushed ginger biscuits with the cooking juices. Stir over medium heat until the mixture thickens.

Slice the meat and serve with the sauce.

Venison Collops

ollops is the Scottish name for what the French (and foodies) call noisettes: the meat from the eye of a chop. In this recipe, meat rounds cut from the loin or leg will do very well. They are cooked quickly, so use a meat hammer to loosen the fibres and flatten the meat, as you would a beef steak. North of the border, rowanberry jelly is traditionally served with game: the bitter-sweet taste is a perfect complement to its vigorous flavours. You can use redcurrant, gooseberry or quince jelly, especially if they aren't too sweet. Mashed potatoes and green or red cabbage are good accompaniments.

SERVES 4

1 tablespoon oil

8 collops, or slices of venison cut across the grain

1 oz (25 g) butter

4 tablespoons rowanberry, redcurrant, gooseberry or quince jelly

1 tablespoon Dijon mustard

5 fl oz (150 ml) single cream

Salt and freshly ground black pepper

Heat a large frying-pan until it is searing hot. Add the oil, then the venison pieces in a single layer. Let them seal for 1 minute, then turn. Add the butter, turn the heat down and cook for 5 minutes more. Add the jelly and let it melt before adding the mustard and cream.

Season the collops, then transfer to plates or a serving dish. Stir the sauce well, boil, and pour over the meat.

MEAT

Meat has not been getting a good press over the last few years. It seems, they say, that red meat, in particular, is not good for our health; the way it's raised is not good for the animals; the way it's killed is not good for our consciences; and what it does to our arteries doesn't bear thinking about. And yet ... and yet ... you only have to visit a pub in the British countryside on a Sunday lunchtime to realise that anything but a traditional roast wouldn't get a look in. There's something about the comfort of a meat dish that (for most people) is unmatched by anything else. And it's not only comfort. The intensity of flavour that you get from meat, especially from the naughty fat that accompanies it, is more than most of our palates, conditioned by millenia of carnivorous evolution, can resist.

Nevertheless, we eat a lot less red meat these days than we did 10 years ago. By 'we' I mean us as a nation, and us as a family at home. Most of the evidence suggests that this trend, combined with eating more fresh fruit, vegetables and fibre, is undoubtedly good for our health – but only to a certain extent. Leaving dedicated vegetarians aside for the moment (the next chapter concentrates on vegetarian food), meat is an important source of nourishment for most of us. But it doesn't have to be consumed in vast quantities three times a day to provide that benefit.

Recent trends in meat-eating are very significant. Organically produced meat and meat orientated to animal welfare is appearing in supermarkets where it is regularly bought despite its premium price. And leaner meat is the order of the day, although it is not always as flavoursome as the fatter kind. People are also increasingly using meat as a part of a meal rather than as the main event, and as a flavouring ingredient rather than as the centrepiece – using it as it's used in countries like China and India and in south-east Asia for its texture as well as its taste, often in surprisingly small quantities. Some of my recipes reflect these new tendencies, some look back to the Sunday roast and the perfect way to make it.

I've brought together my favourite recipes for beef and lamb, and some for much-neglected offal. I love almost all offal except tripe, which I've never managed truly to come to grips with, although I've cooked one or two dishes that just pass the edibility test. Speaking of offal, one of the most amusing stories about the effect *Food and Drink* has had on taste was the report, still unconfirmed, that over 3000 tons of oxtail had to be imported during the week after we used it in the Oxtail casserole recipe on page 121. A whole lot of people who thought that oxen stopped at the rump steak discovered a new delicacy.

There are plenty more delicacies in the recipes that follow. Some are great *Food and Drink* classics like Steak in cream sauce and some are new friends like Venetian liver or Lamb sosaties. There are also a couple of recipes for roast leg of lamb. It may come as a surprise to you, as it certainly did to me, that in a recent magazine survey in France, the majority of men and women voted it their all-time favourite dish. You'll find the French version of it on pages 115 and 116 as Roast lamb with haricot beans. After eating it recently at an old-fashioned Parisian restaurant where the lamb was cut in thick slices and the beans were just seasoned and moistened with its juices, I know why it's so popular. Here, then, are meat dishes to enjoy with no feeling of guilt. The pleasure could be enhanced, perhaps, if they are not served quite so frequently.

BEEF

Steak in Cream Sauce

This technique, using cream as a sauce with sautéd meat, is especially good with steaks but it also works a treat with other meats and other flavours. Sauté chicken breasts, for example, and flavour the cream with chopped chives instead of mustard, or try veal escalopes (make sure the calves were raised in the humane British way) and add juniper berries or poivres rosés to the cream. It's a rich sauce, but you can serve it from time to time without too many pangs of conscience. Just think how much cream you might pour over a fruit salad instead. One thing: don't let on how easy this sauce is to make. No one can ever believe it when they taste it, and I've been getting away with it for years. This is one of the earliest of the crafty cooking recipes from Food and Drink *and it's still one of the all-time favourites.*

FOR EACH PERSON:

Salt and freshly ground black pepper	**A little oil**
1 entrecôte or sirloin steak	**2 tablespoons double cream**
Generous knob of butter	**1 teaspoon grain mustard**

Season the steak. Heat the butter and oil in a heavy frying-pan until they foam. Add the steak and fry on one side for 2 minutes over a high heat. Turn it over, add the cream and stir in the mustard. Cook for 1 minute more and serve.

Pizza Margherita, page 43.

Herbed salmon steak, page 57.

Bili bi, page 64.

Salad of scallops and asparagus, page 69.

Stuffed poussin, page 82.

Peking duck, page 86.

Venison in ginger sauce, page 93.

Beef olives, page 104.

...g lights of British
...ook to 'the original
...sed and degraded. I
...tic Hungarian dish.
...ity paprika. Known
...and rich. It's worth
...ot too difficult a dish
...g casseroles I know.
...meal brown bread and
...little sour cream.

...otatoes, peeled, in
...-sized chunks

...n caraway seeds

...ly ground black pepper

...cornflour (optional)

...wn the meat in it. Add the
onions ... ...ent, stirring from time to
time. Add the tomato pu... ... water to cover. Simmer
covered for 45 minutes. Add the potatoes to the p..., together with the caraway
seeds. Season well and simmer covered for a further 20 minutes. If the sauce is
too thin, thicken it with 1 teaspoon cornflour mixed with a little water – or
mash one or two of the potatoes well and return to the sauce.

Hereford Sausages

When we were doing a Food and Drink *sausage-testing and tasting, so many sausages had to be cooked that we had to call in somebody used to doing them in large quantities. That somebody was an army chef at Aldershot, and his method was a great revelation to me. No pan, no grill, no pricking or prodding. He used a hot oven (gas mark 6, 400°F, 200°C) and wire racks laid over baking tins full of hot water. The sausages went straight on to the racks and into the oven. The heat cooked the skins crisp, while the steam from the water plumped up the bangers and stopped the fat splashing. All in all, a great way to fry (if, indeed, frying it is)! You may only find it worth using if you are cooking a lot of sausages, or if the oven's already hot, but it certainly is an excellent method – and surprisingly similar to the crafty way to cook turkey (see p. 215).*

If you fancy doing something a little more adventurous than just plain sausages, why not try Hereford ones. I'm not sure why this recipe developed in Hereford; maybe it was designed for beef sausages made from Hereford cattle. I certainly prefer beef for this country recipe, which manages to turn sausages and onions into a square meal.

For a dish of scalloped Hereford sausages, cover them with $\frac{1}{4}$ in (5 mm) slices of potato and bake in an oven pre-heated to gas mark 4, 350°F (180°C). Or just serve the sausages plain, with mashed potato.

SERVES 4

1 lb (450 g) beef sausages	Salt and freshly ground black pepper
1 lb (450 g) onions, sliced	10 fl oz (300 ml) apple juice (preferably fresh)
8 oz (225 g) eating apples, cored and sliced	1 teaspoon dried thyme and marjoram, mixed

In a frying-pan, gently fry the sausages in their own fat for 5 minutes. Remove from the pan and set aside. Fry the onions and apples gently for 5 minutes more. Put the sausages back in, add the seasoning, apple juice and herbs and simmer for 40 minutes.

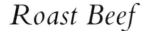

Roast Beef

To roast a joint of beef successfully, whatever the cut, only three things are essential. First, know how much the beef weighs. Second, have an oven that's hot enough to begin with. Third, allow for standing time at the end of the roasting period.

Given a choice of joints, I would choose fore-rib. I am indebted to Jocelyn Dimbleby for this knowledge, and her view is confirmed by all the butchers I've talked to. It's often the joint they keep for themselves because we, the customers, don't know enough to ask for it. A key point about beef for roasting is that it's worth buying a large joint. It's much more economical for a number of reasons, not the least being that you get much less shrinkage than with a small one: the greater ratio of volume to surface area means that you lose less beef in the roasting process, as all meat shrinks as it cooks. You are also almost certain to get better texture, moistness and flavour.

Never try roasting a piece weighing less than about $2\frac{1}{2}$ lb (1.25 kg) by this method. If you do, you're likely to end up with no more than a shrivelled lump. Above that size, allow 12 minutes per 1 lb (450 g) for cooking and another 5 minutes per 1 lb (450 g) for standing afterwards. Stand the beef in a warm place, but not the oven.

Lastly, the greatest virtue of roast beef, for me, is that it's as good cold as it is hot. It's not just left-overs you're left with, but another complete meal.

PRE-HEAT YOUR OVEN TO GAS MARK 7, 425°F (220°C)

Give your oven time to get thoroughly hot at the above temperature, then place the beef on a rack in a roasting tin and put it in the oven on a middle shelf. Immediately turn the oven down to gas mark 4, 350°F (180°C), and allow the temperature to fall with the meat roasting in the oven. The intense high temperature at the beginning seals the meat, preventing loss of juices or flavour, and the declining temperature allows it to cook without burning. The 12 minutes per 1 lb (450 g) I recommend will produce rare roast beef. If you like your meat slightly better done, medium rare, allow 14–15 minutes per 1 lb (450 g), and if you like it pretty well done, allow 17 minutes. More than that, and you'd probably be better off braising the joint, because it will start drying out irretrievably.

When the time is up, take the meat out of the oven and leave it to stand in a warm place for up to 7 minutes per 1 lb (450 g), whatever the length of time you've cooked it. This resting is crucial to produce really tender and succulent beef. Don't be tempted to ignore it, though you can, if pressed, shorten the time a little. The meat continues to cook very gently in its own heat and absorbs its own juices so that it has none of the rubbery texture that roast meat so often has without this crucial resting period. Carve it across the grain for maximum succulence and texture.

Horseradish Cream Sauce

This is a traditional sauce to go with beef in Britain, alongside mustard, but it's too often ignored because it's badly made. At its best it can have a very delicate flavour that doesn't overwhelm the beef in any way. Horseradish is available fresh or dried.

MAKES ABOUT 6 OZ (175 g)

I oz (25 g) fresh horseradish, or ½ oz (15 g) dried horseradish

I tablespoon lemon juice

I teaspoon caster sugar

I x 5 fl oz (150 ml) carton whipping cream

Finely grate the fresh horseradish, if using it, taking care as you do so because it's pretty fiery stuff. To rehydrate dried horseradish, pour on just enough water to cover, leave for 10 minutes, then drain. Make sure that the bits of fresh horseradish are really finely grated. If you're using dried, you may find it useful to stick the rehydrated mixture in a blender or food processor just to make sure it's a smooth purée. Mix the horseradish with the lemon juice and sugar, then let stand for 5 minutes. Whip the cream until it's thick, but not stiff, and fold in the horseradish mixture. Leave the sauce to stand for at least 1 hour before using. It can be put in a sealed jar and kept in the refrigerator for up to 1 week.

The fresh horseradish root, wrapped in cling film, will keep in the bottom of the refrigerator for a couple of weeks.

'Chinese' Yorkshire Pudding

Don't panic at the title of this – it's a Yorkshire pudding that's meant to go with the roast beef and horseradish sauce. But the recipe has an unusual pedigree. Jane Grigson tells the story, gleaned from the then Manchester Guardian, of a Yorkshire pudding competition held in Leeds which was won by the chef of a local Chinese take-away. A wonderful story, and absolutely true. Here is the winning recipe to prove it. It really is an oven-buster, so leave plenty of headroom.

SERVES 4–6
PRE-HEAT THE OVEN TO GAS MARK 7, 425°F (220°C)

4 oz (100 g) plain flour

2 eggs, beaten

Pinch of salt

10 fl oz (300 ml) milk

2 tablespoons beef juices or oil

Whisk the flour, eggs, salt and milk until smooth, and leave to stand for 20–30 minutes. Put a little of the beef juices or oil in patty tins, and heat in the oven for 5 minutes until hot, then take out. Fill the patty tins half full with the batter, and bake for 15 minutes or until well risen and golden.

Great British Braised Beef

Topside is too dry to make a really good roasting joint, but without question it is the best of all choices for roasting's first cousin: braising. The French make a great thing about 'braises', but they are just as traditional on this side of the Channel. The perfect solution for a family who likes its beef moist, but not pink, is a pot roast. This recipe can be adapted to other cuts – the 'aitch' bone, in particular – but topside, with its leanness and its easily sliced shape, is ideal. Mustard, the traditional flavour with beef, is built into this version to add a tang that exactly complements its succulence.

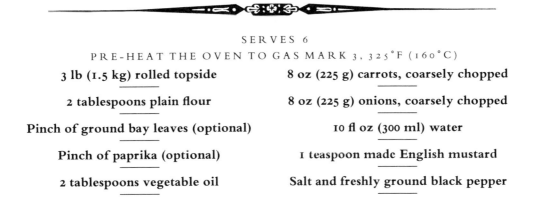

SERVES 6
PRE-HEAT THE OVEN TO GAS MARK 3, 325°F (160°C)

3 lb (1.5 kg) rolled topside	8 oz (225 g) carrots, coarsely chopped
2 tablespoons plain flour	8 oz (225 g) onions, coarsely chopped
Pinch of ground bay leaves (optional)	10 fl oz (300 ml) water
Pinch of paprika (optional)	1 teaspoon made English mustard
2 tablespoons vegetable oil	Salt and freshly ground black pepper

Heat a flameproof casserole (just large enough to hold the beef) until very hot. Rub the beef with the flour, which can have a pinch each of ground bay leaves and paprika in it. Pour the oil into the hot casserole and brown the beef quickly on all sides over a medium heat, then take the beef out and set aside. Brown the carrots and onions for 1 minute in the oil. Place the beef on top, stir the water and mustard together and pour over. Season well, cover, and cook for $1\frac{1}{2}$ hours, until tender.

Serve sliced with the juices and vegetables puréed together (for a sophisticated version) or as they come for a little rustic vigour.

*T*he following three recipes are the result of a *Food and Drink* challenge. The plan was to show that delicious meals can result from buying what's available in the shops, rather than setting off with a preconceived shopping list that takes no account of what is seasonal or cheap. With a shopping basket full of available ingredients, would it be possible to produce a *range* of suitable recipes? The answer was a triumphant YES!

The ingredients we found were the thinly cut beef slices that are now widely available in supermarkets, spring onions and red, green and yellow peppers. They are used in all three recipes, but the dishes are as different as can be. (If you can't find beef slices, slice a piece of lean steak into suitable slices yourself.)

Stir-fry Beef with Peppers

This is good served with rice.

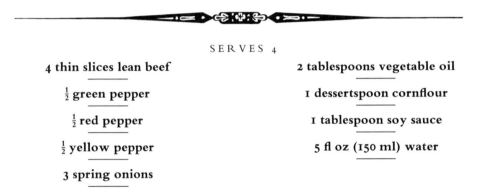

SERVES 4

4 thin slices lean beef	2 tablespoons vegetable oil
$\frac{1}{2}$ green pepper	1 dessertspoon cornflour
$\frac{1}{2}$ red pepper	1 tablespoon soy sauce
$\frac{1}{2}$ yellow pepper	5 fl oz (150 ml) water
3 spring onions	

Chop the beef and vegetables into small strips of equal size about $\frac{1}{2}$ in (1 cm) across. In a wok or frying-pan, heat the oil and add the vegetables. Stir-fry over a high heat for not more than $1\frac{1}{2}$ minutes, remove from the wok and keep warm. Fry the beef over high heat until just browned. Mix the cornflour and soy sauce with the water and add to the beef in the wok. Turn the heat down to medium, and stir until the mixture begins to thicken, then return the vegetables.

Stir all the ingredients, then serve immediately.

Boeuf Stroganoff

*A*lthough I've never been able to confirm the story, Stroganoff is supposed to have been the name of a Russian count who simply adored food cooked in the sour cream that's so much a part of Russian cuisine. This dish is a sort of Slavic stir-fry but until recently, in a slightly more formal version, was a recognised part of haute cuisine. I like it served with buttered flat noodles like tagliatelle.

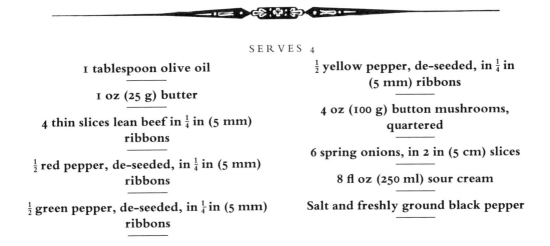

SERVES 4

I tablespoon olive oil

I oz (25 g) butter

4 thin slices lean beef in $\frac{1}{4}$ in (5 mm) ribbons

$\frac{1}{2}$ red pepper, de-seeded, in $\frac{1}{4}$ in (5 mm) ribbons

$\frac{1}{2}$ green pepper, de-seeded, in $\frac{1}{4}$ in (5 mm) ribbons

$\frac{1}{2}$ yellow pepper, de-seeded, in $\frac{1}{4}$ in (5 mm) ribbons

4 oz (100 g) button mushrooms, quartered

6 spring onions, in 2 in (5 cm) slices

8 fl oz (250 ml) sour cream

Salt and freshly ground black pepper

Heat the olive oil in a frying-pan and add the butter. When the butter has stopped foaming, add the beef. Brown on both sides and cook over a high heat for 2 minutes. Add the peppers, mushrooms and spring onions. Cook together another 2 minutes, still over a high heat.

Add the sour cream and salt and pepper, bring to the boil and serve.

Beef Olives

An old-fashioned stuffed beef recipe that's fallen out of fashion. It should be revived immediately. Here's how.

SERVES 8

4 oz (100 g) fresh, soft breadcrumbs

1 egg, beaten

Large pinch of dried thyme

Large pinch of dried marjoram

Salt and freshly ground black pepper

1 small red pepper, de-seeded and finely chopped

1 small green pepper, de-seeded and finely chopped

2 spring onions, finely chopped

A little milk

8 thin slices lean beef

A little oil

3 fl oz (85 ml) water

1 teaspoon tomato purée

Mix the breadcrumbs with the egg, herbs and seasoning, and add the peppers and onions. Mix well, adding a little milk if necessary. Place a small spoonful of the mixture on each slice of beef, and roll up. Secure each 'olive' with a wooden cocktail stick. Fry in the oil in a frying-pan, over a medium heat, until just browned. Remove the frying-pan from the heat. Add the water and the tomato purée and return to the heat. Simmer for 20 minutes, uncovered.

Remove the cocktail sticks before serving – they are very crunchy!

American Meat Loaf (Italian Style)

Meat loaf is to America what roast beef is to Britain — the great Sunday lunch — although they don't make quite such a ceremony of it as we do. An American meat loaf isn't a single recipe. It varies according to the ethnic origins of the people who make it, so the Polish version may include a little chopped sausage; the German American meat loaf may be mixed with a little beer; and the American Italian meat loaf, clearly my favourite, has garlic, oregano and Parmesan cheese as part of its make-up.
It is a terrific and very economical dish which can be sliced and served either with the mashed potatoes and sweetcorn that are traditional or, considering its origins, some shell pasta and an Italian-style tomato sauce (see below).

SERVES 6
PRE-HEAT THE OVEN TO GAS MARK 5, 375°F (190°C)

$1\frac{1}{2}$ lb (750 g) minced beef

1 large onion, finely chopped

4 oz (100 g) breadcrumbs

2 cloves garlic, chopped

Pinch of dried thyme

Pinch of dried oregano

1 heaped tablespoon chopped parsley

2 tablespoons tomato purée

1 heaped tablespoon grated Parmesan cheese

For the tomato sauce:

1 pint (600 ml) passata, or 1 x 14 oz (400 g) tin Italian tomatoes, drained and chopped

8 oz (225 g) mushrooms, sliced

1 clove garlic, chopped

Pinch of dried basil

Pinch of dried thyme

Pinch of dried oregano

Salt and freshly ground black pepper

2 tablespoons olive oil

Mix all the ingredients except the tomato purée and cheese together thoroughly and turn into a 2 lb (1 kg) loaf tin. This is only used as a mould and should be turned upside down on to a baking tray. Give it a good tap and lift off. Spread the top of the loaf with the tomato purée and sprinkle on the Parmesan cheese. Place in the oven for 45–50 minutes.

To make the **tomato sauce,** simply heat all the ingredients together until they reach simmering point. Simmer for 15 minutes, covered, then pour a little of the sauce over the meat loaf. Serve the rest separately.

Boeuf Vigneron

This is beef cooked the way it's prepared in the vineyards during the harvest. It's a rich sustaining casserole that you can make with cheap red wine or with my preferred liquid: the fragrant red grape juice that you can buy in tetra packs and which gives the dish a hint of sweetness to balance the sharpness of the red wine vinegar. It's an autumn dish, or one for full winter, when warmth and richness combine to protect you against autumn chill or winter winds. Serve with boiled potatoes.

SERVE 4–6
PRE-HEAT THE OVEN TO GAS MARK 2, 300°F (150°C)

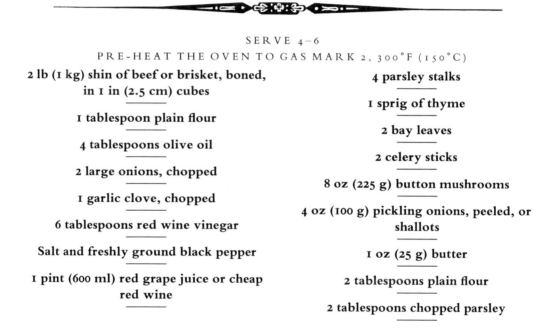

2 lb (1 kg) shin of beef or brisket, boned, in 1 in (2.5 cm) cubes

1 tablespoon plain flour

4 tablespoons olive oil

2 large onions, chopped

1 garlic clove, chopped

6 tablespoons red wine vinegar

Salt and freshly ground black pepper

1 pint (600 ml) red grape juice or cheap red wine

4 parsley stalks

1 sprig of thyme

2 bay leaves

2 celery sticks

8 oz (225 g) button mushrooms

4 oz (100 g) pickling onions, peeled, or shallots

1 oz (25 g) butter

2 tablespoons plain flour

2 tablespoons chopped parsley

Shake the meat in a bag with the flour. Heat the oil in a large flameproof casserole and brown the meat all over. Add the onions and garlic and fry over a high heat for a few moments, then add the vinegar and scrape in all the bits off the bottom of the pan (this is called de-glazing). Season, then add the grape juice or red wine. Make a faggot of herbs by bundling the parsley, thyme and bay leaves between the two celery sticks. Tie with string and add to the casserole. Bring to the boil, cover, and put into the oven for 4 hours. Blanch the mushrooms and onions or shallots for 2 minutes in boiling water, drain and add to the casserole, removing the faggot of herbs. Transfer the casserole to the top of the stove over a gentle heat. Mash the butter and flour together and stir, a teaspoon at a time, into the sauce. It will thicken and go glossy. Check the seasoning, and scatter with parsley.

Spiced Beef

*A*lthough we now tend to eat spiced beef mostly at Christmas, preserving and *flavouring the meat to keep it for the winter dates from the days when refrigeration wasn't available. Don't be tempted to buy a more expensive joint – brisket is the best of all, although silverside does work well. The great trick is to remember to turn the beef every few days, and to have the patience to wait until it's fully matured before cooking it. The delicious smell from the spicing ingredients is mouth-watering long before the beef's ready for the oven. Serve with chutney and baked potatoes.*

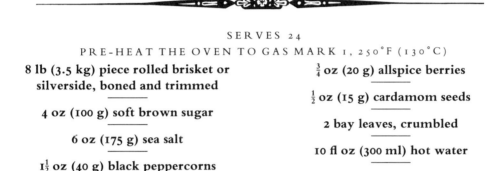

SERVES 24

PRE-HEAT THE OVEN TO GAS MARK 1, 250°F (130°C)

8 lb (3.5 kg) piece rolled brisket or silverside, boned and trimmed

4 oz (100 g) soft brown sugar

6 oz (175 g) sea salt

1½ oz (40 g) black peppercorns

¾ oz (20 g) allspice berries

½ oz (15 g) cardamom seeds

2 bay leaves, crumbled

10 fl oz (300 ml) hot water

Rub the meat with the sugar and place in a large, glazed pan or pot, not aluminium, in which the meat can lie flat. Cover with a cloth and leave in a cool place for 2 days. Crush together the sea salt and all the spices (except the bay leaves) in a blender or with a mortar and pestle, then add the bay leaves. Rub into the meat and leave in a cool place. Turn and baste the beef every 2 days for 12 days.

Take the meat from the pan and wipe clean. Place in a baking pan and add the hot water. Cover with layers of foil or put on a lid. Bake in the oven for 6 hours, then remove. When cool, wrap the beef in greaseproof paper and let it stand for 12 hours. Keep it in a cool place at all times. Slice thinly across the grain to serve.

LAMB

Noisettes with Garlic Sauce

This is a delicate and delicious dish with a hint, rather than a hammer blow, of garlic. If you can't obtain noisettes, cut your own: take out the eyes of thick lamb chops and then split them in half across the grain. To improve the 'healthiness' of the dish, use an oil such as sunflower, soya or olive oil that is low in saturated fats.

I learnt the sauce from an old culinary friend, Nico Laudenis. At the time he was running a great little restaurant in South London; now he is one of the country's top two or three chefs. His speciality is intensity of flavour, and his original version of the sauce used cream rather than skimmed milk. You can revert to the original if you like, but the saturated-fat levels rise dramatically. I think the flavour also improves a little, so it's a moot or even a meat point. This dish is particularly good served with green beans or a tossed green salad.

SERVES 4

1 King Edward potato, diced	2 teaspoons oil
4 cloves garlic, crushed, with the green centres removed	8 lamb noisettes (or chops)
10 fl oz (300 ml) milk (skimmed if preferred)	½ teaspoon dried rosemary
	Salt and freshly ground black pepper

Place the potato in a saucepan with the garlic. Add the milk and cook gently, uncovered, for 15 minutes, or until the potato is soft. Blend, process or sieve the sauce to make a smooth purée.

Meanwhile, heat the oil in a heavy frying-pan until very hot. Fry the noisettes with the rosemary for about 2 minutes on each side, depending on how well-cooked you like your meat. Season when cooked. Pour the sauce on to a serving dish and place the noisettes on top.

*H*ere are three kebab recipes from all over the world. Lamb is, without doubt, the favourite kebab meat. It can be presented in a variety of ways and eaten with a variety of accompaniments – boiled rice or pilau, pitta bread or chapattis. It can be cooked under a grill or on a barbecue. Threading meat on to sticks, skewers or, even as legend has it, on swords, and then grilling it must be one of the oldest ways men have of cooking meat. It's also an up-to-date way because it maximises flavour and minimises fat.

Indian Lamb Kebabs

*I*ndian cookery, or at least the cookery from the northern part of the subcontinent, abounds in varieties of kebabs. Sometimes they're cooked on skewers and sometimes not. Sometimes the meat is in very big pieces and sometimes in tiny bites. This is an average of many of those recipes, but not at all average to the taste. The longer you marinate the meat, up to about 24 hours, the better the flavour when you eat it. If you would like an authentic accompaniment, mix 5 oz (150 g) yoghurt with some chopped cucumber, tomato and mint leaves to serve with either Indian breads or plain boiled rice.

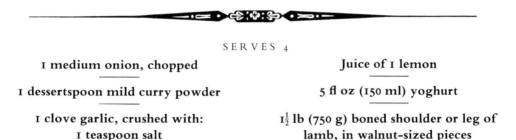

SERVES 4

1 medium onion, chopped	Juice of 1 lemon
1 dessertspoon mild curry powder	5 fl oz (150 ml) yoghurt
1 clove garlic, crushed with: 1 teaspoon salt	1½ lb (750 g) boned shoulder or leg of lamb, in walnut-sized pieces

Mix the onion with the curry powder and the garlic crushed with salt. Add the lemon juice and then beat in the yoghurt. Marinate the lamb in the mixture for at least 2 hours and up to 24 hours. Remove from the marinade, scrape off any bits and pieces and thread on to skewers. Metal ones with flat sides are best for making it easy to turn the meat as it cooks. Pack the meat on to the sharp end so that the handle can stay out from under the heat. Grill under a high heat for 5 minutes then turn the meat 120°, grill another 5 minutes and turn 120°, then grill the last little bit.

Discard the marinade.

Lamb Sosaties

The combination of sweet and sour fruit and meat is surprisingly common all over the world. This is a Cape Malay recipe that combines spices and apricots to produce one of the most delicious forms of kebab I know. The name also has roots in the Malaysian dish, sate. *This version is much more substantial though, like its ancestor, it's on skewers.*

Rice is a traditional accompaniment but I'm very fond of Indian breads like parathas *or* naans *that you can find in most supermarkets.*

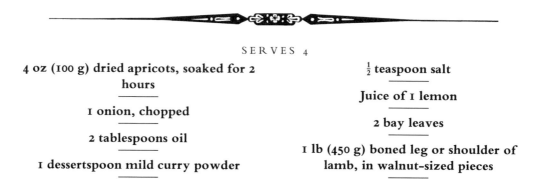

SERVES 4

4 oz (100 g) dried apricots, soaked for 2 hours

1 onion, chopped

2 tablespoons oil

1 dessertspoon mild curry powder

$\frac{1}{2}$ teaspoon salt

Juice of 1 lemon

2 bay leaves

1 lb (450 g) boned leg or shoulder of lamb, in walnut-sized pieces

Stew the dried apricots in a generous cupful of their soaking liquid for about 10 minutes until they're tender. Fry the onion in the oil over a medium heat until it is translucent. Add the curry powder and fry gently for another 2 minutes. Add the apricots and their liquid and cook for a couple of minutes more. Add the salt and either liquidise or purée through a sieve. Add the lemon juice and bay leaves to the resulting mixture and marinate the meat in it for at least 2 hours, and up to 12 hours. Take the meat out of the marinade and thread it on to 4 or 8 skewers, depending on how big your skewers are, bunching the meat together so that it forms a solid mass at the sharp end.

Grill, traditionally over charcoal on a barbecue, or under a kitchen grill that's been very well pre-heated. It's a good idea to line the grill pan with foil to catch the drips. When the meat has been cooked 5 minutes on each side it should be just pink in the middle and crisp on the outside. You can cook it a little longer if you don't like pink meat.

While the meat is grilling, put the marinade in a separate pan and bring to the boil. Simmer for 2–3 minutes until it thickens and begins to bubble. Serve it as a sauce with the crisp kebabs.

Mediterranean Kebabs

The method of cooking kebabs is very similar throughout the eastern Mediterranean and it's also very, very simple. This is a version for eating in summer and preferably outdoors, or at least at a time to recapture the memory of warmer days. Serve the kebabs with a salad made from tomatoes, fetta cheese and herbs, and with hot pittas or crusty flat bread coated in toasted sesame seeds, and even a wet December night in the Midlands can have a whiff of sun-baked hills.

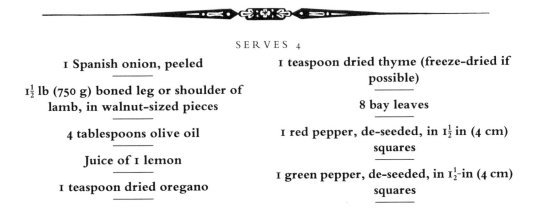

SERVES 4

1 Spanish onion, peeled

1½ lb (750 g) boned leg or shoulder of lamb, in walnut-sized pieces

4 tablespoons olive oil

Juice of 1 lemon

1 teaspoon dried oregano

1 teaspoon dried thyme (freeze-dried if possible)

8 bay leaves

1 red pepper, de-seeded, in 1½ in (4 cm) squares

1 green pepper, de-seeded, in 1½-in (4 cm) squares

Place the onion butt side down and slice ¼ in (5 mm) slices off until you are almost at the middle. Turn the onion through 120° and do the same again, then cut the last third in the same way. You will get a significant number of onion slices that you can thread on to the skewer like the pieces of pepper. Put those pieces aside, and rough chop the remaining onion including the core. Place the chopped onion on the lamb pieces, pour over the olive oil and lemon juice and mix in the oregano and thyme. Leave the lamb to marinate for at least 2 hours, up to 12 hours does no harm at all.

To cook, pre-heat your grill to maximum, line the grill pan with some foil to ease on the washing-up, and thread the assorted lamb and vegetables on to the skewers in an attractive pattern. I start with a bay leaf, then a piece of lamb, then a piece of pepper, another piece of lamb, onion, another piece of lamb, a different-coloured piece of pepper, and so on, ending with another bay leaf (2 bay leaves to a skewer). Pack the meat and vegetables reasonably tight together at the sharp end of the skewer. Grill for 6–7 minutes a side, and baste between turnings with the remaining marinade.

When cooked, the meat should be crisp and brown on the outside but still soft and succulent inside, and the vegetables should be singed but not burned.

Lamb with Egg and Lemon Sauce

Not all the lamb eaten in Greece is on skewers. There are also a number of delicious baked lamb dishes, and this is perhaps my favourite. The adaptation of the Greek avgolemono sauce is absolutely foolproof if you remember not to boil it. Creamy and sharp, it perfectly complements the dense but sweet flavour of the lamb. Rice is good with this dish.

SERVES 6

PRE-HEAT THE OVEN TO GAS MARK 4, 350°F (180°C)

1 carrot, chopped	1 sprig of thyme
1 onion, chopped	Water
Salt and freshly ground black pepper	1 egg
2½–3 lb (1.25–1.5 kg) shoulder of lamb	Juice of 1 lemon
1 bay leaf	

Put the carrot and onion into an oval roasting tin or casserole. Season the lamb and place it, skin up, on the vegetables. Add the herbs and enough water to come up ½ in (1 cm) around the meat. Cover the dish and cook in the oven for 20 minutes per 1 lb (450 g). Remove the lamb and pour off the surplus fat. Reserve and strain the meat juices.

Beat the egg and lemon juice together until frothy. Add 2 tablespoons of the meat juices, mix well, and then pour the mixture into the rest of the juices. Heat over a gentle heat, stirring constantly, until the liquid thickens and coats the back of the spoon. Carve the lamb and pour a little sauce over each portion.

Serve with the rest of the sauce in a jug.

Navarin of Lamb

*L*amb *stews play only a small part in Britain's culinary tradition, but they are a world-wide phenomenon. This one from France was traditionally made in the spring, hence its French name* navarin printanier *(spring lamb stew). That was because spring lamb and the new vegetables arrived at the same time. By my reckoning, that must have been in June, a bit late for the average spring. No matter. The combination of lamb and vegetables is a delicious one. Some versions include new potatoes but I think they're best cooked separately, and eaten in their jackets, as otherwise there's nothing to contrast the flavours against.*

SERVES 6–8

2 lb (1 kg) shoulder or boned breast of lamb, in 2 in x ½ in (5 cm x 1 cm) pieces

8 oz (225 g) onions, in ½ in (1 cm) slices

8 oz (225 g) carrots, in batons

8 oz (225 g) turnips, in batons

2 celery sticks, in ½ in (1 cm) slices

8 oz (225 g) stringless green beans, topped, tailed and cut in half lengthways

Pinch of dried thyme

Pinch of dried marjoram

Salt and freshly ground black pepper

1 tablespoon cornflour

8 fl oz (250 ml) water

1 tablespoon tomato purée

In a sauté pan or flameproof casserole large enough to hold all the ingredients, put the lamb, fat side down. Over a gentle heat brown it in its own fat for about 5 minutes. Add the onions and stir. Add enough water to come half way up, cover and cook gently for 20 minutes, stirring occasionally. Check the liquid to make sure the dish is not drying out, then add the beans, carrots, turnips and celery, and the thyme and marjoram. Season generously and bring to a gentle boil, cover, and simmer for another 10 minutes. Mix the cornflour with the water and tomato purée until smooth. Dish the meat and vegetables into a serving dish with sides.

Make the cooking juices up to about 10 fl oz (300 ml) with water, then add the tomato and cornflour mixture. Bring to the boil, stirring, until it thickens, then pour over the meat. The dish should be quite liquid – it's really a stew.

Cawl (Welsh-style Lamb Stew)

There is one lamb stew in Britain that is worth mentioning – indeed, it's worth more than mentioning, it's worth celebrating. (I don't include Lancashire hot pot as that's really meant to be cooked with mutton.) Cawl is a two-course meal cooked in one pot. Customarily, it was made from scrag end or neck of lamb, but a trimmed, boned and rolled shoulder is ideal for a special occasion. This is food from my Welsh childhood and, for me, it's one of the 'comfort' foods, something I eat when I need to nourish the soul as well as the body. Serve with potatoes boiled in their skins.

SERVES 4

2 lb (1 kg) leeks, trimmed and washed

1 celery stick

1 sprig fresh thyme

2 bay leaves

8 oz (225 g) swede

8 oz (225 g) carrots

2½ lb (1.25 kg) shoulder of lamb, boned and rolled, or 3 lb (1.5 kg) neck of lamb, cut in chops and trimmed of fat

8 oz (225 g) parsnips

Salt and freshly ground black pepper

Chopped parsley

With a piece of string tie half the leeks in a bundle that can be hung over the side of a casserole dish. Cut the celery in half, put the thyme and bay leaves in the hollow of one half, cover with the other half, and tie together with string. Cut the swede, carrots and parsnips into thick pieces. Put the lamb into a large casserole and add all the ingredients except the remaining leeks and the parsley. Cover with water. Simmer for 20 minutes per 1 lb (450 g) lamb. At the end of the cooking time, take the bundle of leeks out and discard. Chop the reserved leeks into 1 in (2.5 cm) pieces, and add to the casserole. Simmer for a further 10–15 minutes. Season.

To serve the first course, fill soup bowls with the broth from the casserole, adding a pinch of chopped parsley. For the second, arrange the meat in the centre of a large serving plate, and surround with the vegetables.

Roast Lamb

We're pretty good at roasting lamb in Britain, and we certainly produce some of the best lamb in the world. But much of our top-quality produce goes abroad, in particular to France, where they too know a thing or two about roasting lamb. My basic recipe is really French-derived in its flavours of rosemary and garlic, but the method is particularly crafty, as it has three special virtues apart from producing delicious roast lamb: it keeps the meat succulent and moist while it cooks; it makes gravy automatically; and washing-up is effortless as there are none of those nasty ground-in, baked-on hard bits to prise out of the roasting tin afterwards. The technique also makes sure that the flavour of the herbs penetrates the meat without overpowering it. I've included three different ways of serving the lamb: a Welsh way with sauce made, amazingly enough, from seaweed – don't laugh, it's wonderful; the way it is served in northern France, with baked haricot beans; and the Mediterranean way, with a kind of ratatouille. Don't forget to allow the meat to stand after roasting to re-absorb its juices and become really tender and moist. Use the same method for a shoulder of lamb, either with the bone in or, if you can persuade your butcher to prepare it, boned and rolled, the way the French like it. If you're cooking a shoulder, roast it for slightly fewer minutes per 1 lb (450 g); it's normally not as bulky as a leg, and will cook through more quickly.

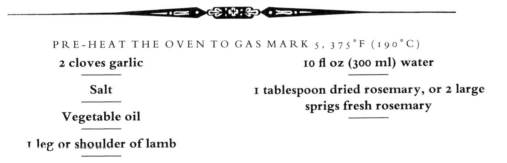

PRE-HEAT THE OVEN TO GAS MARK 5, 375°F (190°C)

2 cloves garlic	**10 fl oz (300 ml) water**
Salt	**1 tablespoon dried rosemary, or 2 large sprigs fresh rosemary**
Vegetable oil	
1 leg or shoulder of lamb	

Crush the garlic cloves with some salt and a little oil. Spread this paste over the top of the lamb as if spreading butter. Place the lamb on a wire rack and set on top of a roasting tin containing the water. Sprinkle over the dried rosemary, or arrange the fresh rosemary around the sides of the lamb. Cook for 20 minutes per 1 lb (450 g); 18 minutes per 1 lb (450 g) if using shoulder. Leave to stand for 5 minutes per 1 lb (450 g) in a warm place before carving.

The cooking juices form the basis of a great gravy.

Laver Sauce for Honey Roast Lamb

If you're going to serve the lamb this Welsh way, you may also like to finish roasting with a method traditional in Wales. When you're preparing the lamb, leave out the rosemary and, 30 minutes before the meat is done, spread 2 tablespoons of clear honey over the lamb. Allow it to form a lovely, rich, caramel-like coating, otherwise proceed exactly as above and serve the Laver sauce with it. Laver is a form of seaweed known and eaten in many parts of the world from Ireland to Japan. A valuable source of vitamins, minerals and flavour, in Britain it's most popular in south Wales, where it's mixed with oatmeal and made into cakes fried at breakfast time. In the eighteenth century it was widely used, particularly as a sauce for lamb and mutton.

1 oz (25 g) butter

8 oz (225 g) laver bread

Finely grated rind and juice of 1 orange
(use organic oranges if you wish to
avoid fungicide wax on the skin)

Pinch of grated nutmeg

Melt the butter in a small, non-stick pan. Add the laver bread and heat through gently, then add the orange rind and juice and stir until smoothly blended. The sauce will be the colour of spinach and slightly shiny. Stir in the nutmeg and serve hot with the roast lamb. Use the sauce as a gravy, rather than a condiment.

Haricot Beans

This is a wonderful dish on its own, but classically it is served with pink roast lamb in the French style to make one of the world's great culinary combinations. You really do need to start with dried haricots – tinned beans which are already cooked don't have the same texture or flavour.

SERVES 6

1 carrot, sliced

3 shallots or 1 small onion, chopped

2 tablespoons olive oil

1 lb (450 g) dried haricot beans, soaked
overnight in plenty of fresh water

1 onion, peeled and studded with
4 cloves

1 bouquet garni (sprig of thyme, parsley,
1 bay leaf, tied between 2 celery sticks)

Salt and freshly ground black pepper

3 celery sticks, finely sliced

1 tablespoon chopped parsley

In a saucepan, fry the carrot and shallots or onion in the olive oil over a medium heat for 10 minutes until they're soft but not brown. Drain the beans and add them to the saucepan with the onion stuck with cloves and the bouquet garni. Cover with fresh water to come at least 1 in (2.5 cm) above the beans. Bring to the boil for 15 minutes then simmer, covered, for 1–1½ hours until the beans are cooked. You can do this in a moderate oven pre-heated to gas mark 4, 350°F (180°C) if you prefer. Once the beans are cooked, that is soft to the tooth, season well. While the joint of lamb is resting, take 10 fl oz (300 ml) of the cooked beans and juice, and the onion (cloves removed), and liquidise or process them until smooth. Strain the remaining beans and mix the processed creamy onion and bean sauce back into the mixture. Add the celery slices and sprinkle generously with parsley before serving with the lamb.

Provençal Sauce for Roast Lamb

The rosemary and garlic flavourings I suggested for the roast leg of lamb are really Provençal. The sauce is a version of ratatouille, transformed into a sauce to go with and enrich the meat. Around Nice, this dish is often eaten with macaroniade, *fairly thick pasta tubes with the lamb juices poured over, instead of potatoes.*
This sauce is equally nice cold with cold meats. Add a small handful of black olives, preferably stoned, in the last 5 minutes of cooking for a true Niçoise flavour.

8 oz (225 g) aubergine, unpeeled, in ½ in (1 cm) dice

Salt and freshly ground black pepper

2 tablespoons olive oil

1 large Spanish onion, finely chopped

2 cloves garlic, finely chopped

2 ripe tomatoes, in ½ in (1 cm) dice

2 tablespoons thick tomato purée

½ teaspoon dried oregano

½ teaspoon dried basil

Sprinkle the aubergine with 2 tablespoons salt and leave for 20 minutes, to drain off its bitter juices. When the aubergine is ready, heat the oil in a large frying-pan. Rinse the aubergine pieces to remove the salt, pat dry with kitchen paper, and fry briskly for 2 minutes. Add the onion and garlic, turn down the heat and simmer for 5 minutes. Add the tomatoes, and the tomato purée thinned to the consistency of double cream with a little water. Turn the heat right down, season with the herbs and some pepper. Be careful about salt as the aubergines have had quite a lot on them already. Cook for 25–30 minutes, until all the vegetables are soft but still distinct.

Serve hot with the sliced lamb.

Grilled Lamb Leg Steaks

As a result of the increased interest in healthy eating, most butchers and supermarkets now sell new lamb cuts – 'leg steaks' are an example – which have a lot less fat than traditional ones. Butchers are also more willing to trim excess fat off cuts such as loin chops. You can buy leg steaks with or without the bone.

The dish gets its character from the strongly aromatic Mediterranean herbs; you can leave the lavender out, but it's a pity, as it gives a gentle, unique hint of rocky, sun-baked hillsides. You can be overcharged for a mixture of dried herbs that includes lavender, rosemary, oregano and thyme; they come in little earthenware pots and are available from specialist herb shops. Or you can make a mixture of your own.

FOR EACH LEG STEAK YOU NEED:

A little olive oil

Pinch of dried lavender

Pinch of dried rosemary

Pinch of dried oregano

Pinch of dried thyme

1 teaspoon quince or redcurrant jelly

Salt and freshly ground black pepper

Pre-heat the grill to high. Trim any fat from the steaks, and brush one side with the oil. Sprinkle with the herbs. Grill for 3–5 minutes. Turn over, lightly coat with jelly and grill for another 3–5 minutes.

Season and serve.

Guard of Honour

If you fancy a more delicate roast than a leg or shoulder, the rack of neck chops, which the French call a carre and we call best end of neck, is ideal. A single rack has eight chops, exactly right for four people. For a larger dinner party, two racks can be combined to form what's known as a 'guard of honour'. For this, ask your butcher to chine the racks so that the chops can be easily separated with a carving knife when they're cooked. Also get him to clean the thin ends of the chop bones, leaving about 2 in (5 cm) of cleaned bone so that you can interlace the two racks of lamb to form the guard-of-honour tunnel. Ask him to take the skin off the racks at the same time.

This cooks very quickly and is nice served with good-quality redcurrant jelly and a collection of lightly cooked or steamed English vegetables.

SERVES 4
PRE-HEAT THE OVEN TO GAS MARK 6, 400°F (200°C)

1 oz (25 g) parsley, finely chopped

3 tablespoons fine white breadcrumbs

Grated rind of 1 lemon

1 8-chop rack of lamb (or 2), chined, trimmed and skinned (see above)

1 egg, beaten

Mix the parsley, breadcrumbs and grated lemon rind together. Brush the skin side of the rack or racks of lamb with the beaten egg and then press on the breadcrumbs to form a coating. This will crisp and brown during roasting and become a kind of external stuffing to each chop. Place the lamb in a roasting tin (if you're using 2 racks, interlace the bones at this stage) and roast in the middle of the oven for 20 minutes for 1 rack, 25 minutes for 2. This will leave the meat a little pink. Add another 5 minutes if you don't like it like that. Allow the lamb to stand for 5 minutes while you dish up the vegetables. To serve, carve downwards between the bones with a sharp knife.

Lamb Chops Milanaise

*L*amb is not much associated with Italy, but this dish is definitely worth mentioning. While hardly a low-fat recipe, it has that very Italian virtue of spreading a small amount of meat a long way. Serve with a green salad and sauté potatoes (if you dare!).

SERVES 2–3

1 lb (450 g) lamb chops, thin cut

1 egg, beaten

6–8 oz (175–225 g) fresh white breadcrumbs

Grated rind of ½ lemon (optional)

4 tablespoons olive oil

1 oz (25 g) butter

Lemon segments (optional)

Dip the chops in the beaten egg, one at a time. Put the breadcrumbs with the lemon rind, if used, in a deep bowl. Place the chops in it and turn until well-coated with the crumbs. Heat the oil in a large frying-pan and fry the chops gently, in a single layer, for 6 minutes each side. Drain the oil from the chops, add the butter, and turn up the heat until the sizzling stops. Remove from the pan and serve. Lemon segments to squeeze over the chops are a nice idea.

OFFAL

I've said it before, but I'll say it again, offal isn't awful. It's used in some of the nicest dishes I know, and here are the recipes to prove it.

One of the problems with modern butchers is that they very often don't stock offal, nor is it easily obtainable in supermarkets. Unfortunately, carcasses are usually delivered with these delicious bits removed for the mysterious purposes of the food-manufacturing industry. We should all demand offal from our butchers – and here are some suggestions as to what we could do with it when we get it home.

Kidneys in Mustard Sauce

Kidneys are traditionally a 'man's dish'. They used to be served for breakfast in the gentleman's clubs around Pall Mall in London, but today, I think, the dictates of healthier eating have elbowed kidneys to lunch, or even dinner. This is a light way of cooking them and even people who have their doubts about this type of offal, enjoy them in this mustard sauce. In the clubs, the dish is served with little crisp triangles of bread fried in butter and with duchesse potatoes. The fried bread can be replaced with triangles of wholemeal toast which add crunch to the richness of the sauce.

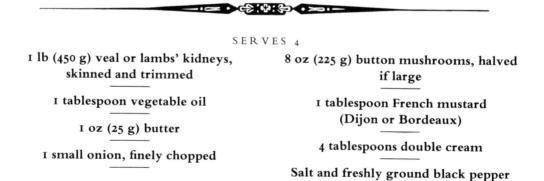

SERVES 4

1 lb (450 g) veal or lambs' kidneys, skinned and trimmed

1 tablespoon vegetable oil

1 oz (25 g) butter

1 small onion, finely chopped

8 oz (225 g) button mushrooms, halved if large

1 tablespoon French mustard (Dijon or Bordeaux)

4 tablespoons double cream

Salt and freshly ground black pepper

Slice the veal kidneys into ½ in (1 cm) pieces or halve the lambs' kidneys. In a frying-pan carefully sauté them in the oil and butter, to brown lightly, then add the onion and cook very gently for 10 minutes. Add the mushrooms and turn in the juice for 3 minutes. Transfer the kidneys, onion and mushrooms to a serving dish with a slotted spoon. Pour the mustard and cream into the pan and stir while bringing to the boil. Pour over the kidneys, and season generously.

Serve at once.

Oxtail Casserole

*I*n the north of Italy there's a famous dish made from shin of veal: osso buco. It is
virtually impossible to obtain this cut in Britain, so I've adapted the Milanaise way
of cooking it to our own oxtail – a very delicious and nutritious cut that deserves far
better than the ubiquitous soup. It's treated very differently in other countries. A French
recipe involves cooking it with grapes, and there is a splendid Indian curry. This
particular recipe has as its special charm the garnish traditionally added in Italy. A
mixture of freshly chopped garlic, lemon rind and parsley, it's called a gremolata. Even
if you're not a garlic-lover, you'll find that the combination of flavours and piquancy it
adds to the long-simmered stew is really worth trying. Yellow rice is the traditional
accompaniment to osso buco, but you could try mashed potatoes, or even pasta.
The majority of good butchers and supermarkets sell oxtail. For this recipe, ask the shop
to slice it through the bone into slices approximately 1 in (2.5 cm) thick.

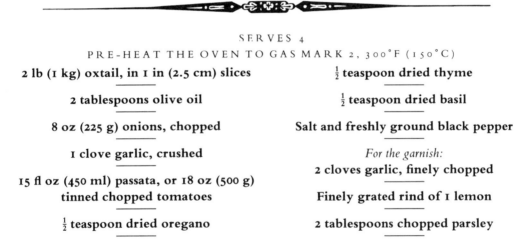

SERVES 4
PRE-HEAT THE OVEN TO GAS MARK 2, 300°F (150°C)

2 lb (1 kg) oxtail, in 1 in (2.5 cm) slices	$\frac{1}{2}$ teaspoon dried thyme
2 tablespoons olive oil	$\frac{1}{2}$ teaspoon dried basil
8 oz (225 g) onions, chopped	Salt and freshly ground black pepper
1 clove garlic, crushed	*For the garnish:*
15 fl oz (450 ml) passata, or 18 oz (500 g) tinned chopped tomatoes	2 cloves garlic, finely chopped
	Finely grated rind of 1 lemon
$\frac{1}{2}$ teaspoon dried oregano	2 tablespoons chopped parsley

In a casserole, fry the oxtail pieces in the olive oil over high heat until browned.
Add the onions, garlic, passata or tomato purée, herbs and seasoning. Cover and
place in the oven for 4 hours. Alternatively, simmer on the top of the stove, also
for 4 hours. You will need to check at regular intervals to ensure it stays moist:
if the casserole starts to dry out, add a little water.

At the end of the cooking time, place the oxtail stew on an oval serving dish,
or serve on a bed of long-grain rice coloured with saffron. Mix the garnish
ingredients and sprinkle over the oxtail.

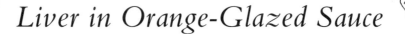

Liver in Orange-Glazed Sauce

*T*his is one of Food and Drink's *great successes. Wherever I go in the country, it is one of the recipes that people mention as having transformed their lives (family's taste, social success or sex life). Use thinly sliced lambs' or calves' liver. Cut out any tubes and, if you wish, remove any skin along the edges of each slice. The liver slices should not overlap while cooking or they will not seal well. If your frying-pan is too small to take four of them, or you want to fry more slices, use two frying-pans.*

SERVES 4

2 oz (50 g) plain flour

½ teaspoon paprika

½ teaspoon ground bay leaf

Salt and freshly ground black pepper

4 x 6 oz (175 g) pieces calves' or lambs' liver, thinly sliced

2 tablespoons olive oil

Worcestershire sauce

2 fl oz (50 ml) high-juice orange squash

Mix the flour, paprika, ground bay leaf, salt and pepper together on a plate. Lightly coat the liver in the flour. Heat the oil until very hot in a frying-pan and add the liver. Cook for 20–30 seconds before turning over. Add a shake of Worcestershire sauce and the orange squash, then fry for another 20–30 seconds. Serve with a little of the sauce. The liver should be just pink in the middle.

Fegato Veneziano

*I*talian-style *liver and onions is quickly cooked and quite different from the British version. Make sure the liver slices are thin and flat. The closer they are in shape to a postcard, the better. In Venice (where it comes from) this dish is eaten with rice cooked with green peas!*

SERVES 4

2 tablespoons olive oil

1 lb (450 g) onions, thinly sliced

4 tablespoons white wine vinegar

1 lb (450 g) lambs' or calves' liver, thinly sliced

Salt and freshly ground black pepper

Heat the oil in a frying-pan and fry the onions very gently until soft but *not* browned, about 10–15 minutes. Turn the heat up, add the vinegar, and, when it boils, add the liver. Cook for only 30 seconds, turn and cook for 1 minute.
  Season and serve.

Liver and Onion Casserole

O*x liver, plenty of onions and thick gravy is the order of the day here – but don't be tempted to revert to the canteen method of flavouring by using a beef cube. This dish has plenty of its own flavour.*
Serve with lots of boiled or mashed potatoes and some crisp cabbage.

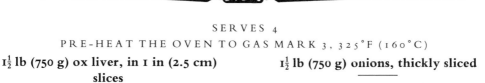

SERVES 4
PRE-HEAT THE OVEN TO GAS MARK 3, 325°F (160°C)

$1\frac{1}{2}$ lb (750 g) ox liver, in 1 in (2.5 cm) slices

6 tablespoons seasoned flour

4 tablespoons oil or beef dripping

$1\frac{1}{2}$ lb (750 g) onions, thickly sliced

1 tablespoon Worcestershire sauce

8 oz (225 g) carrots, sliced

Salt and freshly ground black pepper

Coat the liver in the flour. Heat the oil or dripping in a flameproof casserole and fry the liver steadily over a high heat until well browned. Add the onions and the Worcestershire sauce and cook for 5 minutes. Add the carrots, season, and add enough water to come just below the top of the liver and onion mixture. Bring to the boil and then put in the oven for 1 hour

Liver in Piquant Sauce

*O*ne *of the reasons why liver gets such a bad culinary press is that it is often overcooked. Although lengthy cooking is essential for some types − ox liver in particular tends to be tough − 1 minute is quite enough for a $\frac{1}{2}$ in (1 cm) thick slice of calves' or lambs' liver. You have to serve it very quickly: it is cooked so briefly that it barely heats through and therefore cools down very rapidly.*

A good sharp sauce sets liver off nicely, and the one I suggest is derived from a very easy American way of making gravy for hamburgers and other steaks that have been pan-fried in salt. Don't worry about the salt here; just dip the liver in the seasoned flour and have everything else ready to go as soon as it's cooked. It's 2 minutes from start of play to first bite, so get family or friends seated before you start cooking.

SERVES 4

1 lb (450 g) calves' liver, thinly sliced (lambs' liver will do)

Plain flour seasoned with ground bay leaves, paprika and salt

1 dessertspoon vegetable oil

2 teaspoons Worcestershire sauce

1 tablespoon lemon juice

$\frac{1}{2}$ oz (15 g) butter

Pinch of finely chopped fresh herbs (parsley, sage or thyme, or a mixture)

Coat the liver in the seasoned flour. Heat the oil in a frying-pan and briskly fry the liver for 35–40 seconds on each side. Transfer to a serving dish and keep warm. Add the Worcestershire sauce, lemon juice, butter and herbs to the pan. Stir over a high heat for 30 seconds to amalgamate, then pour over the liver and serve immediately.

Gratin of Sweetbreads

Sweetbreads have rarely enjoyed any kind of culinary success in Britain. This is a great pity: of all offal, they are the most delicate, easily digested and least capable of giving offence. In other countries they are used in a wide variety of ways. Their creamy smoothness sometimes enhances pâtés or terrines; and at other times they are pressed, breadcrumbed and fried to make crispy little cutlets, or threaded on to skewers to make exotic kebabs. Sweetbreads, especially lamb ones, imported from New Zealand, are available in supermarkets.

Prepared in small quantities and baked in tiny gratin or ramekin dishes, this gratin makes a very rich and filling first course for a grand dinner party. As a main dish, I think nothing goes with it quite so well as freshly cooked leaf spinach, lightly buttered and generously peppered.

SERVES 2 AS A MAIN COURSE, 4 AS A STARTER
PRE-HEAT THE OVEN TO GAS MARK 5, 375°F (190°C)

1 lb (450 g) sweetbreads

Salted water

1 tablespoon lemon juice

2 oz (50 g) Cheddar or Gruyère cheese, grated

For the sauce:

10 fl oz (300 ml) milk

1½ tablespoons plain flour

1 oz (25 g) butter

Pinch of English mustard

Wash the sweetbreads carefully and soak in cold water for 10 minutes. Drain, and poach in plenty of salted water with the lemon juice for about 10 minutes, until tender. Drain and cool, then trim and cut into walnut-sized pieces.

Make up a thick white sauce with the milk, flour, butter and mustard, whisking together over heat until the sauce is thick and shiny. Mix the sweetbreads into the sauce and pour into a gratin dish. Sprinkle with the cheese and bake in the top of the oven for about 15 minutes, until brown and bubbling.

Serve immediately.

Vegetarian Dishes

There are claimed to be two million vegetarians in Britain and at least three or four times that number of people are what's known in the trade as 'demi-veg': they don't eat red meat – or sometimes any meat at all – but only a little fish. The days when you could, according to popular mythology, tell vegetarians by the fact that they wore socks with their sandals are certainly long past. I'm not vegetarian but I'm very sympathetic to people who are, especially those who don't eat meat for moral or ethical reasons, and I have a couple of daughters who are in the demi-veg category. With so many of us eating no meat, less meat – or, perhaps, meat less often – main-course dishes without meat or fish become important. At first, especially if you're converting to vegetarianism, it seems an almost impossible task to provide enough variety with vegetables alone. In fact, that's not the case. There are two ways of approaching meatless dishes. The first is the substitution method: chilli without the carne – even, although not in this book, the 'vegeburger'. It's a perfectly good route to go down, especially if some members of the family are not yet convinced that they should give up the use of their canines.

The second is to base dishes on ones from the many cuisines that are vegetarian by choice or provision and effectively ignore the existence of meat (or fish). Vegetable couscous from North Africa, Gado Gado salad from south-east Asia and Potato tortilla from Spain all fit the 'meat – I didn't know it existed!' style of cooking. On *Food and Drink* we tend to concentrate on dishes like these when we answer the increasing requests, indeed demands, for ever more vegetarian dishes.

As vegetarianism has become more widespread, it has become increasingly acceptable. There was a time when people were horrified at the thought of a vegetarian coming to a meal. Today, there are few dinner parties that don't include one or more guests with strong ideas on what they do, or don't, care to eat. This is only a problem if every dish in every course is relentlessly meat-rich: few vegetarians will object to concentrating on the meatless dishes in a meal. However, if you want to serve a main course which everyone, vegetarian or carnivore, will tuck into with enthusiasm, try the Spinach and cheese pancakes or the Vegetarian cassoulet and see how well you get on.

All the dishes in this chapter can be served on their own or, if you wish, be combined with other vegetables or salads to make larger, more substantial – or simply more varied – meals.

Spinach and Cheese Pancakes

These are a meal in their own right: a spectacular dinner-party piece that will feed six ordinary, or four greedy, people. You can cheat a little by buying ready-made French crêpe pancakes, available in packets of 10. They are 15 in (38 cm) across, so the dish really looks astonishing.

SERVES 6

PRE-HEAT THE OVEN TO GAS MARK 6, 400°F (200°C)

2 lb (900 g) fresh spinach, washed, or 1½ lb (750 g) frozen spinach

2 oz (50 g) cornflour

2 oz (50 g) butter

1 pint (600 ml) milk

1 teaspoon French Dijon mustard

8 oz (225 g) Gruyère or Cheddar cheese

Salt and freshly ground black pepper

4 tablespoons grated Parmesan cheese

10 pancakes, 10 in (25 cm) or more across

Cook the fresh spinach in a very little water for 5 minutes. (If using frozen spinach, defrost and heat it.) Make a cheese sauce by whisking the cornflour and butter into the cold milk in a saucepan and continuing to whisk regularly as you bring it to the boil. Add the mustard and Gruyère or Cheddar cheese, season and heat, without boiling, for 2 minutes. Mix half the mixture with the spinach.

On an ovenproof plate at least 1 in (2.5 cm) larger than the pancakes, lay a pancake. Spread it with 3 dessertspoonfuls of the spinach mixture and put another pancake on top. Continue doing this, on and up, finishing with a pancake. Pour the rest of the sauce over the top and spread it as if icing a cake. Sprinkle with the Parmesan cheese and bake for 20 minutes or until heated through and browned on top.

To serve, slice the pancakes into wedges like a cake. This needs nothing with it but a fork and a healthy appetite.

Mushroom and Potato Gratin

This is the ultimate way of stretching mushrooms. A few wild ones will vastly improve this dish, and the combination of golden, creamy potatoes and delicate, earthy mushrooms seems perfect. Eat this with hot French bread, it's far too good to serve with other strongly flavoured food.

Dried mushrooms are available from good delicatessens or Chinese or Indian grocers.

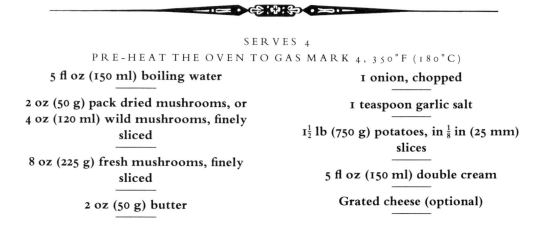

SERVES 4

PRE-HEAT THE OVEN TO GAS MARK 4, 350°F (180°C)

5 fl oz (150 ml) boiling water

2 oz (50 g) pack dried mushrooms, or 4 oz (120 ml) wild mushrooms, finely sliced

8 oz (225 g) fresh mushrooms, finely sliced

2 oz (50 g) butter

1 onion, chopped

1 teaspoon garlic salt

1½ lb (750 g) potatoes, in $\frac{1}{8}$ in (25 mm) slices

5 fl oz (150 ml) double cream

Grated cheese (optional)

Pour the boiling water on to the dried mushrooms and soak for 10 minutes, then drain and reserve the water. Slice finely and fry them, or the wild mushrooms if you are using them, with the fresh mushrooms in the butter, together with the onion and garlic salt, for 2 minutes over a medium heat. Place half the potatoes in a buttered baking dish. Spread the mushroom and onion mixture over the potatoes and then cover this with the remaining potatoes. Mix the mushroom water with the cream and pour it over. Top with grated cheese if desired. Bake for 1 hour.

Stuffed Fennel

Fennel is becoming commonplace in greengrocers and on supermarket shelves. It looks like a plump celery, and has very much the same texture, but its subtle, sweet aniseed flavour is quite different. This type of fennel, also known as Florence fennel, was first grown in Italy and, appropriately enough, this is an Italian way of cooking it. In Italy they'd use riccota, which is occasionally available in supermarkets in this country. Stuffed fennel makes a light first course, or a main course if served in double portions.

PRE-HEAT THE OVEN TO GAS MARK 5, 375°F (190°C)

SERVES 4

1 head fennel, or 2 small heads

1 teaspoon dried oregano

8 oz (225 g) cream cheese or smooth cottage cheese

4 tablespoons breadcrumbs

1 tablespoon olive oil

1 tablespoon grated Parmesan cheese

Trim the fennel and pull it apart into separate stalks. These look like deep spoons with short handles. Place the 4 largest 'bowl up' in a fireproof dish small enough to keep them stable. Mix the oregano, cream or cottage cheese and breadcrumbs and divide into 4. Place each portion in a fennel 'bowl' and sprinkle with the oil and Parmesan cheese. Bake for 20 minutes. Serve either hot or cold.

Tossed Pasta with Three Vegetables

This is a pasta dish in what might be called the new style – served without thick or creamy sauces. Although the flavours of the vegetables aren't extraordinary in themselves, they blend beautifully and add crunch to the pasta. Eat on its own as a main course, followed by a salad and preceded by soup for a contrast in texture.

SERVES 4

1 lb (450 g) pasta shapes (bows or spirals are fine)

1 tablespoon oil

8 oz (225 g) carrots, in 2 in (5 cm) lengths

8 oz (225 g) mange tout, topped and tailed

8 fl oz (250 ml) water

8 oz (225 g) spring onions, in 2 in (5 cm) lengths

2 tablespoons light soy sauce

Cook the pasta until just tender in plenty of water, then drain. In a big frying-pan or wok, heat the oil then add the carrots and mange tout and stir-fry over a high heat for 1 minute. Pour in the water and boil until it evaporates, about 5 minutes. Add the onions and toss. Add the pasta and soy sauce and toss again for 1 minute before serving.

Vegetarian Cassoulet

*C*assoulet is one of the great dishes of French cooking. As with so many of them, it began as a rustic peasant meal in the Languedoc – the south-west of France, near Carcassonne. It is traditionally a meal-in-a-pot, a mixture of haricot beans (dried white beans), various meats, tomatoes and flavourings, baked for several hours to produce a very rich, thick, savoury stew. This version, while maintaining the slow baking and rich savouriness, does not use meat. I replace it with a variety of vegetables and nuts to produce the textures and nutrition the meat normally contributes. I and all my family and friends actually prefer this vegetarian version.

With or without meat, a cassoulet is a filling dish. Serve it in soup plates or bowls, with a little French bread, and nothing much to follow except a salad and perhaps cheese and fruit. For extra spiciness, you could add some Tabasco sauce to the cassoulet.

Be sure to allow yourself enough time to soak the haricot beans and chestnuts; use a large bowl for the beans as they swell to almost double their size.

SERVES 4

PRE-HEAT THE OVEN TO GAS MARK 4, 350°F (180°C)

1 lb (450 g) dried haricot beans, soaked for 6 hours	4 oz (100 g) dried chestnuts, soaked for 4 hours
5 fl oz (150 ml) olive oil	$\frac{1}{2}$ head fennel, sliced, or celery, chopped
4 tablespoons thick tomato purée	8 oz (225 g) button mushrooms
1 medium onion, studded with cloves	1 large beefsteak tomato, chopped
1 clove garlic, crushed	1 tablespoon soft dark brown sugar
Large pinch of dried oregano	$1\frac{1}{2}$ teaspoons salt
Large pinch of dried thyme	Freshly ground black pepper
2 bay leaves	3 tablespoons fresh wholemeal breadcrumbs

Drain the haricot beans, then put in a large saucepan or flameproof casserole. Add the olive oil, tomato purée, onion, garlic, herbs and bay leaves, with water to cover. Bring to the boil for 15 minutes, then cook, covered, for 2–2½ hours. You can, if you like, simmer, covered, over a very low heat on top of the stove for the same length of time. (It is important *not* to add any salt at this stage as it affects the cooking of the beans.)

Remove from the heat and discard the onion. Drain the chestnuts and put in the saucepan with the fennel or celery, button mushrooms, tomato, sugar, salt and pepper to taste. Sprinkle with the breadcrumbs and continue cooking in the oven for 1 hour.

Glamorgan Sausages

It may come as a surprise to find sausages in this chapter, but the recipe contains no meat at all. The sausages are really Welsh cheese rissoles, originally made with the now defunct Glamorgan cheese. Savoury and delicious, they are as appealing to meat-eaters as they are to vegetarians.

I make these sausages with Cheddar or Lancashire cheese; it doesn't matter if it has gone hard, but blue cheeses like Stilton won't do. Use fresh breadcrumbs, or bread soaked in milk: golden crumbs out of a packet are not right for this (or most other recipes).

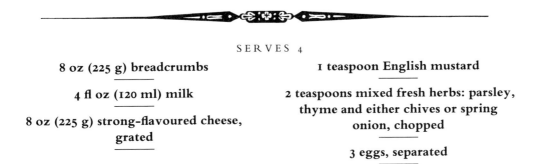

SERVES 4

8 oz (225 g) breadcrumbs

4 fl oz (120 ml) milk

8 oz (225 g) strong-flavoured cheese, grated

1 teaspoon English mustard

2 teaspoons mixed fresh herbs: parsley, thyme and either chives or spring onion, chopped

3 eggs, separated

Soak 6 oz (175 g) of the breadcrumbs in the milk, reserving 2 oz (50 g) for later. Mix the cheese, milk-soaked breadcrumbs, mustard, herbs and egg yolks together. Knead well and divide into 8. Roll into sausage shapes and firm with your hands.

Beat the egg whites, roll the sausages first in them and then in the remaining 2 oz (50 g) crumbs. Leave to set for 10 minutes. Fry for 10–12 minutes over a low heat as for conventional sausages and watch they don't 'catch'.

Savoury Dutch Pancakes

*I*f you thought pancakes were thin, lacy little things (like French crêpes or our slightly
more solid arrangements for Shrove Tuesday), this will dispel those illusions. Holland
regards itself as the home of pancakes, and has a huge variety of them. This one is eaten
very much like a pizza in Italy, or a tortilla in Spain: as a meal cooked on its own,
and in its own right. The method is simple, but getting the batter to the right consistency
can be tricky: the type of flour you use affects the process because some absorb more water
than others. I've suggested a volume of liquid, but you may find that a little less or a
little more is needed to make the 'single cream' consistency for the batter. You can use
wholemeal flour if you want a little more fibre, but it's not traditional in Holland.
To serve, cut the pancake in wedges like a cake and have a green salad to follow. It's
surprisingly solid and filling.

SERVES 4

6 oz (175 g) plain flour	1 oz (25 g) butter
2 eggs	4 oz (100 g) mushrooms, sliced
1 teaspoon vegetable oil	4 oz (100 g) frozen peas
Approximately 10 fl oz (300 ml) water or milk	4 oz (100 g) Gouda cheese, diced
1 shallot or small onion, chopped	1 small green or red pepper, de-seeded and chopped
1 tablespoon vegetable oil	Salt and freshly ground black pepper

To make the batter, mix the flour, eggs and the teaspoon of oil together, then
beat in enough water or milk to make a 'single cream' consistency. Set aside to
rest for 30 minutes.

Fry the shallot or onion in a pan with the remaining oil and the butter for 2
minutes, over a medium heat. Add the batter to the pan, let it cook for 1 minute,
also over a medium heat, then add the mushrooms, peas, cheese and green or
red pepper. Press into the batter, season, cover and cook gently for 6 minutes,
until the batter is set. You can grill the top under a hot grill for 2 minutes, if
you prefer.

Gado Gado

*T*his superb dish comes from Indonesia. While Indonesian food is normally served in one course, with lots of different dishes on the table, Gado Gado is often eaten on its own, although rice cakes are sometimes used to bulk it out. It's really a lunchtime dish or a snack meal. With its spicy, peanut sauce, it is surprisingly filling and satisfying and, as with so many of the 'snack meals' of south-east Asia, is much more accessible to Western palates than some of the main-course dishes with their more intense and fiery flavourings. You can make this dish with whatever vegetables you have to hand; the only essentials are salad greens or blanched cabbage leaves, hard-boiled eggs and the peanut sauce. Bean sprouts, which are now widely available, are a traditional addition; you will need about 4 oz (150 g). If you're going to eat the sprouts raw, make sure you wash them thoroughly and pick off any brown bits. You can eat Gado Gado as a salad or, with other south-east Asian dishes, as part of a large meal.

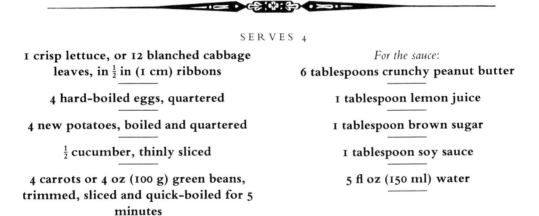

SERVES 4

1 crisp lettuce, or 12 blanched cabbage leaves, in $\frac{1}{2}$ in (1 cm) ribbons

4 hard-boiled eggs, quartered

4 new potatoes, boiled and quartered

$\frac{1}{2}$ cucumber, thinly sliced

4 carrots or 4 oz (100 g) green beans, trimmed, sliced and quick-boiled for 5 minutes

For the sauce:

6 tablespoons crunchy peanut butter

1 tablespoon lemon juice

1 tablespoon brown sugar

1 tablespoon soy sauce

5 fl oz (150 ml) water

Arrange the lettuce or cabbage leaves on a serving plate, with the eggs and potatoes. Decorate with the cucumber and carrots or beans. Chill for 30 minutes. Mix all the sauce ingredients in a saucepan and bring gently to the boil. Don't panic: it becomes a smooth, shiny and scrumptious sauce to pour warm over the salad.

Cheese Fondue

A Swiss-style cheese fondue is a marvellous ice-breaker at a party, to set a happy mood. A large, bubbling pot of rich cheese sauce is set in the middle of the table and guests are given long forks (you can buy special fondue fork sets) with which to spear chunks of French bread or, these days, very often raw vegetables or even fruit, then dip them in the cheese sauce and convey them to their mouths. The old rules used to say that if a gentleman lost his bit of bread in the sauce he had to buy the company a bottle of wine, and if a lady lost hers she had to give all the gentlemen a kiss. That seems sexist to me as I like kissing, and I suggest you make up your own forfeits to add to the fun. Make sure, however, that everybody knows what the rules are before they start dipping, so that they can decide whether or not to lose their bits of bread, etc. Serve with some bread and crispy vegetables such as cauliflower florets, small chunks of carrot and button mushrooms.

Keep the sauce warm on a traditional fondue night-light burner, or in a modern electric frying-pan turned down to the lowest possible heat. If you are using a fondue pan, check that it is secure and firm before people begin dipping in.

SERVES 12–16

12 oz (350 g) Gruyère cheese, grated

12 oz (350 g) Emmental cheese, grated

10 fl oz (300 ml) apple juice

1 teaspoon garlic salt, or 1 garlic clove crushed with salt

1 tablespoon cornflour

10 fl oz (300 ml) milk

In a fondue pan, gently melt the Gruyère and Emmental cheese in the apple juice with the garlic salt or crushed garlic. Whisk the cornflour into the milk and add to the fondue pan when the cheese starts to go runny. Heat gently, stirring, until the sauce thickens and bubbles. Do not overheat.

Potato Tortilla

'*Tortilla*' is the Spanish name for a Spanish omelette. In our family, it's also known as a 'Saturday omelette' because it can use up the bits and pieces that the week has left in the refrigerator. Classically made, it has a robustness and flavour that remind you just how good basic cooking with fine ingredients can be. It's worth finding organic potatoes and onions and using free-range eggs for this. Serve with a salad.

SERVES 4

3 tablespoons olive oil

1 lb (450 g) potatoes, peeled and parboiled for 8 minutes

1 large onion, thinly sliced

1 tablespoon chopped parsley

8 eggs, beaten

Salt and freshly ground black pepper

Heat the oil in a large heavy frying-pan. Add the potatoes, cut into walnut-sized pieces, and fry for 5 minutes. Add the onion and fry gently for another 5 minutes until the whole mixture is soft but not disintegrated. Add half the parsley to the eggs and pour the mixture over the vegetables. Cook over a medium heat, stirring with a fork, until the whole lot starts to set. The potato, onion and egg mixture should be fairly thoroughly mixed. When it starts to set, stop stirring and finish under a hot grill for $1-1\frac{1}{2}$ minutes until the top is starting to brown and bubble. Add the rest of the parsley and season with salt and pepper.

Put the pan on the table (on a heat-proof pad) and cut the tortilla into wedges like a cake.

Vegetarian Couscous

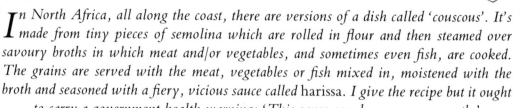

*I*n North Africa, all along the coast, there are versions of a dish called 'couscous'. It's made from tiny pieces of semolina which are rolled in flour and then steamed over savoury broths in which meat and/or vegetables, and sometimes even fish, are cooked. The grains are served with the meat, vegetables or fish mixed in, moistened with the broth and seasoned with a fiery, vicious sauce called harissa. I give the recipe but it ought to carry a government health warning: 'This sauce can damage your mouth.'
Different towns, different families and, especially, different countries use different ingredients for their couscous sauces and broths. This vegetarian version is traditional in Algeria, but some of the vegetables have been replaced with ones we can find more easily in Britain. Although it originates in a hot country, it's a warming dish for our colder climate and makes a marvellous party centrepiece. It can be cooked in large quantities without too much effort or expense. Authentic equipment is available but the method I describe below – using a saucepan and a colander – will do just as well.
To eat, take a portion of the couscous, a selection of the vegetables, a pinch of harissa and enough stock to moisten it to your taste. Some people like eating it very runny like a soup, others very dry. Either way, it's an amazing combination of richness and delicacy.

SERVES 4–6

6 oz (175 g) chick peas, soaked for 4 hours, drained and boiled for 1 hour until tender

1 lb (450 g) onions, chopped

8 oz (225 g) carrots, chopped

8 oz (225 g) green beans, chopped

8 oz (225 g) courgettes, chopped

8 oz (225 g) tomatoes, chopped

1 clove garlic, crushed

1 teaspoon turmeric

1 teaspoon salt

1 teaspoon freshly ground black pepper

A little oil (optional)

1 lb (450 g) couscous (this can be bought in health food shops, usually 'pre-cooked')

3 tablespoons olive oil

18 fl oz (550 ml) warm water

For the harissa:
2 cloves garlic

2 teaspoons chilli powder

$\frac{1}{2}$ teaspoon ground cumin

Choose a large saucepan into which a colander (or sieve) will fit comfortably, leaving at least 6 in (15 cm) underneath. Put the chick peas, onions, carrots, green beans, courgettes, tomatoes, garlic, turmeric and salt and pepper into the saucepan. Cover with at least 2 in (5 cm) water. (If you want a very rich dish, fry the onions and garlic first for 3–4 minutes in a little oil, then add the other vegetables.) Put the colander on top of the saucepan. In a separate bowl, stir the couscous with the olive oil and 10 fl oz (300 ml) of the warm water. The couscous will absorb the water remarkably easily and start to swell up. Keep stirring it so it doesn't go lumpy but forms a smooth mixture, then pour into the colander. (Don't worry, it won't fall through the holes.) Put the saucepan and colander over a fairly high heat until the vegetable mixture boils, then put a tightly fitting lid or tea towel over the top and steam for 30 minutes, until the couscous is thoroughly hot.

Take the couscous out of the colander and stir in the remaining 8 fl oz (225 ml) warm water, which it will again absorb. Return to the colander and steam for another 10 minutes. (The couscous should now be the size of rice grains.)

To serve, put the couscous in a large pile on a serving dish and make a big well in the middle. Drain the vegetables, reserving their stock and place in the well. Moisten the couscous with some of the stock.

To make the **harissa**, mix 8 fl oz (225 ml) of the stock with the garlic, chilli powder and cumin in a blender or food processor until thoroughly smooth. Serve in a separate bowl.

Vegetable Lasagne

Many lasagnes made in Italy contain no meat at all. Some are made with fish and some with vegetables, but all combine a white, creamy sauce and a red, spicy one with the broad sheets of pasta that give the dish its name. The chunks of vegetables in my vegetarian version are great for adding a substantial bite to what can sometimes, even in the meat version, be a rather insubstantial dish.

SERVES 4

PRE-HEAT THE OVEN TO GAS MARK 5, 375°F (190°C)

12 oz (350 g) green lasagne

1 pint (600 ml) semi-skimmed milk

$2\frac{1}{2}$ oz (65 g) butter

$2\frac{1}{2}$ tablespoons flour

Salt and freshly ground black pepper

Pinch of ground nutmeg (optional)

1 large onion, chopped

1 clove garlic, chopped

2 tablespoons olive oil

1 x 14 oz (400 g) tin Italian chopped tomatoes

1 heaped tablespoon concentrated tomato purée

Pinch of dried basil or oregano

1 head fennel, finely chopped

1 lb (450 g) cauliflower florets

4 oz (100 g) grated cheese (preferably Parmesan)

Put the lasagne into a flat baking dish and pour a kettle of boiling water over them: this avoids the tedious business of having to boil the pasta. To make the white sauce, put the milk, butter and flour together in a non-stick pan. Whisk briskly while still cold and heat rapidly, whisking as you go, until the sauce thickens and goes smooth and shiny. Check for seasoning and, if you like, add a little nutmeg for extra flavour.

Fry the onion and garlic in the olive oil. Add the Italian tomatoes and tomato purée and the basil or oregano. Add the fennel to the tomato sauce. Simmer, uncovered, for 10 minutes.

In a large baking dish, at least 1 in (2.5 cm) deep, spread the cauliflower florets across the base and pour over half the white sauce. Put on a layer of lasagne, taking it from the water which should have made it reasonably soft and pliable. On top of the lasagne, put half the tomato and fennel sauce, another layer of lasagne, another layer of tomato and fennel, and the last half of the white sauce directly on top of that. Sprinkle with the cheese and bake for 30 minutes.

Vegetable Curry

*A*s most of the population of India is vegetarian, or inclined to vegetarianism, vegetable curries are hardly a surprise. However, in Britain we tend to regard them only as an accompaniment to one of the meat dishes that are part of every high street Indian restaurant's repertoire. In fact, many of them are extremely nutritious, as well as delicious. The one I've chosen has potatoes and chick peas as its main ingredients with spices and one or two side-note vegetables. Serve the curry with plenty of rice, either boiled or pilau (that is, fried in a little butter before the water is added), chutney and a cucumber and mint salad on the side. A few crispy poppadoms make a terrific texture contrast; ready-made ones are widely available in supermarkets.

SERVES 4

1 large onion, finely chopped

1 clove garlic, finely chopped

2 tablespoons oil

2 teaspoons ground coriander

1 teaspoon ground cumin

1 teaspoon ground ginger

1 teaspoon turmeric

1 teaspoon garam masala

(or substitute for the spices, 1 tablespoon mild curry powder)

10 fl oz (300 ml) water

1 lb (450 g) potatoes, in 1 in (2.5 cm) dice

6 oz (175 g) chick peas, soaked for 4 hours and cooked for 1½ hours in plenty of water, then drained

6 oz (175 g) Italian tomatoes in juice

Juice of ½ lemon

1 dessertspoon soft brown sugar

Fry the onion and garlic in the oil for 2–3 minutes over a medium heat, then add the spices. Turn the heat down low and fry gently, stirring for 2–3 minutes. Add the water, bring to a fast boil and continue boiling until the water has evaporated and the onions, garlic and spices are frying again. Add the potato pieces and turn in the spice mixture. Add the chick peas and the tomatoes, which you should break up with a wooden spoon. The liquid part of the mixture should have the consistency of single cream and should cover the potatoes. If necessary, add a little water until you achieve the correct consistency. Simmer gently, partly covered, for 10–15 minutes until the potatoes are cooked but not dissolved. Stir in the lemon juice and brown sugar and check for seasoning.

This dish can be cooked and kept overnight to be re-heated the next day with some advantage.

THE THREE-STAR VEGETARIAN MEAL

This trio of matching vegetarian dishes is designed as a complementary package of flavours and textures to make up a complete meal. You can, of course, serve them independently, but the contrasts of colour, texture and flavour are intended to work as a team. If you get the opportunity, do serve them together. They are not difficult to make, and a food processor makes them easy-peasy.

Each dish serves six people as a starter and four as part of a main meal.

Potato and Leek Quiche

*T*he unique feature of this is that the potato is the 'pastry', or at least a substantial part of it, and the filling doubles as a sauce for this bulky part of the dish.

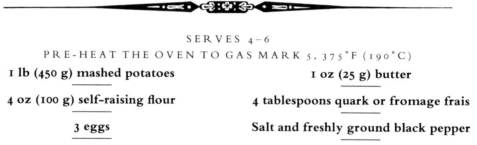

SERVES 4–6
PRE-HEAT THE OVEN TO GAS MARK 5, 375°F (190°C)

1 lb (450 g) mashed potatoes	1 oz (25 g) butter
4 oz (100 g) self-raising flour	4 tablespoons quark or fromage frais
3 eggs	Salt and freshly ground black pepper
8 oz (225 g) leeks, washed, in thin ribbons	

Mix the mashed potato, self-raising flour and one of the eggs together and knead to form a firm potato dough. Press this by hand into an 8 in (20 cm) flan tin; it will be a fairly thick pastry-type filling. Fry the leeks lightly in the butter for about 3 minutes. Remove and cool a little. Beat the remaining 2 eggs and the quark or fromage frais together. Add the leek pieces, season generously, and pour into the potato pastry mould. Bake for 20–25 minutes. Serve cut in wedges.

Spinach and Pine Nuts

*P*ine nuts are tiny crunchy morsels, the shape of a grain of rice and about four times the size. They come from a member of the evergreen pine family, but don't have a resinous flavour. The nuts are wonderful toasted, or lightly fried until golden-brown. Here they're combined with creamy, nutmeg-flavoured spinach to provide a perfect foil for the other two dishes in the three-star meal.

SERVES 4–6

1½ lb (750 g) spinach, washed	2 oz (50 g) pine nuts
1 oz (25 g) butter	½ teaspoon ground nutmeg
1 tablespoon oil	1 lemon, quartered

Plunge the spinach into plenty of boiling salted water, bring back to the boil and cook for approximately 2 minutes. It should still be bright green, but thoroughly soft. Drain, then put in a colander or sieve and make 1 or 2 cuts across the leaves with a knife to help all the surplus water run out. Heat the butter gently in a pan and turn the spinach in the butter. In a separate pan, put the oil and the pine nuts and cook gently until the nuts are gold in colour – do not let them burn or cook too long. Allow to cool slightly. Mix the nutmeg into the spinach and put into an oval or round, shallow gratin-style dish.

Sprinkle the pine nuts over the top and serve with lemon quarters for guests to squeeze over the delicious confection.

Carrot and Cashew Gratin

This is bright, crunchy, very good for you – and extremely easy to make. It is also a good accompaniment to roast meat if you're in carnivorous mode.

SERVES 4–6

1½ lb (750 g) carrots, in small chunks	2 oz (50 g) salted or unsalted cashew nuts, roasted
2 oz (50 g) butter, softened	
Salt and freshly ground black pepper	

Boil the carrots in plenty of salted water until they're well done, about 12–15 minutes. Drain and put in a food processor with the butter and plenty of seasoning (but be careful with the salt if you're using salted cashew nuts). Purée until smooth, add half the cashew nuts and purée again until the nuts are rough-chopped through the mixture. Pour into a gratin dish, sprinkle the rest of the cashew nuts over the top and pop under a grill for 5 mintues to brown off the top coating before serving.

VEGETABLES

There are so many different and wonderful kinds of vegetables that it is difficult to know where to begin. *Food and Drink* has always abounded with vegetable recipes and, indeed, with advice on vegetables. One of the marvellous things about working on the programme is the opportunities I have to add to my knowledge. I've had a chance to learn about, and test, the cooking qualities of different varieties of potatoes, old and new; to see a whole range of new mushrooms come on the market; and to watch tropical vegetables like sweet potatoes and yams, plantains and chilli peppers become commonplace in super-markets and greengrocers all over the country. The enormous explosion in the variety of vegetables available throughout the year – thanks to new methods of growing in places like Spain and Kenya, and transportation in chilled vehicles – has been extraordinary. And flavour hasn't been totally neglected. The return of the cherry tomato that actually tastes like a tomato has been a feature of the last couple of years. So, too, has the introduction of different kinds of lettuces, including the never-to-be-forgotten 'Lollo rosso' from the television adver-tisement for cream cheese.

A most interesting development in the last couple of years has been world-wide research that suggests that a daily consumption of fresh fruit and vegetables – 8 oz (225 g) is a recommended minimum – provides us with vitamins and minerals that can help prevent heart disease and some cancers.

When I looked at the vegetable department of my local supermarket today, I saw kohlrabi and bean sprouts, baby sweetcorn and mange tout, three kinds of beans, aubergines, four kinds of peppers, courgettes ... plus the standard vegetables like onions, carrots, potatoes, broccoli and cauliflower. In case you think I'm talking about high summer, this was the beginning of April.

And cooking methods have improved, along with this increase in variety. The day of the cottonwool carrot, the bean you could bend double, and the crunchless cauliflower seem to have gone for ever, except in one or two bastions of old-fashioned cooking. We've learnt to enjoy lightly cooked vegetables with their colour, flavour and texture pretty well intact. And learned to enjoy them for their own sake and not just as accompaniments to meat.

It's this new, fresh approach that I hope to celebrate here. There are vegetable dishes from all over the world: hot and cold; vegetables on their own and as accompaniments to other dishes. With all the varieties available now, no general programme or book can hope to deal with them comprehensively. What I hope you'll find here are ideas, methods, and combinations of taste that will help you to enjoy the traditional 'two veg' – or even three, or more – in new ways.

Brussels Sprouts Polonaise

If you think that the name of a nineteenth-century dance combines uneasily with Brussels sprouts, let me reassure you. Polonaise is just the French culinary term for food finished in what they believe is the Polish way: that is, with butter-fried breadcrumbs and chopped hard-boiled egg. In fact, that's exactly the combination that transforms Brussels sprouts into something very special. So special, indeed, that I often serve this as a vegetable course on its own rather than merely as a subordinate dish to meat or fish. It is substantial, and a revelation to people for whom sprouts are a burden to be borne every Christmas.

SERVES 4

1 lb (450 g) small sprouts, trimmed

2 oz (50 g) butter

4 oz (100 g) soft white or wholemeal breadcrumbs

2 hard-boiled eggs, shelled with whites and yolks separated

Salt and freshly ground black pepper

Plunge the sprouts into boiling water and cook for 7–8 minutes until cooked through but still bright green and firm. Drain, then run a little cold water over them to stop them going khaki. In a large frying-pan, melt the butter and fry the breadcrumbs over a medium heat until light brown. Add the sprouts and allow them to heat through and become partially coated with the breadcrumbs. Chop the egg whites finely and add those to the pan. Check for seasoning, and pour the mixture into a serving dish. Mash the egg yolks with a fork until they're crumbly then sprinkle over the dish.

Serve immediately.

Stir-fry Fennel

I always think that Florentine fennel looks like rather overweight celery with the sticks cut off. It's widely available and very good raw and in salads. Its crisp texture and aniseed flavour also make it an ideal candidate for Chinese-style stir-frying. Have all the ingredients ready to hand before you start, and cook them very quickly. This dish is good either as part of a Chinese meal, or served as a vegetable with lamb chops.

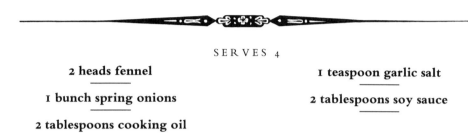

SERVES 4

2 heads fennel

1 bunch spring onions

2 tablespoons cooking oil

1 teaspoon garlic salt

2 tablespoons soy sauce

Trim the fennel and onions and slice into thin strips across the grain. Keep the white and the green parts of the onions separate. Heat a frying-pan or wok, add the oil and the white parts of the onions, then the fennel. Fry on a high heat for 1 minute, tossing the vegetables with a spatula. Add the garlic salt and soy sauce, toss for 30 seconds more and serve sprinkled with the green parts of the onions.

Red Cabbage with Apples

This is a vegetarian winter casserole that can be served on its own or with some granary bread. In Europe, it is traditionally eaten with game like venison or hare. Cooked for a longish time, as in this recipe, the cabbage loses its bright red, pickled colour and turns a dark, rich purple. It looks fine and tastes terrific, but don't let it go anywhere near a cream sauce: the combination can be visually disastrous.

SERVES 4

1–1½ lb (450–750 g) head red cabbage, trimmed, in ½ in (1 cm) slices

1 large onion, finely chopped

1 cooking apple, cored and finely chopped

2 tablespoons oil

2 teaspoons vinegar

2 teaspoons brown sugar

½ teaspoon ground cloves

10 fl oz (300 ml) water

Sauté the cabbage, onion and apple in the oil over a medium heat in a big saucepan, until they glisten. Add the remaining ingredients, then cover and simmer on the lowest heat for at least 40 minutes and preferably 1 hour. This is great re-heated.

Exotic Stir-fry

*T*his Chinese-style dish teams up two newcomers with an established exotic vegetable: the red pepper, a sweet relative of the fiery chilli. The first newcomer is snow peas. Similar to mange tout, they're delicate and never develop much 'pea', but their pods are delicious. They can be cooked in boiling water for 5 minutes and eaten like peas, or stir-fried as here.

The other ingredient is mooli, which looks like a white carrot, but is actually a giant radish. It can be grated in salads, or used as a hot vegetable. It is very low in calories but good on flavour. The colours of this stir-fry are so bright and attractive that it's worth serving it on its own as a separate course. It's simple but exciting, both to cook and eat.

SERVES 4

1 tablespoon cooking oil

1 teaspoon finely chopped fresh ginger

1 clove garlic, crushed

8 oz (225 g) snow peas

8 oz (225 g) mooli, peeled

1 red pepper, de-seeded

Pinch of salt

1 dessertspoon soy sauce

Pour the oil into a hot, heavy-based frying-pan or wok. When the oil has heated up, add the ginger and garlic and leave to fry over a high heat for 1 minute.

Meanwhile, string the snow peas (as you would runner beans) and chop the mooli and red pepper into pieces the same size as the peas. (The vegetables take the same amount of time to cook if they are all the same size.)

Put all the vegetables into the hot frying-pan or wok and stir, gently and continuously, over a high heat, for 1–1½ minutes. Add the salt and soy sauce. Continue stirring for 1 minute, and serve while the vegetables still have a crisp bite to them.

Purée of Celeriac and Potatoes

The celery flavour of celeriac can turn one of our everyday dishes, mashed potato, into a gourmet treat. Serve the purée with rich foods such as pheasant casserole or rosemary-flavoured roast lamb. The almost nutty celeriac flavour comes through strongly but is not overwhelming.

SERVES 4

1 lb (450 g) celeriac, peeled, in 1 in (2.5 cm) cubes

2 lb (900 g) potatoes, in 1 in (2.5 cm) cubes

5 fl oz (150 ml) semi-skimmed milk, heated

2 tablespoons fromage frais, or 2 oz (50 g) butter

Salt and freshly ground black pepper

Boil the celeriac and potatoes in salted water for 15 minutes. Mash thoroughly and add the heated milk and then the fromage frais or butter. Whisk well until smooth and season lightly.

Roast Parsnips

Roast parsnips seem to be everybody's favourite. In fact, I find that, like prawns, I never have enough of them. The following method of roasting them is very similar to the right way to get perfect roast potatoes, and involves a little parboiling. This ensures that the insides are soft before the outsides are baked hard, so that the pleasure of eating them is not replaced by the problem of entry. Be careful about the timing and make sure the parsnips are reasonably bulky when you cut them up – they're not meant to be as thin as chips. If you have tiny parsnips leave them whole: they cook perfectly well this way.

SERVES 6

PRE-HEAT THE OVEN TO GAS MARK 4, 350°F (180°C)

$1\frac{1}{2}$ lb (750 g) parsnips, peeled and cut lengthways in 3 x $1\frac{1}{2}$ in (7.5 x 4 cm) pieces

4 tablespoons vegetable oil

Parboil the parsnips for 5 minutes, then drain carefully. Pre-heat the oil in a baking tin, then add the parsnips. Roll them in the oil and bake for 30 minutes, turning at least once.

Leeks in White Sauce

*L*eeks, in white sauce, are one of the many vegetables that were ruined for me when I was at school. They can be absolutely atrocious if boiled until they turn khaki. But if you cook the leeks gently, and make the white sauce carefully, this can be one of the most delicious of dishes.

Be careful when cleaning leeks: they are almost always very gritty with sand and dirt trapped inside their folds. To get as much grit out as possible as easily as possible, cut the leeks into 1 in (2.5 cm) pieces and wash them in a bowl of water. Don't be tempted to cook them for more than 3 minutes, or the colour will make you think you're back at school – or in the army.

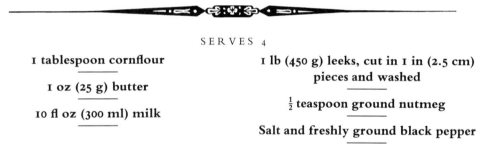

SERVES 4

1 tablespoon cornflour

1 oz (25 g) butter

10 fl oz (300 ml) milk

1 lb (450 g) leeks, cut in 1 in (2.5 cm) pieces and washed

$\frac{1}{2}$ teaspoon ground nutmeg

Salt and freshly ground black pepper

To make the white sauce, whisk the cornflour, butter and milk together with a wire whisk, then heat to boiling, whisking constantly. Simmer for 3 minutes, then remove from the heat.

Blanch the leeks for 3 minutes in boiling water, then drain well. Add to the white sauce and stir, coating the leeks with the sauce. Add the nutmeg and seasoning before serving.

Serve hot.

Classic Cabbage

A variation of this recipe produces 'caraway cabbage' and requires, in addition to the basic recipe, a teaspoon of caraway seeds. Add these 1 minute before the cabbage has finished cooking and give the pan an extra good shake. Caraway cabbage is particularly good with Middle-European dishes like goulash and the Venison with ginger sauce on p. 93. Please trust me for the timing!

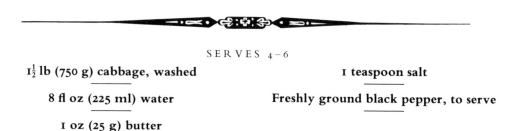

SERVES 4–6

1½ lb (750 g) cabbage, washed

8 fl oz (225 ml) water

1 oz (25 g) butter

1 teaspoon salt

Freshly ground black pepper, to serve

Just before you're ready to cook, trim and cut the cabbage into 1 in (2.5 cm) ribbons, using a sharp knife. Mix the water and butter together in a saucepan big enough to take all the cabbage at once, with a good tight-fitting lid. Bring to the boil, then add the cabbage and salt. Stir quickly over maximum heat, cover and leave for 1 minute. Give the pan a thorough shake, holding the lid on tightly with your other hand. Put back on the heat for 30 seconds, then serve. Season with the pepper. The cabbage will be crisp, hot, aromatic and buttery. Don't let it sit around before you eat.

Aniseed Carrots

Carrots are often disregarded as being ordinary, everyday vegetables, and, indeed, they are cheap, convenient and brightly coloured. It also turns out that they are extraordinarily good for you. But ordinary they are not! The classic French way of cooking them, known as Carrots Vichy, involves a pinch each of sugar and salt, a little knob of butter, and just enough water to boil away by the time the carrots are done but still have a little bite to them.

This recipe follows that pattern and adds an exotic note: the flavour of star anise, a Far Eastern spice which is a version of aniseed. The combination of carrots and the aniseed flavour is unexpectedly blissful, and goes as well as an accompaniment to a roast dinner as it does to a group of dishes for a Chinese meal. Do find the proper star anise, though. It's available from all oriental or Chinese-style supermarkets, and European aniseed doesn't have the same intensity of flavour.

SERVES 4

1 lb (450 g) carrots, peeled	6 segments (or 1 complete star) star anise
½ teaspoon sugar	½ oz (15 g) butter
½ teaspoon salt	

Slice the carrots carefully across the grain into diagonal ½ in (1 cm) slices. Place in a thick-based saucepan with the sugar, salt, star anise and butter, and just enough water to come below the topmost carrots. Bring to the boil and cook for 10–12 minutes depending on whether the carrots are young or old. They should still have a little bite in them when you test one and the water should have just about vanished, leaving a little butter and star anise sauce. You can take out the bigger bits of the spice before you serve.

PROVENÇAL VEGETABLES

The people of Provence have a very special way with vegetables. It's based on the use of garlic and olive oil, and also on vegetables that grow particularly well in the Provençal climate and conditions. Here are three of my favourite recipes. Very crafty and simple to make, they provide a real taste of the south.

Courgettes and Tomatoes Provençal

This reflects my liking for hot, but crisp, vegetables. The technique of stir-shaking works well for any vegetable that you can eat and enjoy raw. Courgettes are one: if you're doubtful, try them sliced thinly in salad.

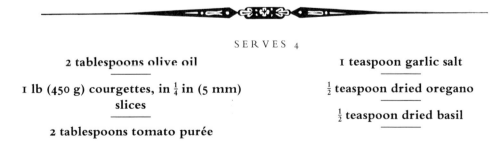

SERVES 4

2 tablespoons olive oil	1 teaspoon garlic salt
1 lb (450 g) courgettes, in ¼ in (5 mm) slices	½ teaspoon dried oregano
	½ teaspoon dried basil
2 tablespoons tomato purée	

Heat the oil until very hot in a frying-pan with a lid. Throw in the courgettes, cover the pan and shake. Add the tomato purée, garlic salt, oregano and basil. Cover and shake again. Cook for 1 minute and serve.

Jerusalem Artichokes Provençal

Jerusalem artichokes look like a knobbly potato, and have a crisp texture and slightly nutty flavour. They are very easy to cook: peel them, then either boil them like potatoes, or, better still, cook them in a sauce, which they absorb very readily. After peeling to prevent discolouration, put the artichokes into a bowl of water to which lemon juice has been added. Another advantage, apart from their texture and flavour, is that although they look like potatoes and, to a certain extent, have the same kind of role to play in a meal, they aren't fattening because our bodies don't absorb the kind of starch they contain. This can make them a little 'windy' but, then, nothing in life is perfect.

SERVES 4

1 tablespoon oil (preferably olive)

1 lb (450 g) Jerusalem artichokes, peeled and sliced

1 small onion, chopped

$\frac{1}{2}$ teaspoon garlic salt

8 oz (225 g) ripe tomatoes, sliced

Heat the oil in a frying-pan and stir in the artichokes. Make sure they are coated in hot oil, then add the onion, garlic salt and tomatoes. Stir well and cook gently for 10–15 minutes, until the artichokes are softened.

Grilled Tomatoes Provençal

In the south of France grilled tomatoes are a course on their own, often at lunchtime. They must, however, be the giant Marmande or beef tomatoes, weighing up to 1 lb (450 g) each and must be generously seasoned, then grilled until the top is almost black and the whole vegetable is hot and juicy.

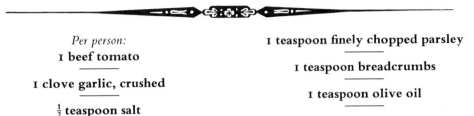

Per person:
1 beef tomato

1 clove garlic, crushed

½ teaspoon salt

1 teaspoon finely chopped parsley

1 teaspoon breadcrumbs

1 teaspoon olive oil

Cut the tomato in half across its equator. Place both halves (skinside down) in a shallow earthenware grilling dish. Score their cut sides with a sharp knife in a criss-cross pattern, to allow the flavours to penetrate while cooking.

Mix the garlic and salt together and spread equal amounts on each half of the tomato. Then put the finely chopped parsley and breadcrumbs over the top. Lastly, pour a half teaspoon oil over each half. Press down to firm the topping.

Pre-heat the grill for 5 minutes, then grill the tomato for 10 minutes under high heat until the top is blackened. Eat quickly while hot!

POTATOES

Potatoes are our most eaten and least valued vegetable. They still remain the best budget food of all. It is only very recently, and because of legislation, that retailers have started to name the varieties. Don't make the mistake of thinking it doesn't matter which one you buy – it does! Different types of potato differ in taste at least as much as apples, and they have widely varying cooking characteristics. The following guide is not totally comprehensive, but includes the varieties most widely available.

King Edward is good for roasting, mashing and making chips. It absorbs slightly less fat than other varieties.

Maris Piper is particularly good for making chips, as it absorbs less fat than other varieties.

Desiree is best for roasting and good for baking.

Cara is best for baking, as it has a neat shape and good size and flavour.

Wilja is a good boiling potato that keeps its shape well.

Estima is a boiling potato and is particularly good in potato salads.

Romano is good for mashing and for boiling in its skin.

Pentlands is a prefix for a number of varieties. All are good for boiling and mashing. In recent tests, *Pentland Squire* was voted the best all-round potato. It is great for mash.

Crafty Mashed Potatoes

*M*ashed potatoes have suddenly acquired a fashionable cachet. Top French restaurants are serving them as a speciality dish, sometimes mashed with olive oil, with added saffron, and a whole lot of other refinements. Here's my crafty way with mashed potatoes, which I hope will turn them into a speciality dish in your house too.

SERVES 4

2 lb (1 kg) King Edward, Romano or, best of all, Pentland Squire potatoes

4 fl oz (120 ml) hot milk

1 oz (25 g) butter

$\frac{1}{2}$ teaspoon ground nutmeg

Salt and freshly ground black pepper

Peel the potatoes, cut them evenly and boil, covered, until completely soft but not disintegrated. Drain thoroughly and allow to dry in the warm saucepan with the lid off for 2 minutes. Add the warm milk and mash thoroughly. When smooth, add the butter, nutmeg and seasoning. Whip vigorously until the mash is light and fluffy.

Serve immediately.

Champ

This is the Irish version of mashed potatoes – the Irish, after all, do know quite a lot about this particular vegetable. That's not just hearsay. Every time I've been to Ireland I've been struck by the quality of, and the interest in, potatoes. Properly, this has melted butter, and not fromage frais, in the middle. Even more delicious, but ...

SERVES 4

2 tablespoons spring onion, finely chopped

1 lb (450 g) hot mashed potatoes

4 tablespoons fromage frais

Stir the spring onion into the potatoes, and arrange the mixture in nests on 4 individual plates. Make a well in the middle of each nest and fill with 1 tablespoon fromage frais.

Serve immediately. Use spoons to eat the potato and dip each spoonful into the fromage frais.

Chips

Chips are here to stay, and quite right too. They may not be my idea of everyday food but, well made, they can be a great delicacy and a gourmet pleasure. Here is how to produce non-greasy, super-crisp chips.

1 Use clean or filtered *oil*.
2 Get the oil hot but not smoking. (An electric, thermostatically controlled frier is best.)
3 Cut, wash, and drain the chips in advance so there is no excess moisture to make the oil foam.
4 Cook until pale brown, then drain.
5 Let the oil regain its temperature (about 1 minute).
6 Put the chips back in the oil for about 45 seconds. Drain, season and serve.

Perfect Roast Potatoes

Four hints for really great roast potatoes. The kind you use is important: you want a potato that will go crisp on the outside but stay fluffy inside. The general consensus seems to be that the red-skinned Desiree are the best.

1 Make sure all the peeled potatoes are the same size.
2 Cover with water, bring to the boil and simmer for 8 minutes.
3 Drain and turn in 2 tablespoons oil heated in a roasting tin in an oven that has been pre-heated to gas mark 5, 375°F (190°C).
4 Roast for approximately 45 minutes, turning once. Very large potatoes will need longer.

Danish Roast Potatoes

This is a Scandinavian twist on our roast potatoes, which I think is worth trying. It's designed to produce the maximum amount of surface on each potato to get the maximum amount of crunch – rather like the principle used to get lots of crust on French bread. Use a good roasting potato for this: Desiree, one of the Pentlands or King Edward.

SERVES 4
PRE-HEAT THE OVEN TO GAS MARK 5, 375°F (190°C)

8 medium potatoes, peeled	**2 tablespoons fresh breadcrumbs**
6 tablespoons vegetable oil (preferably olive)	**Salt and freshly ground black pepper**

Make incisions across each potato at about $\frac{1}{2}$ in (1 cm) intervals and cut three-quarters of the way through the potato. Be sure not to cut all the way through. Put in cold salted water, bring to the boil and parboil for 5 minutes. Drain thoroughly. Heat the oil in a roasting tin until it is almost smoking. Put in the potatoes, cut side up, and spoon hot oil over each of them. Roast for 25 minutes. Sprinkle the breadcrumbs over the potatoes, season and baste, then roast for a further 10 minutes.

Baked Potatoes

*T*he great trick with baked potatoes is to push a thick metal skewer through the length of each potato after you have scrubbed it. This will conduct heat to its centre, so that the inside is baked before the outside dries out. Devices with four or six prongs to hold the potatoes are available.

Pommes de Terre Dauphinoise

A dish from France that's become a classic in that country of classic recipes, and is one of my, and Food and Drink's, absolute favourites. This way of cooking potatoes makes them a dish to be savoured on its own, though it's often served with roast lamb or beef, or grilled veal kidneys.

Although the recipe is rich, each person gets only 2 tablespoons of cream and 1 dessertspoon of butter if the dish is served to four people. Not too bad for something that tastes as superbly self-indulgent as this dish.

Whether or not you're a vegetarian, try this as a main course, perhaps with one or two other vegetables to set it off – or just salad and wholemeal bread.

SERVES 4
PRE-HEAT THE OVEN TO GAS MARK 6, 400°F (200°C)

1 clove garlic, cut in half

Salt and freshly ground black pepper

1 butter paper

2 oz (50 g) butter

1⅓ lb (750 g) King Edward, Pentland Squire or Cara potatoes, thinly sliced

5 fl oz (150 ml) double cream

5 fl oz (150 ml) semi-skimmed milk

Rub the inside of an earthenware baking dish with the cut sides of the garlic clove and leave to dry. Then grease the dish with the butter paper. Place a layer of potato slices in the dish. Add seasoning and spread a little of the butter over the top. Repeat this process until all the potatoes have been used up and are evenly layered. Then mix the double cream and milk together and pour over the potatoes. Dot with remaining butter. Cook for 30 minutes, reduce the oven to gas mark 4, 350°F (180°C) and cook for another 30 minutes.

After 1 hour, the potatoes should be browned on the surface and golden and creamy on the inside.

SALADS

Salads have always been a feature of *Food and Drink*. Not only are they delicious ways of eating those most healthy of foods, raw vegetables, they also have some of the most interesting textures as well as flavours. Over the years, I've gathered and shown salad recipes from all over the world, and a selection of these is represented here. Some are sufficiently substantial to make meals in their own right: Salad fermier from France or Caesar salad from America make splendid centrepieces for a light lunch. All of them provide the pleasure and freshness on the palate that is unique to salads.

Chinese Cabbage Salad

This lovely winter salad, made from the cos lettuce look-alike sold in most supermarkets as Chinese leaves, is a splendid colour combination as well as a midwinter treat. It's a Boxing Day special in our house.

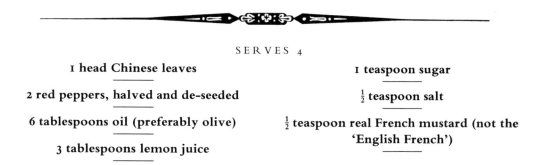

SERVES 4

1 head Chinese leaves

2 red peppers, halved and de-seeded

6 tablespoons oil (preferably olive)

3 tablespoons lemon juice

1 teaspoon sugar

$\frac{1}{2}$ teaspoon salt

$\frac{1}{2}$ teaspoon real French mustard (not the 'English French')

Split the head of Chinese leaves lengthwise, then cut out the hard core and discard it. Cut the leaves lengthwise into quarters. Slice these across (like cutting bread) into $\frac{1}{2}$ in (1 cm) slices and crumble them into a salad bowl. Cut the peppers into $\frac{1}{8}$ in (3 mm) slices across. Mix the peppers with the Chinese leaves. Mix the remaining ingredients and use to dress the salad. Toss thoroughly to blend the light-red and pale-green vegetables with the piquant dressing.

Ultimate Coleslaw

In the last couple of years, detailed research, particularly in America, Japan and Britain, has suggested that some foods have an incredibly beneficent effect on our health, not curing what ails us but preventing what might ail us from doing so. In particular, there is a group of vegetables and fruits that seem to have specific effects on specific diseases. Some of this research is still controversial, but there is growing evidence to suggest that, while no one can guarantee that those foods will keep you free of a disease, they certainly seem to help. And, as it happens, they taste pretty good! I've devised this coleslaw recipe to use as many as possible of these foods, that are widely available, in a single dish. If the research is right, it will help to prevent such varied problems as arthritis, stomach cancer, lung cancer, high blood pressure, heart disease and cholesterol in the arteries. Thank goodness it tastes as good as it does.

SERVES 4–6

1 lb (450 g) white cabbage

8 oz (225 g) carrots, coarsely grated

4 oz (100 g) spring onions, chopped (both white and green parts)

1 red apple, cut into small pieces

For the dressing:
4 fl oz (120 ml) olive oil

2 fl oz (50 ml) grapeseed oil (or any other kind of oil – olive oil alone is too strong and overwhelming)

Juice of 1 lemon

1 garlic clove, crushed

1 heaped tablespoon runny honey

1 teaspoon Dijon mustard

Salt and freshly ground black pepper

Cut the cabbage into quarters, cut away the thick core and finely shred the leaves with a sharp knife. Mix the cabbage, carrots, spring onions and apple together thoroughly in a large bowl.

To make the dressing, simply combine all the ingredients together in a blender or whisk in a bowl. Pour over the vegetables and mix well.

This salad is best refrigerated for a few hours before serving.

Wild Mushroom Salad

This salad was on the first film I ever made for Food and Drink *at the beginning of the 1980s. It followed a mushroom-gathering session in the Hampshire woods, and was a revelation both for its taste and as a reminder of our 'wild' resources. Although the recipe requires wild mushrooms, the salad can be made with some of the new cultivated varieties now available — especially oyster or champignon mushrooms, which are half-way between real wild ones and old-fashioned domesticated ones.*
The salad is smashing with grilled meat, but also good as a course on its own.

SERVES 4

1 lb (450 g) wild mushrooms, washed but not peeled

4 tablespoons olive oil

1 clove garlic, chopped

2 tablespoons lemon juice

$\frac{1}{2}$ teaspoon caster sugar

Salt and freshly ground black pepper

Lettuce, radishes and sorrel leaves (for the salad base)

1 teaspoon chopped parsley

1 teaspoon chopped chives

Slice the mushrooms into attractive shapes. Heat 2 tablespoons of the oil in a frying-pan, add the mushrooms and garlic and sauté them in hot oil for 2 minutes. Do not let them burn. Mix the lemon juice with the caster sugar, stirring until the sugar has dissolved. Place the mushrooms in a bowl and, while still warm, toss with the remaining oil, and the lemon juice. Season, then cool.

To serve, make beds of shredded lettuce, radishes and sorrel leaves. Put a quarter of the mushrooms on each bed and sprinkle the herbs over them.

Potato Salad

This recipe is extremely simple but it can be one of the most delicious of all potato dishes if you use the right potatoes. They need to be small, yellow-fleshed and unblemished. Jersey Royal is the best kind readily available in Britain. If you grow your own, try to get some seed of the Pink Fir Apple: it makes an excellent salad. To appreciate the full flavour of the potatoes, eat this dish with the simplest of cold meats or poached fish, or on its own.

SERVES 4

1 lb (450 g) waxy potatoes

2 tablespoons lemon juice

4 tablespoons olive or sunflower oil

$\frac{1}{2}$ teaspoon salt

$\frac{1}{2}$ teaspoon freshly ground black pepper

1 tablespoon chopped chives

Scrub the potatoes and cut into equal-sized pieces. Put them in a pan with cold water and bring to the boil. Simmer until they are just tender, which will take about 10 minutes. Drain, and sprinkle while hot with 1 tablespoon of the lemon juice. Leave to cool and then dress with the oil, remaining lemon juice, salt and pepper. Don't refrigerate them unless you have to.

Add the chives just before serving, sprinkled on the top.

Hot Potato Salad

Here's an alternative way of serving a potato salad: hot. It's an American tradition, usually eaten with food like salt beef sandwiches, but it's a great favourite in our house, especially with young people.

SERVES 4

1 lb (450 g) potatoes, freshly boiled

1 tablespoon cider vinegar

$\frac{1}{2}$ teaspoon salt

4 tablespoons mayonnaise

1 bunch spring onions, finely chopped

Chop the boiled potatoes and sprinkle with the cider vinegar and salt. Stir in the mayonnaise and spring onions. Serve hot.

Green Salad with Lemonette Dressing

Choose any of the enormous range of salad greens available these days: oak leaved, iceberg and mini-cos lettuces in the summer; radicchio and frilly lettuces in the autumn; and Chinese leaves, chicory and endive in the winter and spring. Aim to vary flavour and texture as well as colour. Wash the leaves, tear them into small pieces and put them in a salad bowl. Dress the salad just before you serve it, and toss thoroughly.

FOR THE LEMONETTE DRESSING:

Juice of 1 lemon

1 teaspoon caster sugar

$\frac{1}{2}$ teaspoon salt

5 fl oz (150 ml) olive or other salad oil

Whisk or liquidise all the ingredients until thick and pour over the salad so that the leaves are coated. Serve immediately.

Chicory and Orange Salad

You can make this crisp and tangy salad with the little bullet-shaped chicory or the bigger-leafed 'sugar loaf' kind that is now sometimes available, especially in winter.

SERVES 1

1 large orange, peeled and quartered

2 tablespoons lemon juice

2 heads chicory, or 1 loose-leaf sugar loaf, in $\frac{1}{2}$ in (1 cm) rounds

1 teaspoon caster sugar

$\frac{1}{2}$ teaspoon salt

For the vinaigrette dressing:
2 tablespoons cider or wine vinegar

8 tablespoons salad oil (ideally half olive, half sunflower)

Cut each orange quarter into 5 slices across and mix with the chicory. Whisk the dressing together and pour over. This salad improves with being left for 1 hour before serving.

Lamb sosatie (left), page 110; Mediterranean kebab (right), page 111.

Chicken tikka, page 242.

Caesar Salad

Caesar salad, one of the world's greatest salads, can be eaten with meat or fish dishes but is wonderful on its own. The classic dressing is made with a 1-minute boiled egg (rather like an unthickened mayonnaise) but with recent salmonella scares in mind, you may wish to play safe and substitute a little yoghurt or fromage frais.

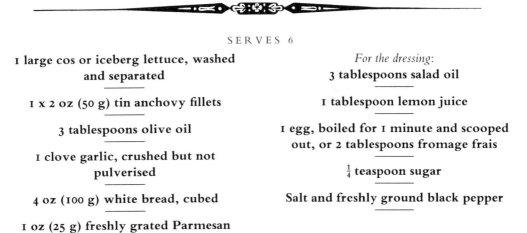

SERVES 6

1 large cos or iceberg lettuce, washed and separated

1 x 2 oz (50 g) tin anchovy fillets

3 tablespoons olive oil

1 clove garlic, crushed but not pulverised

4 oz (100 g) white bread, cubed

1 oz (25 g) freshly grated Parmesan cheese

For the dressing:

3 tablespoons salad oil

1 tablespoon lemon juice

1 egg, boiled for 1 minute and scooped out, or 2 tablespoons fromage frais

$\frac{1}{4}$ teaspoon sugar

Salt and freshly ground black pepper

Break the lettuce into bite-sized pieces. Cut up the anchovy fillets and add to the lettuce. Heat the oil in a frying-pan and add the garlic and bread. Fry the croûtons over a medium heat for 2 minutes until they're golden and crisp and then drain them on kitchen paper. Discard the garlic.

Put the dressing ingredients into a bowl and whisk well until they're thick and creamy. Pour the dressing over the salad, add the croûtons and then sprinkle over the Parmesan cheese.

Toss well before serving.

Salad Fermier

*T*he farm salad has suddenly become fashionable again in France – although it never really went out of fashion in the more rural parts of the country. It is essentially a mixture of vegetables and seasonings that are readily available and is therefore an ideal part of home cooking. It varies from place to place, containing Roquefort near where that wonderful cheese is produced; lardons of bacon in Lorraine, where they're also used in the well-known quiche; and pine nuts in the south. My version is essentially a vegetarian one, but maintains the combination of bitter leaves and crisp additions. A really super vinaigrette combines the two. It's eatable as a light lunch, or as a first course for a meal which contains a substantial main dish or pudding.
Serve in individual bowls or soup plates in the French style with plenty of crusty bread.

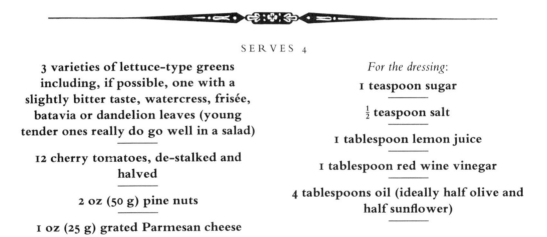

SERVES 4

3 varieties of lettuce-type greens including, if possible, one with a slightly bitter taste, watercress, frisée, batavia or dandelion leaves (young tender ones really do go well in a salad)

12 cherry tomatoes, de-stalked and halved

2 oz (50 g) pine nuts

1 oz (25 g) grated Parmesan cheese

For the dressing:

1 teaspoon sugar

$\frac{1}{2}$ teaspoon salt

1 tablespoon lemon juice

1 tablespoon red wine vinegar

4 tablespoons oil (ideally half olive and half sunflower)

Wash the greens and dry them thoroughly. Tear the leaves into playing-card-sized pieces and place in a salad bowl. Sprinkle the cherry tomatoes over the leaves. Put the pine nuts into a small, lightly oiled frying-pan, and cook over a medium heat until lightly browned – this will only take $1\frac{1}{2}$ minutes. Toss or stir the pine nuts while they are browning. Set aside and allow to cool.

Whisk together the sugar, salt, lemon juice and vinegar and add the oil, whisking again until thoroughly mixed. Sprinkle the cooled pine nuts over the salad, then the Parmesan cheese. Just before serving, pour over the dressing and toss thoroughly.

Bean Sprout Salad

This is dressed in a way very different to the way we normally dress salads in Britain. The dressing is a pattern of flavours that's used all over China and southeast Asia. Very simple, it is particularly appealing with crunchy ingredients like the bean sprouts and peppers I use here. It can be used on a wide variety of other vegetables provided they have a combination of freshness and crunch to marry with the dressing.

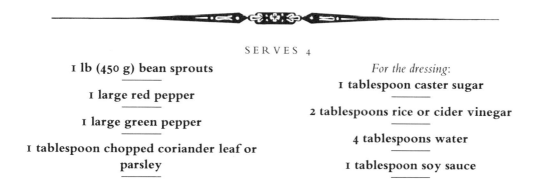

SERVES 4

1 lb (450 g) bean sprouts

1 large red pepper

1 large green pepper

1 tablespoon chopped coriander leaf or parsley

For the dressing:

1 tablespoon caster sugar

2 tablespoons rice or cider vinegar

4 tablespoons water

1 tablespoon soy sauce

Wash the bean sprouts thoroughly, removing any brown tips. Halve the peppers, remove the core and seeds, and slice them across the grain into the thinnest possible strips. Mix with the bean sprouts.

Stir the sugar into the vinegar and water until fully dissolved. Add the soy sauce and check for balance. The sauce should be sweet and sour with a hint of saltiness from the soy. Not than more than 10 minutes before you are ready to eat, add this to the bean sprouts and peppers and toss thoroughly.

Sprinkle the coriander or parsley over just before serving.

RICE

Rice is the most popular food grain in the world. Not surprising really when you think that it is the staple diet in China, India and the whole of south-east Asia, the three most heavily populated parts of the world. But there are many different kinds of rice and the ways in which it can be eaten vary enormously. Every time I go into my favourite wholefood shop at least one other variety has been added to a list that is already in double figures.

My ideas for rice include basic ways of cooking it for Chinese and Indian food, and some rather more specialist dishes. In most cases, of course, rice is intended to be a background or accompaniment to other foods and that's the case with all of these recipes. However, the stir-frying technique the Chinese have developed for left-over rice makes wonderful meals.

Chinese Techniques

The Chinese don't use the long-grain rice normally used in westernised Indian food, but a medium grain that has a little stickiness so that it can easily be picked up with chopsticks when it's cooked.
Any medium-grain rice, other than pudding rice, can be used.

Measure the rice into a cup or container. You need about 2 oz (50 g) per person: a 10 fl oz (300 ml) mug will contain about the right amount for four people. Put the rice into a saucepan with a good tight-fitting lid and measure twice the volume of water, using the same mug. Pour on to the rice, then add a good pinch of salt and a couple of drops of cooking oil. Stir together, bring to the boil and turn the heat down to the absolute minimum.

Cover the pan carefully with a folded tea towel, which will absorb the steam and avoid the rice getting too soggy. Be sure to keep the tea towel well away from the heat source. Put the lid on and leave to simmer for about 20 minutes.

When the rice is cooked, it will have absorbed all the water and have little vent-holes on its surface. You can keep it warm by turning the heat off and leaving the lid on for up to another 15 minutes or so without any harm.

To serve, break the rice up with a fork so that the grains separate a little, but leave enough residual stickiness to make it perfect for eating with chopsticks.

Indian Techniques

The people of the Indian subcontinent use long-grain rice almost exclusively. There are various grades, the grandest being Basmati with a fragrance all its own. However, many other varieties are sold here under the general name Patna even though they're often grown in the United States. If you're cooking long-grain rice the method is very different from the Chinese one.

Use about 2 oz (50 g) dry rice per person, put it in a sieve or colander and wash under running cold water until the water runs pretty well clear. Put the rice into a large saucepan, cover with at least three times its depth of cold water and add a pinch of salt and a drop of oil. Bring to the boil, then turn down and simmer for 9–11 minutes. Test the rice. It will swell considerably, and should be cooked through, with no hard bite, but not yet mushy.

As soon as the rice is done, tip it back into the sieve or colander and run approximately 1 pint (600 ml) hot water (from a tap or kettle) through the rice. Shake it dry, return it to the dry empty pan and let it rest for 2–3 minutes to steam itself. It will come up fluffy with the individual grains quite separated. You can stir a little butter in at the end if you like to add flavour.

Mexican Rice

This is a crafty version of Mexican rice. To make it properly, you should start with a whole range of fresh vegetables, but when they've been cooked for 20 minutes with rice it's difficult to tell them from one of the more exotic packs of frozen ones. I suggest you use the latter. Mexican rice goes nicely with some of the more robust Mexican and South American dishes that can stand up to its competitive flavours.

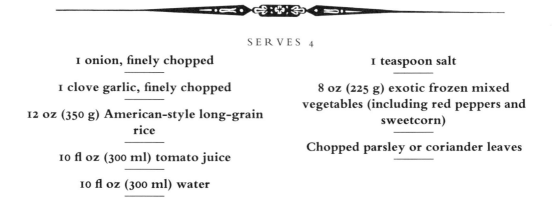

SERVES 4

1 onion, finely chopped

1 clove garlic, finely chopped

12 oz (350 g) American-style long-grain rice

10 fl oz (300 ml) tomato juice

10 fl oz (300 ml) water

1 teaspoon salt

8 oz (225 g) exotic frozen mixed vegetables (including red peppers and sweetcorn)

Chopped parsley or coriander leaves

Add the onion and garlic to the rice with the tomato juice, water and salt. Stir thoroughly and bring to the boil. Add the mixed frozen vegetables, check for seasoning and boil for 3–4 minutes. Turn the heat down and partly cover the rice, allowing some steam to escape. Cook for another 10–12 minutes. By this time all the liquid should have been absorbed and the rice should look dry. Tip the rice out into a serving dish, giving it a quick stir to break up any lumps. Serve sprinkled with a little chopped parsley or coriander leaves.

Risotto alla Milanaise

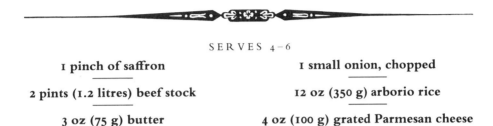

*I*talian risottos are made by cooking Italy's own unusual rice, arborio, in an unusual way. The final texture of the dish is crucial: it should be slightly moist, even creamy, and each grain should be separate with just a little bite. Don't stint on the saffron as it makes all the difference. Risotto is not worth making if you can't find the right ingredients.

SERVES 4–6

1 pinch of saffron	1 small onion, chopped
2 pints (1.2 litres) beef stock	12 oz (350 g) arborio rice
3 oz (75 g) butter	4 oz (100 g) grated Parmesan cheese

Steep the saffron in 2 tablespoons of warmed stock for 5 minutes or so. Heat half the butter in a heavy pan – a deep frying-pan or a shallow saucepan – then add the onion and cook gently until it is very light yellow in colour. Put in the saffron stock and the rice, stirring constantly with a wooden spoon until blended thoroughly. Add the rest of the stock, a ladleful at a time. Always wait until the rice has absorbed the previous ladleful and stir gently. When the stock is used up and the rice is translucent, add the cheese and remaining butter.

Stir well and serve hot.

TARTS AND PIES

---

*T*he British have an extraordinary love affair with pies. A couple of years ago, I prepared a range of what I thought was quite special food for a New Year's Eve party, including Wild duck with pickled quinces and other exotica. I was a bit worried that there might not be enough for a hearty appetite or two, and so I made a Christmas pie. It's a simple dish, made in a cake tin and just slightly decorated, and was intended to be a back-stop in case people stayed hungry. You can imagine my chagrin when nobody touched the special food until the pie had completely vanished. I don't know why this should be; possibly it's the sense of comfort and warmth that old-fashioned pies give. Certainly, there's no question that their bright, glazed, golden pastry is as appetising to the eye as it is to the palate.

We also like sweet pies, or tarts, but the savoury versions seem to be what catches our fancy. I have a small selection of savoury pies here, some pastry- and some potato-covered, as well as some of my favourite sweet ones. The latter include one of the great *Food and Drink* recipes, Pear and almond tart. This is also known by the wonderful name of Frangipani, after a tropical sweet-flowering tree: the aroma of the pie is said to be similar to its scent. And don't miss out on Mince tart royale. It's a super dish for Christmas, but just as toothsome at other times of the year with its combination of crisp meringue and succulent filling.

PASTRIES

I make all my pastry in a food processor, not least because I have hot hands, which are traditionally the bane of good pastry-makers. It is also much easier to make pastry this way. You can make both the shortcrust and the sweet Pâté sablée recipes by hand if you're a purist.

Basic Shortcrust Pastry

A general use 'British' pastry for savoury and sweet fillings.

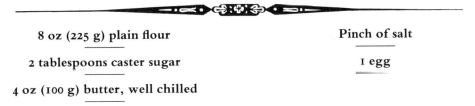

8 oz (225 g) plain flour

1 tablespoon icing sugar

½ teaspoon salt

4 oz (100 g) butter or white fat like Trex, or 2 oz (50 g) each

2–3 tablespoons water

Put the flour, sugar and salt into a food processor. Cut the butter and/or fat, which should be quite soft, into cubes and add that. Process until the mixture forms fine breadcrumbs, about 10 seconds. Add the water 1 tablespoon at a time. Different flours take up water at different speeds, and the trick is to stop as soon as the dough forms a ball around the blade. Take the dough out, press it together to cohere tidily, wrap it in cling film and put it in the refrigerator for 30 minutes.

By hand, work the flour, butter and/or fat, sugar and salt together until the mixture resembles fine breadcrumbs. Gradually add the water until the dough clings firmly, then wrap in cling film and chill in the refrigerator for 30 minutes.

Pâté Sablée

This is the ultimate French sweet pastry – literally 'sandy pastry', because it crumbles under your tongue when you eat it.

8 oz (225 g) plain flour

2 tablespoons caster sugar

4 oz (100 g) butter, well chilled

Pinch of salt

1 egg

If you're using a food processor, put all the ingredients, except the egg, in together. Switch on, then add the egg and – gradually – enough water for the dough to form a coherent ball around the blade of the processor. About half an eggshell is right.

By hand, work the flour, sugar and butter together with the salt until the mixture resembles fine breadcrumbs. Work in the egg and about half an eggshell of water, until the pastry clings firmly.

Knead briefly, roll into a ball and allow to rest in the refrigerator for 30 minutes before using.

SAVOURY PIES

Game Pie

*C*ooking game frightens people and this recipe is a marvellous introduction to how easy it is. It's also a very good introduction for people who haven't eaten game before and are reluctant to try it. The pie looks so appetising, and is so cheering and comforting to eat, that it easily wins over doubters. Use any kind of game; this is an ancient recipe, designed to use up what is available. Venison, hare, wild rabbit, wild duck, pigeon, pheasant and even grouse or partridge can go into it. You need about $2\frac{1}{2}$ lb (1.25 kg) for the pie and, if pushed, you can use one kind of game – a pigeon, for example – and bulk it out with stewing steak. This was a traditional English custom when times were hard on the game front.

This is a hot game pie, not the kind you leave to get cold and serve in slices, and should be served as a main course in autumn or winter. It's nicest if you can find a moment to take the bones out of the meat, either before or after cooking. You can make your own puff pastry, but I suggest you buy the ready-made version. Serve this with Mashed potato (see p. 152) and Red cabbage (see p. 144).

SERVES 4
PRE-HEAT THE OVEN TO GAS MARK 4, 350°F (180°C)

$2\frac{1}{2}$ lb (1.25 kg) assorted game, or game bulked with stewing steak

1 tablespoon olive or vegetable oil

1 onion, studded with cloves

2 bay leaves

$1\frac{1}{2}$ pints (900 ml) water

2 tablespoons cornflour

1 level tablespoon made mustard (grain, Dijon or English)

4 oz (100 g) baby onions (frozen are fine)

8 oz (225 g) button mushrooms

Salt and freshly ground black pepper

1 x 8 oz (225 g) packet puff pastry, thawed if frozen

Beaten egg, to glaze

Cut the game into small pieces and remove the bones. (Alternatively, this can be done after the meat has been cooked but before the pastry is added.) Sauté the game in the oil, over a medium heat, for 5–10 minutes until brown, then put in a deep pie dish with a flat rim. Add the onion, bay leaves and water, cover with foil and cook in the oven for about 2 hours if using venison in the pie. Wild duck, pigeon and pheasant will cook more quickly – check them after about 1 hour.

When the meat is cooked, take the pie dish out of the oven and remove the onion and bay leaves. Mix the cornflour and mustard with a little water and stir into the cooked game stock. Add the baby onions and mushrooms and mix. Season with salt and pepper. Roll out the pastry. Rub the flat rim of the pie dish with a little water to moisten it and cover with the pastry, pressing into the wetted rim. (This will help it stick.) Trim off the surplus pastry and use to make leaf or flower decorations. Brush with a little beaten egg and make a cut in the centre. Turn the oven up to gas mark 7, 425°F (220°C), and bake the pie for about 30 minutes, until the pastry is golden.

Beef and Kidney Pie

This is the pie version of one of the great British dishes. If you make it in a suet crust in a pudding basin it becomes a steak and kidney pudding. I've a liking for both, but the pie is a little lighter and, therefore, more suited to everyday eating. You do need a good lie-down after a large steak and kidney pudding in my experience – not that I'm averse to lying down when the opportunity arises.
This is wonderful winter food and needs to be served with plenty of mashed potato and a good green vegetable.

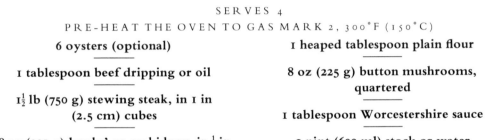

SERVES 4
PRE-HEAT THE OVEN TO GAS MARK 2, 300°F (150°C)

6 oysters (optional)

1 tablespoon beef dripping or oil

1½ lb (750 g) stewing steak, in 1 in (2.5 cm) cubes

8 oz (225 g) lambs' or ox kidney, in ½ in (1 cm) cubes

1 large onion, chopped

1 heaped tablespoon plain flour

8 oz (225 g) button mushrooms, quartered

1 tablespoon Worcestershire sauce

1 pint (600 ml) stock or water

Salt and freshly ground black pepper

1 measure shortcrust pastry (see page 169)

Open the oysters, if you're using them (You may find it's easier, if you are going to use shellfish, to get your fishmonger to do that for you and to put the resulting fish and their juices into a tub to bring home.) Put the beef dripping or oil into a saucepan and brown the meat in that over a medium heat. Add the onion and turn over for 1–2 minutes, then sprinkle on the flour, stirring so that it takes up the juices. If you're using the oysters, add them at this stage with the mushrooms and the Worcestershire sauce and enough of the stock or water to just cover the meat. Season generously and cook for 30 minutes.

Transfer to a pie dish, check for seasoning and cover with the pastry in the following manner. Roll the pastry out to approximately the size it needs to fit over the pie dish, cut a strip ½ in (1 cm) wide and, dampening the edge of the pie dish, place that all around the rim. Lay the rolled-out pastry over the top of that, crimping down to hold the lid on. Slash a couple of holes in the middle, decorate if you like with the off-cuts of the pastry, and brush with beaten egg before baking for 1½ hours. You may want to put a piece of greaseproof paper over the top of the pastry after the first 30 minutes to prevent it browning too quickly before the meat cooks.

French Sausage Pie

This is a crafty version of a dish eaten in the Berry area of France, particularly at Easter. The ingredients vary, depending upon which village you're close to. What is universal is that the pie is very wide and very flat: only about 1 in (2.5 cm) thick at best, it can be 2 ft (60 cm) across! It's very economical and, because of its size, quite spectacular — if you can find a cooking utensil big enough to cope. You can use an oblong baking tin, which is more efficient, but the finished pie is less impressive.

SERVES 8

PRE-HEAT THE OVEN TO GAS MARK 4, 350°F (180°C)

2 measures shortcrust pastry (see p. 169)

1 clove garlic, chopped

4 oz (100 g) chopped parsley

2 bunches spring onions, chopped

4 eggs

1½ lb (750 g) minced beef

1 lb (450 g) minced turkey (widely available these days, veal in some of the originals)

Salt and freshly ground black pepper

1 teaspoon ground allspice

8 hard-boiled eggs, halved

8 oz (225 g) button mushrooms, quartered

Beaten egg or milk, to glaze

Roll out the pastry into a ring at least 18 in (45 cm) across if you've got the dish for it, or to fit your baking tin, and line the dish or tin with it. Mix the garlic, parsley and spring onions with the eggs and minced beef and turkey. Add plenty of black pepper, salt and the allspice. Put half of it into the pastry case. Place the halved hard-boiled eggs in a neat pattern on the meat and fill the spaces between them with the mushrooms. Cover with the remaining meat. Roll out the remaining pastry to cover, and place over the filling, carefully crimping the edges. Cut a series of slits decoratively around the pie You can use the remaining off-cuts of pastry for leaves and other decorations if you choose. Brush with milk or beaten egg and bake for 1½ hours. This pie is normally served warm. It's eaten in large wedges, often in the hand as outdoor food.

Shepherd's Pie

A crafty version of the well-loved favourite. There aren't many surprises in this recipe, but it's sometimes useful to be reminded just how good old-fashioned food can be. Shepherd's pie, just for the record, is made with lamb and mashed potato whereas Cottage pie, made in almost exactly the same manner, uses beef and slices of potato which are laid across the top in overlapping patterns as in a Cobbler. This tastes particularly wonderful served with carrots and crispy cooked cabbage.

SERVES 4

PRE-HEAT THE OVEN TO GAS MARK 4, 350°F (180°C)

$1\frac{1}{2}$ lb (750 g) minced lamb	1 tablespoon soy sauce
1 lb (450 g) onions, chopped	1 tablespoon plain flour
1 teaspoon marjoram	Salt and freshly ground black pepper
1 teaspoon dried rosemary	$1\frac{1}{2}$ lb (750 g) potatoes, cooked and mashed with 5 fl oz (150 ml) milk
2 tablespoons tomato purée	
2 tablespoons Worcestershire sauce	2 oz (50 g) grated Cheddar or Lancashire cheese

Fry the mince in its own fat over a medium heat until well browned. Stir in the onion, marjoram, rosemary, tomato purée, Worcestershire and soy sauce and 6 tablespoons water. Add the flour, which will take up some of the juices. Season well with salt and pepper and put into an ovenproof dish. Top the meat with the mashed potato. Mark the surface with a fork, sprinkle with the cheese and bake for 35 minutes until golden-brown. That's all there is to it.

Crafty Fish Pie

This is a great family favourite which is why I have to make plenty: everyone always has seconds. This particular version is unusual in that it mixes fresh and smoked fish but the flavour combinations are terrific and complement each other. You can vary the fish you use according to what's available.

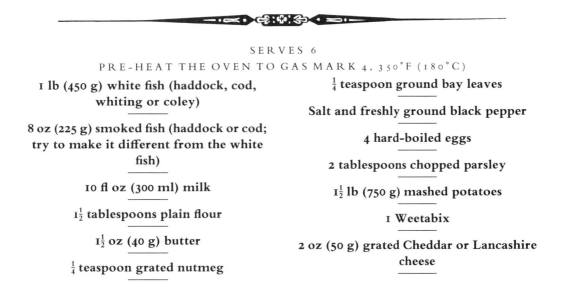

SERVES 6

PRE-HEAT THE OVEN TO GAS MARK 4, 350°F (180°C)

1 lb (450 g) white fish (haddock, cod, whiting or coley)

8 oz (225 g) smoked fish (haddock or cod; try to make it different from the white fish)

10 fl oz (300 ml) milk

1½ tablespoons plain flour

1½ oz (40 g) butter

¼ teaspoon grated nutmeg

¼ teaspoon ground bay leaves

Salt and freshly ground black pepper

4 hard-boiled eggs

2 tablespoons chopped parsley

1½ lb (750 g) mashed potatoes

1 Weetabix

2 oz (50 g) grated Cheddar or Lancashire cheese

Poach both kinds of fish in the milk for about 10 minutes until they flake. Skin the fish, remove any bones and separate into pieces. Put the milk into a non-stick saucepan, whisk in the flour and butter and bring gently to the boil, whisking as the mixture thickens. Put in the nutmeg and bay leaves, season generously and add the fish pieces. Spoon the mixture into a pie dish or baking dish. Shell and halve the hard-boiled eggs and put them on top, cut side down. Sprinkle with the parsley and top with the mashed potatoes. Crumble the Weetabix, mix with the cheese and sprinkle over the potato. Bake for 30–35 minutes until nicely browned.

SWEET PIES

Pumpkin Pie

Pumpkin pie is the classic American dish for Hallowe'en: All-Hallows Eve, the night before All Saints' Day, when ghosties and ghoulies are supposed to be about. America's Hallowe'en traditions – 'Trick or Treat' and lanterns made from hollowed-out pumpkins – seem to be catching on in Britain, and I hope Pumpkin pie will as well. It's very rich, golden-brown in colour and resembles our own Treacle tart in texture and taste. You won't need a whole pumpkin. One slice weighing about 1 lb (450 g) will do fine: you can find pumpkin in many supermarkets and most ethnic food markets.

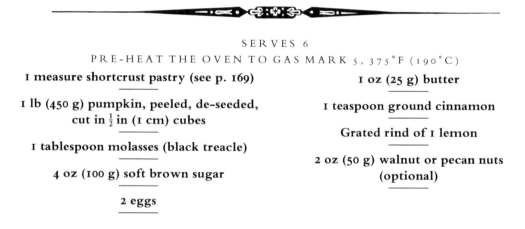

SERVES 6
PRE-HEAT THE OVEN TO GAS MARK 5, 375°F (190°C)

I measure shortcrust pastry (see p. 169)

1 lb (450 g) pumpkin, peeled, de-seeded, cut in $\frac{1}{2}$ in (1 cm) cubes

1 tablespoon molasses (black treacle)

4 oz (100 g) soft brown sugar

2 eggs

1 oz (25 g) butter

1 teaspoon ground cinnamon

Grated rind of 1 lemon

2 oz (50 g) walnut or pecan nuts (optional)

Line an 8 in (20 cm) pie tin with the pastry. Boil the pumpkin in water until soft – about 20 minutes. Drain and mash the pumpkin and add all the other ingredients except the nuts. Fill the pastry case with the pumpkin mixture, and decorate with the nuts, if you are using them. Bake for 35–40 minutes. Check with a skewer to make sure it's baked evenly: the skewer should come out clean, wherever you insert it in the pie. Allow to cool for 5 minutes before serving. Do not refrigerate; the pie will go soggy.

American Apple Pie

There's a strong suspicion that many years ago, in the days when the Pilgrim Fathers set up shop across the water, we made our apple pies in a very similar way to this. But then we changed, and began to make them more and more shallow, often with pastry only on the top of the pie. This recipe returns to the older tradition and the ingredients include the American addition of cornflour, so that the slices are thick and succulent, not floppy and runny.

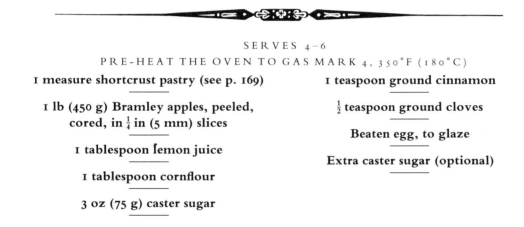

SERVES 4–6

PRE-HEAT THE OVEN TO GAS MARK 4, 350°F (180°C)

1 measure shortcrust pastry (see p. 169)

1 lb (450 g) Bramley apples, peeled, cored, in $\frac{1}{4}$ in (5 mm) slices

1 tablespoon lemon juice

1 tablespoon cornflour

3 oz (75 g) caster sugar

1 teaspoon ground cinnamon

$\frac{1}{2}$ teaspoon ground cloves

Beaten egg, to glaze

Extra caster sugar (optional)

Thinly roll out half the pastry on a lightly floured surface to about $\frac{1}{4}$ in (5 mm) thick. Line a greased $1\frac{1}{2}$ pint (900 ml) pie dish with the pastry. Put the apples into a bowl, add the lemon juice, cornflour, sugar, cinnamon and cloves and gently mix together. Pile into the pastry case, making a mound in the centre to keep the pastry lid from sinking. Cover with the remaining pastry, pressing the edges to seal. Make 2 incisions in the centre of the lid for the steam to escape. Trim the edges and glaze with the beaten egg. (The trimmings can be used to make decorations.) Sprinkle a little caster sugar on the top to give a crunchy texture to the pastry, if desired. Bake for 35–45 minutes until golden.

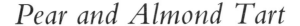

Pear and Almond Tart

This is a French-style tart with a double filling: almond frangipani and poached pears. You can use tinned pears at a pinch, but it's much better to prepare your own. Peel, halve and core the pears, then poach them for about 10 minutes in a syrup made from 4 oz (100 g) sugar and 10 fl oz (300 ml) water.

The tart is very spectacular and should be served with a whole pear-half in the centre of each slice. It's delicious warm and scrumptious cold.

SERVES 8

PRE-HEAT THE OVEN TO GAS MARK 7, 425°F (220°C)

I measure Pâté sablée (see p. 169)

2 oz (50 g) butter

2 oz (50 g) caster sugar

2 oz (50 g) ground almonds

I oz (25 g) self-raising flour

½ teaspoon almond essence

I egg

4 pears, peeled, cored, halved and poached (see above), then cooled

Thinly roll out the pastry on a lightly floured surface to about ¼ in (5 mm) thick. Use to line a 10 in (25 cm) flan tin. Cream the butter and sugar together. Add the ground almonds, flour, almond essence and egg and knead together. Fill the pastry case with the mixture. Place the poached pear halves on top like spokes of a wheel, pointed ends to the middle. Bake for 25–30 minutes until the pastry is crisp and the pears are tender.

Apple Ring Tart

This is the craftiest tart I know. It's so simple to make it's almost outrageous, yet everybody seems to love it. You can make grander versions adding crème pâtisserie (or even fresh cream) to the jam and then covering it with sumer fruits like fresh strawberries, raspberries or peaches. I keep coming back, however, to this very simple apple version. I first ate it in the French-speaking area of Switzerland so many years ago that ski-boots (which is why I was there) were ordinary leather boots that stayed on the skis even when you had fallen off them.

SERVES 12
PRE-HEAT THE OVEN TO GAS MARK 6, 400°F (200°C)

1 measure shortcrust pastry (see p. 169)

2 tablespoons apricot jam

2 red eating apples, cored and sliced into thin rings

2 green eating apples, cored and sliced into thin rings

A little caster sugar

Roll out the pastry to make a 12 in (30 cm) circle. Prick the pastry. Bake blind for 5 minutes. Spread the flan with the jam and layer with overlapping apple rings. Sprinkle with sugar. Bake for a further 20 minutes. Serve warm or cool, but don't refrigerate.

Mince Tart Royale

*T*his is a very grand mince pie made in an 8 in (20 cm) flan tin, but you can use individual mince pie moulds. I prefer this style of mince pie to the ones covered in flaky pastry where the filling always seems to have shrunk away, leaving more air than flavour. The meringue is piled up into swoops and swirls on top of the pie.

SERVES 6
PRE-HEAT THE OVEN TO GAS MARK 4, 350°F (180°C)

1 measure Pâté sablée (see p. 169)

8 oz (225 g) mincemeat, home-made (see p. 225) or bought

3 egg whites

3 oz (75 g) caster sugar

1 teaspoon white wine or cider vinegar

Roll out the pastry and use it to line an 8 in (20 cm) flan tin. I like to use one with a removable base because it makes serving very much easier. Fill the pastry with the mincemeat and smooth off. Whisk the egg whites in a bowl until they're stiff enough to hold a peak. Whisk 1 tablespoon of the caster sugar into the egg whites until the peaks re-form, then add a second tablespoon of the sugar and once again whisk until the egg whites form peaks. Add the vinegar to the mixture and fold in the remaining caster sugar. Use a spoon, and don't whisk. Pile on top of the mincemeat, covering it completely. Bake for 45–50 minutes. The meringue should be set and just starting to turn gold.

Serve hot or allow to cool.

Treacle Tart

This is an adaptation of a traditional English recipe: the walnuts add a little crunch. It can be served warm or cold, but my preference is for warm, with lots of pouring cream to go with it. About a million calories an ounce, and worth every one of them.

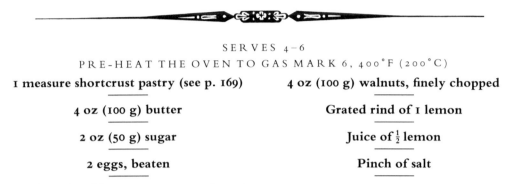

SERVES 4–6

PRE-HEAT THE OVEN TO GAS MARK 6, 400°F (200°C)

1 measure shortcrust pastry (see p. 169)

4 oz (100 g) butter

2 oz (50 g) sugar

2 eggs, beaten

6 oz (175 g) golden syrup, or 4 oz (100 g) golden syrup and 2 oz (50 g) treacle

4 oz (100 g) walnuts, finely chopped

Grated rind of 1 lemon

Juice of $\frac{1}{2}$ lemon

Pinch of salt

Roll out the pastry and use it to line an 8 in (20 cm) tin with straight sides. Cover the base of the pastry with kitchen foil to stop it bubbling in the middle, and bake in the oven for about 10 minutes. Turn the oven down to gas mark 4, 350°F (180°C) when you take out the pastry case. Mix together the butter and sugar until they are smooth and beat in the eggs and syrup (warm the syrup gently in a saucepan if it's too cold to pour). Add the walnuts, the grated rind and juice of the lemon and the salt. Turn the mixture into the pastry case, having first removed the kitchen foil. Bake for 45–55 minutes, until the top is brown, crispy and scented. Try and let it cool enough not to burn your mouth! It tastes best warm or cold.

Bakewell Tart

This is another confection with an ancient lineage – the use of almonds is an indication of its medieval origins – and one of the most popular pies I know. I make quite a thin version in a big 12 in (30 cm) flan tin, but you can make a much thicker one using the same quantities in an 8 in (20 cm) tin. It's smashing for high tea, but people also enjoy it as a pudding after a light meal.

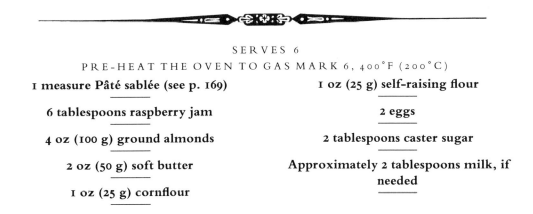

SERVES 6
PRE-HEAT THE OVEN TO GAS MARK 6, 400°F (200°C)

1 measure Pâté sablée (see p. 169)	**1 oz (25 g) self-raising flour**
6 tablespoons raspberry jam	**2 eggs**
4 oz (100 g) ground almonds	**2 tablespoons caster sugar**
2 oz (50 g) soft butter	**Approximately 2 tablespoons milk, if needed**
1 oz (25 g) cornflour	

Roll out the pastry and use it to line an 8 in or 12 in (20 cm or 30 cm) flan tin. Spread the jam over the base of the pastry. Mix the remaining ingredients together, either in a food processor or by hand. The mixture should be like very thick cream. If it's thicker than that, loosen it with about 2 tablespoons milk. Pour the mixture into the flan tin, making sure it comes at least $\frac{1}{2}$ in (1 cm) below the rim. Bake for 35–45 minutes until a skewer inserted into the almond mixture comes out clean. Allow to cool for at least 20 minutes before eating.

Puddings

*A*s you'll see when you glance through this chapter, I'm in favour of puddings that are on the lighter side of life, and often ones that are based on fruit. My esteemed colleague, Chris Kelly, once joined the 'Pudding Club' on behalf of *Food and Drink*. He was pretty doubtful until it was explained to him that this is just an organisation in the west of England that specialises in dinner parties consisting almost entirely of a choice of puddings. And old-fashioned puddings at that: steamed suets and dishes covered in butterscotch and full of chocolate. While I can understand their appeal, they're not my scene and in the following pages you'll find oranges and apples, blackberries, rhubarb, pears and pineapples, turned into a variety of delicious but simple desserts. There is a suet pudding, but it is stuffed with a whole lemon!

I'm a devotee of fruit salad, and have included a recipe for one. But to start with, here are my two fundamental fruit salad rules. The first is to use four fruits in combinations based on the regions of the world – four tropical fruits or four temperate ones – or even on the seasons: four summer or four winter fruits. Very basic salads can be wonderful: apple, orange, pear and grapes for autumn or peaches, nectarines, raspberries and redcurrants for summer. You don't even need as many as four kinds of fruit. Strawberries and raspberries go wonderfully together, particularly if the raspberries are puréed with a little sugar to make a sauce for the strawberries. Of the exotic fruits, a mixture of mango, guava, pineapple and kiwi produces a lovely colour combination as well as a delicious blend of flavours. My second rule is that fruit salads need a binding medium. This can be simple orange or apple juice, or it can be a syrup made from a little sugar boiled fiercely in water until it thickens. When the liquid chills it adds a certain amount of texture as well as sweetness to the salad.

There are times when something grander than a fruit salad is called for. My Oranges in caramel, Chocolate mousse and the Burnt cream or Baked pears recipes suit these occasions very well. But all of them round off a meal without leaving you feeling too rounded off as well.

By the way, if you are being really grand and also serving cheese, I favour the French method of serving it before the pudding (in very small quantities), so that you're left with a sweet finish to the meal.

Apple Clafoutis

A clafoutis is a giant fruit pancake and really must be eaten hot to be appreciated. It owes its high reputation in French gastronomy to the brief period when the huge, bitter-sweet black cherries of south-west France are in season. If you can get the great big, sweet, black cherries that come from Kent for about 2 or 3 weeks of the year, do make it with those.

Clafoutis is also traditionally made with apples. In France, they use a variety called 'Reinette', but most British cooking apples can be used with great success. My favourite is the Howgate Wonder, a cross between a Blenheim Orange and other apples, with a flavour and scent that are unique. Although cream isn't usually served in France it is, I think, a smashing addition. So, too, is a rich, plain yoghurt like Greek yoghurt.

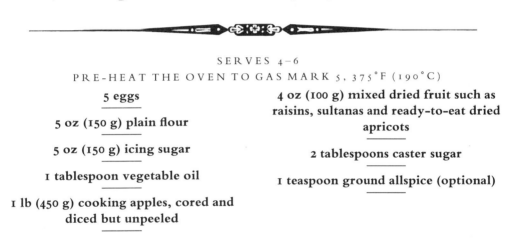

SERVES 4–6
PRE-HEAT THE OVEN TO GAS MARK 5, 375°F (190°C)

5 eggs

5 oz (150 g) plain flour

5 oz (150 g) icing sugar

1 tablespoon vegetable oil

1 lb (450 g) cooking apples, cored and diced but unpeeled

4 oz (100 g) mixed dried fruit such as raisins, sultanas and ready-to-eat dried apricots

2 tablespoons caster sugar

1 teaspoon ground allspice (optional)

Beat the eggs, flour and icing sugar together, or blend in a food processor, until the mixture resembles a batter. Add the oil and mix the batter again. Pour the mixture into a greased oval or round gratin dish that is deep enough to take the fruit: the mixture will rise, so use a dish at least 1.5 in (4 cm) deep. Combine the apples, dried fruit and caster sugar and distribute evenly over the top of the batter. If using allspice, sprinkle it on top of this mixture. Cook for 30–40 minutes until risen and golden on top.

Serve hot.

Baked Apple Meringue

This dish is served in one of Britain's most highly commended restaurants, where it is extremely expensive. It's easy to make, much cheaper – and just as good – at home!

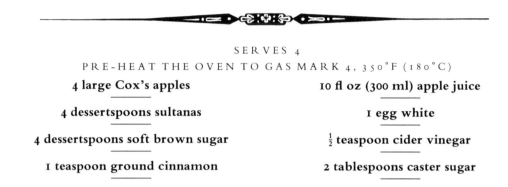

SERVES 4
PRE-HEAT THE OVEN TO GAS MARK 4, 350°F (180°C)

4 large Cox's apples	10 fl oz (300 ml) apple juice
4 dessertspoons sultanas	1 egg white
4 dessertspoons soft brown sugar	$\frac{1}{2}$ teaspoon cider vinegar
1 teaspoon ground cinnamon	2 tablespoons caster sugar

Wipe the apples and core them without piercing the base. Scoop out the top of each apple and fill with 1 dessertspoon each of sultanas and soft brown sugar. Sprinkle with the ground cinnamon, then place the apples in a baking dish. Pour the apple juice into the dish. Whisk the egg white until stiff, and beat in the cider vinegar. Fold in the sugar, and beat until smooth.

Top each apple with a quarter of the meringue mixture and bake for 35 minutes.

Oranges in Caramel

*W*e often take for granted food that was once a luxury and, conversely, regard as a luxury that which used to be commonplace. When oranges first arrived in the United Kingdom they were highly prized and carefully handled. Today we hardly notice them, but they deserve better and we really should treat them with a little old-fashioned courtesy again. Thick-peeled juicy Jaffas; red-skinned blood oranges from Malta; Moroccan navels; the bitter Sevilles from Spain. Even the names are romantic.

One of the most delicious ways of using these fruits is for Oranges in caramel: glowing, golden globes in a dark sauce that is always tart and refreshing and, at its best, fragrant and luxurious. It's very important to make sure you stop the caramel cooking when it's light brown. If you don't you'll have to start again and also be faced with an impossible mess to get out of the saucepan.

SERVES 4–6

Peel (no pith) of 2 oranges

6 oz (175 g) caster sugar

10 fl oz (300 ml) water

1 cinnamon stick

4 large oranges, peeled, and cut across the grain in $\frac{1}{4}$ in (5 mm) slices

Cut the orange peel into matchsticks. Blanch it in boiling water twice. (This is best done by pouring the boiling water from a kettle over the peel placed in a deep bowl.) Melt the sugar in a thick saucepan over a medium heat until it bubbles and goes light brown. This will take about $2\frac{1}{2}$ minutes. Take from the heat immediately and carefully add the water. Stir to dissolve the caramel. Add the cinnamon, oranges and peel and simmer for just 3 minutes. Pour into a serving bowl and chill. Be sure to serve some peel matchsticks with each orange.

As an alternative, you can cook small oranges whole, and slice them on serving or give each person a knife and fork as well as a spoon.

Chocolate and Orange Mousse

The association of orange and chocolate is surely one of the greatest of gastronomic affaires. The richness of chocolate and the zest of citrus balance each other magnificently. This mousse is perfect for an intimate late-night supper, and also good for conventional dinner parties. It's simple to make and, despite its smoothness, contains no cream. Buy the bitterest chocolate you can find: British 'dark' chocolate is often very sweet compared to Continental brands, so it's worth checking it for taste.
This is especially nice with crisp, orange-flavoured biscuits.

SERVES 4

Juice and grated rind of 1 orange

4 oz (100 g) bitter, dark chocolate

2 oz (50 g) butter, unsalted if possible

4 large eggs, separated

Put the juice of the orange into a heavy-based saucepan. Break up the chocolate, add it to the juice in the saucepan, and melt it gently over a low heat, stirring regularly. When it's smooth, add the butter and the grated rind of the orange. Stir while the butter melts, then beat the mixture until thick. Take the pan off the heat, stir in the egg yolks and heat briefly until the mixture is thick again.

Be careful: too much heat gives you chocolate scrambled eggs.

Leave to cool. Beat the egg whites until stiff, and fold the chocolate mixture into them. Pour into custard cups or wine glasses, and chill for at least 2 hours.

Pears Baked in Honey

The main difference between these pears and the ones in the following recipe, apart from the slight one of flavour and spicing, is that the finished dishes are different colours. These ones, baked in honey, are bright gold, and the pears in red wine – or red grape juice which is my preference – are dark cornelian red. I often make both versions for a grand party: if you use small pears, each person can have one of each kind. If you're serving them individually, they look particularly pretty standing up in wine glasses, with the juice forming a pool at the bottom of the glass. Serve the cream separately.

SERVES 6
PRE-HEAT THE OVEN TO GAS MARK 6, 400°F (200°C)

6 firm pears

6 cloves

8 cardamom seeds, cracked

2 cinnamon sticks

For the honey syrup:

2 tablespoons caster sugar

4–6 tablespoons clear honey

10–15 fl oz (300–450 ml) boiling water

Peel the pears, leaving the stalks in place and remove the cores. Stick a clove in each pear and lay the pears on their sides in an ovenproof dish. Scatter the cardamom seeds and cinnamon sticks on top of the pears.

To make the honey syrup, dissolve the sugar and honey in the boiling water. Pour over the pears, which should be half-covered in liquid. Bake for about 1 hour or until tender, basting and turning occasionally.

Serve hot, or let the pears cool in the honey syrup.

Pears Baked in Red Wine

SERVES 6
PRE-HEAT THE OVEN TO GAS MARK $\frac{1}{2}$, 250°F (120°C)

6 firm pears

8 oz (225 g) sugar

1 teaspoon ground allspice

2 teaspoons ground ginger

10–15 fl oz (300–450 ml) red wine or grape juice

Peel the pears, leaving on the stalks and place in an ovenproof dish. Sprinkle with the sugar, allspice and ground ginger. Half-cover with red grape juice or wine, and top up with water to cover the pears. Bake in the oven for 5–7 hours, turning pears frequently. They will turn a mahogany colour and the wine will reduce to a rich syrup. Alternatively, poach the pears on top of the stove for $1\frac{1}{2}$ hours. Remove with a slotted spoon and rapidly boil the liquid until it has reduced to a light syrup. Pour over the pears and leave to cool.

To serve, pile the pears up in a pyramid, stalks uppermost, in a shallow bowl.

Blackberry Cobbler

*F*ruit cobblers are an ancient country tradition in Britain, and a frugal one: a hot, baked pudding with a topping made from stale bread. The cut-up bread, waiting to be used and lying in rows like the leather heels in a cobbler's shop, gave the dish its name. Here is a tasty fruit filling.

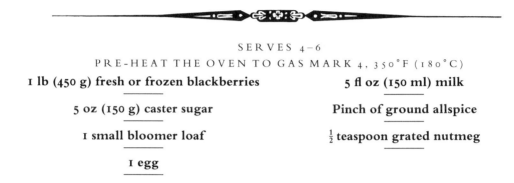

SERVES 4–6
PRE-HEAT THE OVEN TO GAS MARK 4, 350°F (180°C)

1 lb (450 g) fresh or frozen blackberries

5 fl oz (150 ml) milk

5 oz (150 g) caster sugar

Pinch of ground allspice

1 small bloomer loaf

$\frac{1}{2}$ teaspoon grated nutmeg

1 egg

Wash or defrost the blackberries, and put them in a $1\frac{1}{2}$ pint (900 ml) pie dish. Mix with 4 oz (100 g) of the sugar. Cut the bloomer loaf in half lengthwise and cut one of the halves into $\frac{1}{2}$ in (1 cm) slices to make the 'cobbles'. Beat the egg and milk with a pinch of allspice, and dip the bread pieces in the mixture. Place them over the top of the blackberries, carefully overlapping them to form the cobbled effect. Sprinkle with the remaining sugar and the grated nutmeg. Bake for 20 minutes or until golden brown.

Real Egg Custard

*F*or the finishing touch, serve your Cobbler with real custard, the original version of that great British favourite. It is slightly paler and less sweet than powdered custards, and infinitely more delicious.

SERVES 4–6

3 egg yolks

1 teaspoon vanilla essence

2 dessertspoons caster sugar

10 fl oz (300 ml) milk

1 teaspoon cornflour

Whisk the egg yolks, sugar, cornflour and vanilla essence. Gently heat the milk to boiling point, and add to the other ingredients. Whisk and pour into a saucepan. Simmer the custard gently, stirring continuously, until thickened.

Pour over your fruit pudding and eat immediately!

Crème Caramel

The French have another version of real custard that has proven enduringly popular on this side of the Channel. For a perfect end to a sophisticated meal, Crème caramel – custard with its own sauce – has few rivals.

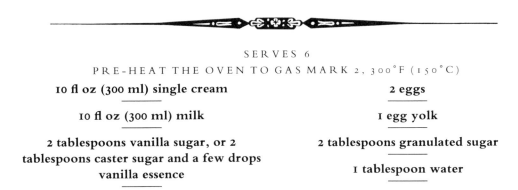

SERVES 6
PRE-HEAT THE OVEN TO GAS MARK 2, 300°F (150°C)

10 fl oz (300 ml) single cream	2 eggs
10 fl oz (300 ml) milk	1 egg yolk
2 tablespoons vanilla sugar, or 2 tablespoons caster sugar and a few drops vanilla essence	2 tablespoons granulated sugar
	1 tablespoon water

Gently heat the cream and milk in a saucepan with the vanilla sugar, or the caster sugar and vanilla essence, until the sugar has dissolved, taking care not to bring the mixture to the boil. Cool slightly, then beat the eggs and egg yolk and whisk them into the mixture. In a separate saucepan, dissolve the granulated sugar and water. Heat until the solution thickens and turns golden-brown. Do not overboil. Pour the caramel into 6 small ramekins. Allow to cool, then strain the custard mixture on to the caramel through a sieve. Place in a bain-marie, or roasting tin filled with water to come half-way up the ramekins, and bake for 45–50 minutes. Remove from the oven and leave to cool.

To turn out, loosen the edges with a palette knife, put a small plate over the top of each ramekin, and turn over. Give the bottom of the ramekin a sharp tap to loosen the little custard cup.

Burnt Cream

This is the grandest of all egg custards, known in France as Crème brûlée. There are very early manuscript versions of this in England, where it is said to have originated in a Cambridge college. Trinity may claim it, but versions can be traced back to more than 200 years before their one. 'Burnt cream' is not to be taken too literally: the coating must be pale caramel brown and not singed.

SERVES 12

PRE-HEAT THE OVEN TO GAS MARK 4, 350°F (180°C)

1 pint (600 ml) double cream

10 fl oz (300 ml) single cream

10 fl oz (300 ml) milk

6 oz (175 g) caster sugar

1 teaspoon vanilla essence

6 eggs

6 egg yolks

1 tablespoon cornflour, blended with 4 tablespoons water

8 oz (225 g) granulated sugar

2 tablespoons water

Heat the creams, milk, caster sugar and vanilla essence together until the sugar has dissolved. Bring to the boil and leave to cool. Whisk in the eggs and egg yolks and cornflour blended with water. Strain into 12 ramekins, place in a baking tin filled with 1 in (2.5 cm) water and bake for 20 minutes or until the custard is firm. In a non-stick saucepan, melt the granulated sugar in the water until pale golden-brown and caramelised. Make sure that it doesn't burn. Allow the caramel to cool for 3 minutes, then pour over the custard in the ramekins.

Leave to set, but don't refrigerate.

Home-made Ice-Cream

Home-made ice-cream often seems to be a matter of enormous complication, involving special machines, putting the mixture in the freezer and taking it out again, beatings and bashings. This is the simplest ice-cream I've ever discovered. And not only is it the simplest; it is also, without question, the most delicious. In France, it's known as a parfait *or, as we would say, 'perfect'. Strangely enough, I first discovered it in a Chinese take-away. It's foolproof, needs no special equipment, contains no crunchy bits of ice and tastes fabulous.*

SERVES 4–6

3 eggs

3 tablespoons icing sugar

5 fl oz (150 ml) double cream

1 teaspoon vanilla essence

Up to 5 oz (150 g) flavourings (optional; see method)

Whisk the eggs until they are lemon-coloured, frothy and thick. Whisk in the sugar, spoonful by spoonful, until it is absorbed. In a separate bowl, beat the cream until it is thick but not stiff. Add the vanilla to the egg mixture, and then fold in the cream – gently, so that you don't knock all the air out. At this stage you can add up to 5 oz (150 g) crushed fruit like strawberries or peaches, or other flavourings like $2\frac{1}{2}$ fl oz (65 ml) strong coffee or $2\frac{1}{2}$ oz (65 g) grated chocolate. Pour into a container and freeze for at least 4 hours. The ice-cream does not need stirring, but benefits from 30 minutes softening in the refrigerator before serving.

Ginger Ice-Cream

To commemorate the Chinese take-away of parfait fame, here's a version of Home-made ice-cream that contains honey and ginger. It's as simple to make as the vanilla one, but the ginger gives it the added advantages of a little more crunch.

SERVES 4–6

3 eggs

1 tablespoon icing sugar

1 tablespoon honey

5 fl oz (150 ml) double cream

3 oz (75 g) stem ginger in syrup, finely chopped

Whisk the eggs together until they're lemon-coloured and frothy. Whisk in the sugar and then the honey, making sure that the mixture stays as bubbly as possible. In a separate bowl, beat the cream until it's thick but not stiff. Add the ginger and syrup to the cream and then fold in the egg mixture, keeping it as full of air as you can. Put into a plastic container and freeze for at least $2\frac{1}{2}$–3 hours. The ice-cream needs to soften for about 30 minutes in the refrigerator before serving.

Rhubarb Fool

Rhubarb is a joke to many of us: the shape, the name – even the teeth-furring qualities of unripe rhubarb seem to evoke mirth. It's a pity, because it's diverted us from the delicious quality of this vegetable-cum-fruit. In Yorkshire, where many things are different, it is taken seriously. The specially forced, pale pink rhubarb grown there is best for this dish, both for its lovely colour and its delicate flavour. It isn't expensive, so make the most of its short season.

SERVES 4

1 lb (450 g) forced rhubarb, in 1 in (2 cm) pieces

4 oz (100 g) granulated sugar

8 oz (225 g) low-fat fromage frais

4 oz (100 g) set yoghurt

2 tablespoons roughly chopped stem ginger (optional)

Put the rhubarb in a saucepan with the sugar and cook gently, covered, until the rhubarb is soft. Leave to cool, and in the meantime beat the fromage frais and yoghurt together in a bowl. Whiz the rhubarb in a blender or food processor until smooth, add the stem ginger if using it, and whiz for a few seconds more; the ginger should be in small pieces. Fold the rhubarb into the fromage frais and yoghurt, creating a pretty rippled effect.

Spoon into bowls or glasses and chill for at least 1 hour before serving.

Junket

Junkets are an old, if forgotten, tradition in Britain, and were probably brought over the Channel by the French when they invaded us under William the Conqueror. The name comes from the rush-basket colanders used to drain the dish in Normandy. Try it for its delicate and refreshing taste. You can make junkets with semi-skimmed milk if you want an even lighter version. Flavourings can be anything from the traditional 1 tablespoon brandy to (my preference) lemon or raspberry juice or vanilla essence – only 1 teaspoon. In Devon they top this with clotted cream and toasted almonds. It makes a very rich treat. Vegetarian rennets are now available in health food shops.

SERVES 4

1 pint (600 ml) milk

2 tablespoons sugar

1 teaspoon rennet

½ teaspoon ground nutmeg

Clotted cream (optional)

Toasted almonds (optional)

Optional flavourings:
1 teaspoon vanilla essence, or 1
tablespoon lemon or raspberry juice

Heat the milk until it is hot but you can still dip a finger in it without screaming (be careful). Dissolve the sugar in the milk and add the rennet and nutmeg or other flavourings. Put in a pretty basin and leave to set out of the refrigerator for 4 hours. Then chill for an hour and top with clotted cream and toasted almonds if you fancy it.

Raspberry Fool

I developed this recipe as part of the Good Food Show Food and Drink did at the Ideal Home Exhibition in the spring of 1991. I cooked a three-course meal for four people in 25 minutes, from a standing start. It was a challenge but also great fun, because I believe that some of the most convenient foods are already prepared by nature and can be turned into almost instant dishes. This pudding is a wonderful example of how that can be done.

SERVES 4

8 oz (225 g) fresh or frozen raspberries

2 oz (50 g) caster sugar

5 fl oz (150 ml) double cream

5 oz (150 g) plain yoghurt

Mint leaves, to decorate

Crush the raspberries with a fork and mix them with the sugar. Put them aside to let the juices run for a moment. Beat the double cream with a whisk until it's thick and peaking, then beat in the yoghurt spoonful by spoonful. You'll find that if you whisk between times the cream doesn't lose its thickness and you have twice the quantity of whipped cream but only half the amount of fat. Mix the raspberries into the cream and yoghurt, stirring so that you get a marbled effect. Pile into 4 wine glasses, decorate with mint leaves and, if you have them, a couple of extra raspberries. Chill for 30 minutes before serving.

Pineapple Surprise

*P*resentation is as important as the ingredients in this dish. It uses the wonderful abundance of mini-pineapples that are available through the year. Comparatively cheap, they would fit into a large soup plate. They form the basis of, and the containers for, a lovely, multicoloured, multi-flavoured tropical fruit salad. A dish for special occasions, it never fails to delight the eye as well as the taste buds.

SERVES 4

2 small pineapples complete with green plumes

1 papaya (paw paw)

1 star fruit or kiwi fruit

1 mango

4 fl oz (120 ml) mango juice or mango and apple juice

With a large sharp knife, cut the pineapples, including the green plumes, in half lengthwise. Lay them cut side up on a work surface and score the flesh of each pineapple with a noughts-and-crosses board of cubes about $\frac{1}{2}$ in (1 cm) square, cutting down to the skin but not through it. Cut a ring round the outside of the noughts-and-crosses board, but inside the skin of the pineapple, as though you were preparing a grapefruit, then, with a strong spoon, pop the cubes out into a mixing bowl. This last part of the exercise is surprisingly easy once you have cut the pattern into the pineapple flesh. Cut the papaya in half, scoop out the black seeds and, using a large teaspoon, scoop out the flesh into the bowl with the pineapple cubes. Trim the star fruit or, if you're using a kiwi fruit, peel it and cut it into thin slices to show its colour and shape as much as possible. Cut the cheeks off the mango, score the flesh with a $\frac{1}{2}$ in (1 cm) cube pattern, and pop the cubes off into the mixing bowl. Stir all the fruit together with the juice, reserving some slices of star fruit or kiwi fruit for decoration. Pile the fruit mixture back into the boat-like bowls that the pineapple shells now form. Put these into appropriate-sized individual serving dishes, decorate with the reserved slices of fruit, and refrigerate for 30 minutes before serving. This dish is as spectacular as it is delicious.

Sussex Pond Pudding

There are two versions of this solid suet pudding from south-east England, one from Sussex and one from Kent. The only difference seems to be that the Kent one (called a Kentish Well pudding) includes dried fruit, particularly currants, whereas the Sussex one doesn't. Either way, they're an unusual twist on the old concept of suet pudding. While the pastry is suet, the predominant flavour is the scent and bitter-sweetness of the lemon, an unexpected centrepiece. In the light of new information about fungicide waxes, you may wish to use an organic lemon, or one that hasn't been waxed, to make this pudding. Serve with Real egg custard (see p. 188).

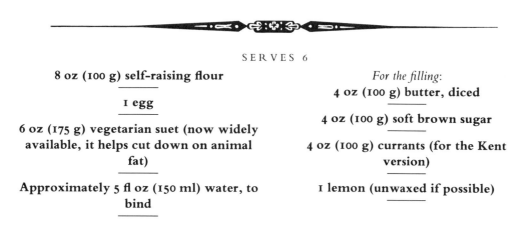

SERVES 6

8 oz (100 g) self-raising flour

1 egg

6 oz (175 g) vegetarian suet (now widely available, it helps cut down on animal fat)

Approximately 5 fl oz (150 ml) water, to bind

For the filling:

4 oz (100 g) butter, diced

4 oz (100 g) soft brown sugar

4 oz (100 g) currants (for the Kent version)

1 lemon (unwaxed if possible)

By hand, or in a blender or food processor, mix the flour, egg and suet with just enough water to make a soft malleable dough. Roll out on a lightly floured board to $\frac{1}{4}$ in (5 mm) thick. Using two-thirds of the dough, line a 2 pint (1.2 litre) pudding basin, keeping the rest for a lid. Fill the basin with half the butter and brown sugar, and the currants if you are using them. Then, using a sharp, thin instrument (a hat pin is ideal), pierce the lemon all over and stand in the pudding on the filling mixture. Top with the remaining filling ingredients so that the lemon is covered. Cover with the pastry lid and seal firmly round the edges. Cover the basin in buttered foil, pleated to allow for steam expansion during cooking. Tie up with enough string to leave a handle on top for easy removal, then steam for 3 hours in a saucepan, or 1 hour in a pressure cooker.

Remove the foil from the pudding basin. To turn out the pudding, put a serving bowl over the basin and turn both upside down. Make a cut in the suet pastry so that the juice flows out, forming a 'pond'.

Serve with custard.

PANCAKES

There are all kinds of pancakes from all over the world: a batter mixture spread on a hot griddle is an almost universal food. The key to geographical differences is the flour and liquid used: maize and water for tortillas in Mexico, wheat and water for Peking pancakes in China. In Europe, white wheatflour is normally used, but we add eggs and a variety of liquids: milk in Britain and water or fruit juice in France, for instance.

It's worth remembering how adaptable the basic mixture can be. The batter can be made with orange juice for pancakes to be eaten with honey and garnished with an orange section, or with chicken stock for pancakes filled with mushrooms and cream. Remember, too, that when you make pancakes the first one always goes wrong, and the others get better as you go on. So don't panic!

Basic Method

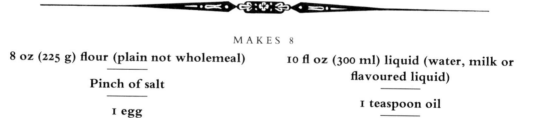

MAKES 8

8 oz (225 g) flour (plain not wholemeal)

Pinch of salt

1 egg

10 fl oz (300 ml) liquid (water, milk or flavoured liquid)

1 teaspoon oil

Combine the flour and salt, stir in the egg and mix. Beat in the liquid until the consistency is like single cream. Add the oil, stir, and leave to rest for up to 30 minutes. Heat a heavy pan and oil it lightly. Pour a ladle of batter into the pan and swirl around. When bubbles appear, after $1\frac{1}{2}$–2 minutes, flip or turn the pancake and cook for 1 minute more.

The pancakes will keep stacked with greaseproof paper between them.

Oat Pancakes

*M*y *own version of a recipe long cooked in Scotland and in parts of England, these pancakes are filling and deliciously nutty.*

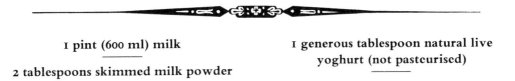

MAKES 8

4 oz (100 g) fine oatmeal

2 oz (50 g) self-raising flour

Good pinch of salt

1 tablespoon oil or melted butter

10 fl oz (300 ml) water mixed with 2 tablespoons plain yoghurt

For the topping
Heather honey

5 fl oz (150 ml) double cream, lightly whipped

Mix the oatmeal, flour and salt together, then mix the oil or butter and watered yoghurt together. Combine and stir well. Leave to mature for at least 20 minutes. Heat a heavy pan and wipe thoroughly with oil. Drop the pancake mixture into the pan (by the tablespoonful), cook for 2 minutes a side and serve with the honey and cream.

Home-made Yoghurt

*I*f *you're making yoghurt, be careful to choose the right starter. Some varieties, particularly imports from Greece, have been pasteurised to improve their keeping qualities. This means they are 'dead' with no live bacteria to start your batch.*

1 pint (600 ml) milk

2 tablespoons skimmed milk powder

1 generous tablespoon natural live yoghurt (not pasteurised)

Boil the milk with the skimmed milk powder stirred in for 5 minutes. Allow to cool to blood heat (cool enough to put your little finger in the milk for 10 seconds without screaming). Stir in the yoghurt. Place in a covered bowl in a warm place for 6 hours. A wide-necked insulated flask is ideal for this process. The yoghurt will make itself. All you have to do is refrigerate and eat it.

The two recipes that follow are simple, super-quick ways of flavouring plain yoghurt. Both are infinitely adaptable: you can substitute ingredients, change quantities and add your own touches for individual tastes and textures. This flexibility apart, one of the greatest benefits of making your own flavoured yoghurts is that you know what's in them, and can control the amount of sugar that's added.

The first recipe, with honey and walnuts, is based on flavours I always associate with Turkey, where thick, golden yoghurt made from sheep's milk, wonderful dark thyme-scented honey and fresh walnuts combine to make the most wonderful breakfast. Good cow's milk yoghurt, a little runny honey and a few nuts make a passably satisfactory substitute.

Honey and Walnut Yoghurt

SERVES 4

3 tablespoons runny honey

18 fl oz (550 ml) natural yoghurt

3 tablespoons crushed walnuts

Warm the honey until it's fairly liquid, then stir into the yoghurt. If the yoghurt is one of the pre-set kinds, beat it until it's a little liquid before adding the honey, or they won't mix satisfactorily. Mix in 2 tablespoons of the walnuts and pour into pretty stemmed glasses. Decorate with the remaining walnuts.

Quick Fruit Yoghurt

Ideally, use home-made jam for this. Not only will the flavour and texture be more delicious, but you will know what's in it. However, if you don't make your own jam, some very good, low-sugar, high-fruit jams are available. Even nicer jams, described as conserves, are made in the softer European style: the fruit is often in large pieces, and the jelly quite thin by our standards. Conserves are particularly good for flavouring. Serve the yoghurt in glasses, with thin, crisp biscuits to give it a special appeal.

SERVES 4

**6 tablespoons good-quality home-made
jam or high-fruit conserve**

18 fl oz (550 ml) natural yoghurt

Beat the jam into the yoghurt. (If the jam is a little stiff, melt it over a low heat first.) Allow to set in the refrigerator for 30 minutes if possible before serving.

BREAD AND CAKES

*T*he fresh bread counter is one of the most exciting sights in a supermarket today – and some of the signs you see on it are even more exciting: 'unbleached flour', 'made without animal fats', 'stone-ground organic' … These really do show how our taste in bread has changed in the last 10–15 years. We've come to realise the amazing range of flavours, textures and health benefits that it provides. Flavour and fibre go hand in hand, not just in solid wholemeals, but in the newly developed soft grain breads and the range of seed and Turkistan and nut-flavoured loaves that are available, not just in supermarkets but in many small bakers as well. Bread with a meal is almost essential to me, unless the food is ethnic, from a country where bread's never been heard of – and there aren't many of those. And I don't just mean a raised loaf. Mexican tortillas, Mediterranean pittas and Indian chapatis, all have their part to play. I've always had a soft spot for the Food and Wine Society ever since it stated in the preamble to one of its recipe books that it, 'took for granted good water and fine bread' on the table without having to mention it in every menu.

Very recently, *Food and Drink* did a major tasting of breads from supermarkets all over the country. It took place in a sandwich bar at the Royal Exchange in the City of London late in the evening, after the daytime customers had departed. It lasted about 4 hours and was extraordinarily revealing, not for the individual winners and losers (losers attempt to improve their products and winners don't always maintain standards), but because the tasting demonstrated the huge range of different breads available. Very different from the time, not so many years ago, when finding more than a couple of kinds of loaves, plus Hovis, was like discovering a treasure trove.

I've given a variety of recipes for making bread here. Some, like the Soda bread, are very quick and easy to make, and some take a little longer because they're yeast-risen (but there are crafty techniques to speed the process up). Either way, the time it takes *you* to make bread, as opposed to the time it takes for the bread to get on with it itself, is never more than 10–15 minutes – absolutely worth it for the wonderful flavours.

When making bread, always remember that the absorbent qualities of different flours vary; the amount of water used depends very much on the flour.

I also give recipes for using the bread once you've made it. Some unusual sandwiches and some delicious cheese-on-toast ideas are a reminder of how, given good basic ingredients to start with, crafty cookery doesn't have to be in any way complicated.

Later on in the chapter, I give recipes for a few, very simple, cakes. I'm not a committed cake cook myself, although a slice of something sweet and scrumptious with a cup of tea is hard to resist at around 4pm. The chocolate cake is particularly suitable and ridiculously easy to make. Let me commend it to you – and also let me commend the banana bread, which is a family favourite. We always seem to have left-over, slightly too brown bananas in the house and this is the most wonderful way of using them up. You can, of course, use perfectly ordinary bananas but a few recipes acknowledging that we don't all have perfect household management skills are very useful, in any cookery book.

BREADS

Soda bread is often thought of as a poor relation to yeast-risen bread, but it isn't. It's different, both in texture and taste: more spongy – particularly the white version – slightly sweeter, and a lot quicker to make. These two versions are great as alternatives to traditional bread. They are best eaten the same day, if possible while still warm from the oven. Do remember that baking *soda*, used in the first recipe, is different from baking *powder*, used in the second.

White Soda Bread

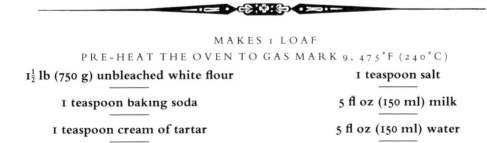

MAKES 1 LOAF
PRE-HEAT THE OVEN TO GAS MARK 9, 475°F (240°C)

1½ lb (750 g) unbleached white flour	1 teaspoon salt
1 teaspoon baking soda	5 fl oz (150 ml) milk
1 teaspoon cream of tartar	5 fl oz (150 ml) water

Mix the flour, baking soda, cream of tartar and salt together thoroughly. Mix the milk and water together and add to the dry ingredients. Knead lightly for 1 minute until thoroughly blended. Shape into a large round ball and place on a greased baking sheet. Make a pattern of slits on the top of the dough and cover with a pudding pasin big enough not to touch the dough. Bake for 30 minutes. Take off the basin and bake for a further 10 minutes until the loaf sounds hollow when tapped on the bottom. Cool on a wire rack.

Brown Soda Bread

MAKES 2 SMALL LOAVES
PRE-HEAT THE OVEN TO GAS MARK 8, 450°F (230°C)

$1\frac{1}{4}$ lb (550 g) wholemeal or granary flour

2 teaspoons baking powder

1 teaspoon salt

1 teaspoon cooking oil

10 fl oz (300 ml) buttermilk, or 5 fl oz (150 ml) water and 5 fl oz (150 ml) natural yoghurt, mixed

Mix all the ingredients into a dough, quickly but thoroughly. Then simply divide the mixture into 2 equal-sized, round loaves and place on a greased baking sheet. Bake for 30–40 minutes. The loaves are done when they sound hollow when you tap them on the bottom. Cool on a wire rack.

Seed Bread

When I first began to make bread regularly, wholemeal bread was a real problem as it never seemed to rise satisfactorily and, while the texture was doubtless good for you, it was a little heavy on the jaw. I then discovered the beneficial effects of Vitamin C in bread-making. It's the only addition that French bakers are ever allowed to use to help their bread develop its aerated inside and crisp crust. It transforms wholemeal bread-making and, I think, allows you to experiment in interesting ways. This loaf includes a whole range of seeds which give it an even more interesting texture and a delicious nutty flavour. Leave out the seeds, and you have perfect plain wholemeal.

MAKES 2 LOAVES
PRE-HEAT THE OVEN TO GAS MARK 7, 425°F (220°C)

2 lb (1 kg) stoneground wholemeal bread flour

$\frac{1}{4}$ teaspoon (really!) Vitamin C or ascorbic acid powder

1 teaspoon salt

1 oz (25 g) fresh yeast

1 dessertspoon brown sugar

1 pint (600 ml) warm water

2 tablespoons soya or olive oil

2 oz (50 g) pumpkin seeds, shelled

2 oz (50 g) sesame seeds

2 oz (50 g) sunflower seeds

Put the flour, Vitamin C or ascorbic acid powder and salt together in a large basin. (If you are using a dough-kneader machine, place these ingredients in the appropriate bowl.) Mix the yeast, the sugar and 5 fl oz (150 ml) of the water in a basin and leave for 10 minutes until frothy. Put the oil into the flour and add the yeast mixture and the remaining warm water, which should be at approximately blood heat. Knead thoroughly for 2–3 minutes until you feel the dough change texture and become elastic. If it proves sticky towards the end of this time, add a little sprinkling of flour to help its handling qualities. Pour a little more oil into the bowl and roll the dough in it to prevent it sticking to the sides. Cover the bowl with cling film or a tea towel, and put it in a warm place to rise for 30 minutes to 1 hour, depending on how rapidly the yeast works on your flour. When it has risen satisfactorily, that is, it has doubled in volume, sprinkle on the pumpkin, sesame and sunflower seeds, knock the dough down with the back of your hand, and knead again until the seeds are thoroughly incorporated. Divide the dough in half and put into 2 greased 2 lb (1 kg) bread tins and allow to rise in a warm place for another 20–25 minutes, by which time it should have reached the top of the tins or even peaked above them. Bake for 5 minutes, then turn the oven down to gas mark 4, 350°F (180°C). Bake for another 45–55 minutes. Tip one of the loaves out of its tin and tap it on the bottom. It should sound hollow. If it doesn't, return it to the oven without the tin, lay it on its side, and bake for another 5 minutes or so, then tap again. Take the other loaf out of its tin and let it also bake on its side for 5 minutes. Cool on a rack for at least 4 hours before eating, no matter how wonderful the smell.

White Unbleached Bread

Unbleached flour is white flour that hasn't had any artificial or chemical bleaching agent added, so it has a creamy colour and produces a loaf that tastes amazingly rich to people used to white bread that has been treated. It also has a nice texture, producing a rather firmer and slightly chewier crumb. The method here is very easy and I suggest a couple of alternatives to simply putting the dough in a loaf tin. If you want to follow one of them, use just two-thirds of the dough for standard loaves.

MAKES 2–3 LOAVES
PRE-HEAT THE OVEN TO GAS MARK 7, 425°F (220°C)

1 oz (25 g) fresh yeast

1 dessertspoon brown sugar

1½ pints (900 ml) warm water

3¼ lb (1.5 kg) unbleached white flour (for bread-making)

1 teaspoon salt

2 tablespoons oil

¼ teaspoon Vitamin C or ascorbic acid powder

Milk (optional)

Mix the yeast and brown sugar together in a bowl and add 5 fl oz (150 ml) of the warm water. Stir and leave to froth (about 10 minutes). Mix the flour, salt and oil together in a warm bowl with the Vitamin C or ascorbic acid powder. Add the yeast mixture and the remaining water, which should be at approximately blood heat. Knead thoroughly for about 2–3 minutes. You'll feel the texture change and start to become elastic. You can do this with an electric mixer or in a food processor. When the dough is elastic, add a little more oil to the bowl and roll the dough in it so that it doesn't stick. Put to rise in a warm place for about 30–35 minutes. It should double in bulk. Knock it down with the back of your hand and knead it again briefly. Put two-thirds of the dough into 2 greased 2 lb (1 kg) bread tins (or use 3 tins for all the dough). Allow to rise in a warm place for 20–25 minutes. Dust with a little flour or brush with milk and put into the oven. Immediately lower the temperature to gas mark 4, 350°F (180°C) and bake for 40–45 minutes. To test whether it is done, take one of the loaves out of its tin and tap the bottom. It should sound hollow – if it doesn't, return it to the oven, on its side, for another 5 minutes. Take the other loaf out of its tin and bake it on its side for 5 minutes. Cool on a wire rack before slicing and eating.

Focaccio

This is an Italian way of cooking bread and is marvellous as a first course with some tomato salad or a seafood cocktail.

MAKES 2 FLAT LOAVES
PRE-HEAT THE OVEN TO GAS MARK 6, 400°F (200°C)

$\frac{1}{3}$ **measure White unbleached bread dough (see opposite), after 1st rising**

4 tablespoons olive oil

1 teaspoon coarse salt

Rosemary or sage leaves (optional)

Put the dough into a bowl and add the olive oil. Knead thoroughly until the oil is absorbed. Cut the quantity of dough in half and spread each half into a flat loaf, the size of a dinner plate, on a greased baking sheet. Sprinkle with the coarse salt and a few rosemary or sage leaves if you have them. Allow to rise for another 10 minutes and then bake in the oven for 15–20 minutes. The bread should be golden but not too brown on the top.

Fruit Loaf

MAKES 1 LOAF
PRE-HEAT THE OVEN TO GAS MARK 4, 350°F (180°C)

2 oz (50 g) softened butter

4 oz (100 g) sultanas

2 oz (50 g) raisins

2 oz (50 g) candied peel

1 oz (25 g) sugar, plus 1 tablespoon for glazing

$\frac{1}{3}$ **measure White unbleached bread dough (see opposite), after 1st rising**

1 tablespoon water

Knead the butter, sultanas, raisins, candied peel and 1 oz (25 g) sugar into the dough. Put into a greased 2 lb (1 kg) loaf tin and put in a warm place to rise for 20 minutes. Mix the tablespoon of sugar and the water and melt in a saucepan over a gentle heat, making sure it doesn't go brown. Brush the top of the loaf with the glaze and bake for 45 minutes until the bottom of the loaf sounds hollow when it is tapped. Cool on a rack.

Garlic Bread

*H*ere *is my own special recipe for garlic bread. The addition of lemon and parsley goes a long way to transforming this pungent parcel into a rather more refined experience. It's safer if everyone at the meal eats it — a dissenter can feel pretty isolated. You can prepare it a day in advance, and keep it refrigerated until it's time to bake it.*

PRE-HEAT THE OVEN TO GAS MARK 5, 375°F (190°C)

1 French loaf

2 oz (50 g) butter

2 cloves garlic, crushed

Juice of $\frac{1}{2}$ lemon

1 oz (25 g) parsley, finely chopped

Slice the French loaf three-quarters of the way through, at $1\frac{1}{2}$ in (4 cm) intervals. Blend the garlic with the parsley, butter and lemon juice, either in a food processor or by hand. Spread the mixture on to the slices in the loaf, wrap loosely in foil and bake for 20 minutes. Serve hot.

SANDWICHES

Only too often, sandwiches are last-minute concoctions put together without any special care or thought. This is a real pity because we eat more and more of them in our busy lives, and they really benefit from a little care and fresh ingredients. Here are two traditional sandwiches with a little twist, and two unexpected combinations, that make use of some of the delicious breads that are now so widely available.

Wholemeal Baps with Egg and Cress

*I*deal *for school lunch-boxes or a quick, delicious snack lunch. This recipe has a double twist on the classic egg and cress: added texture from the hard-boiled egg, and bite from the peppery watercress.*

MAKES 4

3 eggs

1 oz (25 g) butter

2 tablespoons real mayonnaise
(see Crafty mayonnaise, p. 65)

1 bunch watercress, chopped

4 wholemeal baps, split and buttered

Hard-boil one egg and then cool, shell and chop it. Scramble the other 2 eggs in the butter and add the hard-boiled egg and the mayonnaise. Leave to cool. Add the watercress to the egg mixture, divide into 4 and fill the baps.

Chopped Herring on Black Rye

*A*n *unexpected combination – black rye bread looks very dark but tastes quite mild. Chopped herring pâté from a delicatessen looks grey and bleak, but has a lively, spicy taste.*

MAKES 4

4 oz (100 g) chopped herring pâté

8 slices black rye bread, buttered

1 crisp eating apple

Divide the herring mixture into 4 and spread on 4 slices of the bread. Core the apple and slice into thin rings. Place on top of the herring mixture. Cover with the remaining 4 slices of bread. Press the sandwiches gently together, then slice into strips.

Cheese and Salami on Granary

*T*hese are really filling sandwiches with bags of flavour and staying-power. I find them ideal for car journeys and travelling lunches of all kinds. My favourite salami is the very garlicky Kosher and a good cheese to use is Gruyère, though you can use other kinds and flavours if you prefer.

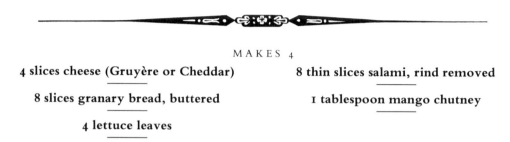

MAKES 4

4 slices cheese (Gruyère or Cheddar)

8 slices granary bread, buttered

4 lettuce leaves

8 thin slices salami, rind removed

1 tablespoon mango chutney

Place one slice of cheese on each of 4 bread slices, then a lettuce leaf and 2 slices of salami. Spread with chutney, top with a bread slice and press together firmly.

Hunters' Loaf

*T*his is said to have been a traditional pocket lunch for French hunters, always careful to look after the inner homme *even when at la chasse. Even if you don't hunt,* find an excuse to make this. It's scrumptious, travels well and can satisfy the most voracious appetites. Don't neglect to 'press' it as directed: it makes a lot of difference.

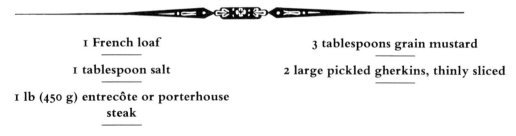

1 French loaf

1 tablespoon salt

1 lb (450 g) entrecôte or porterhouse steak

3 tablespoons grain mustard

2 large pickled gherkins, thinly sliced

Cut the loaf in half lengthways so that you have 2 'canoes' of bread. Scoop out and discard some of the crumb. Heat a dry pan until it's very hot. Sprinkle it with the salt and cook the steak $1\frac{1}{2}$ minutes on one side, and then turn and cook for a further $2\frac{1}{2}$ minutes. Cut the steak into strips to fit the bread. Spread the lower half of the loaf with the mustard (no butter), put the steak in and cover it with the slices of gherkin. Cover with the other half loaf, wrap in foil and press under telephone directories or other weights for 2 hours. To eat, slice into 2 in (5 cm) pieces.

TOASTED CHEESE IN FOUR GUISES

The English call it Welsh Rarebit, the Welsh call it Caws Enllyn and the French call their version *croque-monsieur*. Whatever its name, it's loved everywhere. Now, with the variety of breads, cheeses and relishes that are available, the changes that can be rung on toasted cheese make this quick snack a meal in its own right.

Cheddar and Anchovy Toast

MAKES 4

4 slices granary bread

8 slices Cheddar cheese

1 x 2 oz (50 g) tin anchovies in oil

Toast the bread on one side only. Put the cheese (2 slices per piece) on the untoasted side. Place 2 anchovy fillets in the shape of a cross over each, and toast until the cheese bubbles.

French Toast

MAKES 2

6 oz (175 g) Gruyère cheese, grated

2 tablespoons Dijon mustard

½ French loaf

Mix the cheese and mustard together. Split the loaf lengthways and toast the crust sides for 1½ minutes until they are hot. Spread the cheese and mustard mixture on the cut side of the bread making sure it covers the entire surface. Grill until the cheese mixture is melted and golden.

Pitta and Haloumi

A *Middle-Eastern version of cheese on toast, using pitta bread and a white, salty cheese which melts most satisfactorily. You can use other cheese but Haloumi is worth seeking out in delicatessens.*

MAKES 2

2 pittas

4 oz (100 g) Haloumi, thinly sliced

8 black olives, stoned

Heat the pittas for about 2 minutes under a medium-hot grill, then split lengthways along one edge into halves. Lay the Haloumi on the inside surfaces of the pittas and dot the olives over the cheese. Grill until the cheese bubbles and the bread is just beginning to scorch. Eat hot.

Stilton and Mango Toasts

A *new style with the classic combination of cheese and chutney. You can use other blue cheeses, but Stilton has that special bite.*

MAKES 4

4 slices good white bread

4 tablespoons mango chutney

8 oz (225 g) Blue Stilton

Toast and butter each slice normally. Spread one side of each slice with the mango chutney. Crumble the Stilton and spread over the chutney. Press gently down, then grill the toasts until the Stilton melts and begins to bubble.

CAKES

Crafty Chocolate Cake

*T*his is my and my family's favourite chocolate cake. It's dark, yummy and moist, easy to ice and even easier to eat! The method may sound extraordinary but do trust me. It has a health bonus too: the oil can be polyunsaturated. Remember: don't be tempted to use drinking chocolate instead of cocoa – you need the bitter chocolate tang for maximum success. On Food and Drink *we compared how long it took to make this chocolate cake and a chocolate cake mix handled by one of the Women's Institute's leading bakers. I'm glad to say that not only was mine about 2 minutes faster (the whole exercise takes only about 3 or 4 minutes altogether) but everyone agreed that it also tasted a lot better.*

PRE-HEAT THE OVEN TO GAS MARK 3, 325°F (160°C)

6 oz (175 g) self-raising flour

4 heaped tablespoons cocoa powder

1 heaped teaspoon baking powder

4 oz (100 g) caster sugar

1 dessertspoon black treacle

5 fl oz (150 ml) sunflower oil

5 fl oz (150 ml) milk

2 large eggs

For the filling and topping:
12 fl oz (350 ml) fromage frais

5 fl oz (150 ml) double cream

4 tablespoons black cherry jam

Place all the cake ingredients in a food processor and blend together (or put them in a large bowl and mix with a wooden spoon). When the mixture has turned dark brown and creamy, divide it in half and spoon evenly into 2 x 7 in (18 cm) greased sandwich tins. Bake for 45 minutes, then remove from the oven and take the cakes out of their tins. Allow to cool. Meanwhile, beat the fromage frais into the double cream until it is thick. When the cakes have cooled, spread one of them with the cherry jam, followed by a third of the cream mixture. Sandwich both cakes carefully together. Spread the remaining cream mixture on top and, using a fork, bring up into peaks. This cake can be refrigerated for up to 24 hours before serving. Do make sure you use the correct size of sandwich tins. The wrong size could lead either to a biscuit or a gooey mess.

Apple Cake

More of a pudding than a cake, this dish comes originally from Sweden but has been adapted all over the world. It resembles a cold version of our apple crumble, but it's spicier and more exotic. Served without cream, it makes a refreshing end to a rich winter meal.

SERVES 4–6

PRE-HEAT THE OVEN TO GAS MARK 2, 300°F (150°C)

2 lb (1 kg) cooking apples, peeled, cored, in $\frac{1}{4}$ in (5 mm) slices

8 oz (225 g) brown sugar

$\frac{1}{2}$ teaspoon ground cinnamon

$\frac{1}{2}$ teaspoon ground cloves

1 lb (450 g) fresh brown breadcrumbs (these can be made in a blender or food processor)

Put the apples in a frying-pan with 6 oz (175 g) of the sugar and cook over a medium heat until soft and translucent. Stir in the cinnamon and cloves and leave to cool. Mix the breadcrumbs with the remaining 2 oz (50 g) sugar and heat together in the oven, or on top of the stove, for 5 minutes. Allow the breadcrumb mixture to cool. Divide the 2 separate mixtures into 3 parts each and place them in layers in a bowl. Start with apple and finish with breadcrumbs. Use a glass bowl if possible, to show off the layers. Chill for 2 hours in a refrigerator. The contrasts of texture and flavour are really intriguing.

Chocolate Brownies

Sometimes known as fudge brownies, these are half-way between a pudding and confectionery. They are almost as gooey to cook as to eat, so non-stick baking paper (widely available) is a good idea and saves quite dramatically on the washing-up. They are very tempting, but don't cut the squares too big: they're quite filling, too. Unlike most cakes, they can be eaten hot, almost straight out of the oven – but they don't acquire their really tooth-sticking quality until they are cool.

PRE-HEAT THE OVEN TO GAS MARK 4, 350°F (180°C)

6 oz (175 g) butter or margarine	2 eggs
2 oz (50 g) cocoa	2 oz (50 g) self-raising flour
6 oz (175 g) soft brown sugar	2 oz (50 g) walnuts, chopped

Melt a third of the butter and add the cocoa. Cream the rest of the butter with the sugar. Add the eggs and flour and then beat in the butter and cocoa mixture. Grease and line a 7 in (18 cm) square tin. Mix the walnuts with the other ingredients and pour into the tin. Bake for about 35 minutes. Leave for 5 minutes, then cut into squares. The cakes can be eaten hot or cold and are often iced, usually before they're completely cool, with a fudge mixture.

If you want to use a food processor for this recipe, melt the cocoa with a third of the butter, then put in all the ingredients except the walnuts and zip for 5 seconds. Add the walnuts before pouring the mixture into the tin.

Banana Bread

This is surprisingly banana-tasting, but because it's full of other goodies as well it's really quite rich. When I'm feeling abstemious I eat it in slices on its own. When I'm feeling really self-indulgent, I have been known to butter it.

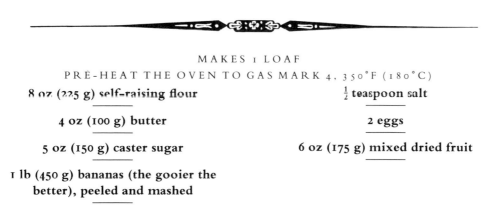

MAKES 1 LOAF
PRE-HEAT THE OVEN TO GAS MARK 4, 350°F (180°C)

8 oz (225 g) self-raising flour	$\frac{1}{2}$ teaspoon salt
4 oz (100 g) butter	2 eggs
5 oz (150 g) caster sugar	6 oz (175 g) mixed dried fruit
1 lb (450 g) bananas (the gooier the better), peeled and mashed	

Mix all the ingredients except the dried fruit together. You can do this in a food processor or by hand in a basin. When they're all thoroughly mixed, add the dried fruit. Spoon the mixture into a 2 lb (1 kg) non-stick loaf tin, spread it out evenly and bake it for $1\frac{1}{2}$ hours. The loaf is done when a skewer pushed into its middle comes out clean. Cool on a wire rack before slicing.

Marmalade Cake

This is a real store-cupboard cake that is a great family favourite. You can make it from ingredients most of us have in the refrigerator or larder. I cook it in a long loaf tin, rather than a round cake tin. It makes it easier to cut and allows one of the ultimate self-indulgences: lightly toasted slices of marmalade cake spread with a little butter at tea-time ... Don't be tempted, by the way, to add more marmalade – it sinks to the bottom and doesn't add much to the flavour.

MAKES 1 LOAF

PRE-HEAT THE OVEN TO GAS MARK 5, 375°F (190°C)

4 oz (100 g) butter or soft margarine	2 eggs
8 oz (225 g) self-raising flour	Grated rind and juice of 1 orange
1 teaspoon baking powder	Grated rind and juice of 1 lemon
3½ oz (90 g) caster sugar	3 tablespoons marmalade

If you've got a food processor, put all the ingredients except the marmalade into it and mix the cake in 30 seconds. If mixing by hand, make sure the butter or margarine is soft, then add to the flour, baking powder, caster sugar, eggs and orange and lemon rind and juice and beat with a wooden spoon until creamy. Add the marmalade and pour into a non-stick 2 lb (1 kg) loaf tin. Bake for 45–50 minutes, until a skewer pushed into the middle of the cake comes out clean. Cool on a wire rack for at least 3 hours before eating.

CHRISTMAS

---

*F*or Christmas on *Food and Drink* we've always rung the changes on what we do and the way we do it. For a couple of years, there was the *Food and Drink* quiz, a light-hearted game of tastings and challenges, which went on to become a successful television series in its own right. But the most important feature of *Food and Drink* Christmases hasn't been the trips to Devon villages, the surprise guests and the mixing with audiences. Rather, it is the healthy approach to festive eating that's become a hallmark of the programme.

Christmas is a time for enjoying yourself, but you shouldn't finish feeling worse than when you started. I'm not referring only to the consumption of alcohol, but to the rich foods with which we sometimes abuse ourselves over the holiday period. I've devised, and am happy to bring together for the first time below, a whole range of crafty Christmas recipes. They range from turkey-roasting techniques which save on washing-up as well as producing the most wonderful bird, through low-fat Christmas puddings and vegetarian mince pies to the most delicious Christmas cake I know. The recipes here can be used to produce a complete *Food and Drink* Christmas; or just substitute one or two of them for your own dishes and traditions. And, because it is always important to make sure the cook gets a chance to enjoy herself (or himself), these methods are also crafty in terms of effort.

Crafty Roast Turkey

*R*oasting a turkey often seems a matter of guesswork. To get the legs properly cooked while keeping the breast moist isn't always easy. Well, there's a crafty way of doing this that makes the gravy at the same time and saves on washing-up. It's only fair to admit that, although this is a very healthy way to roast a turkey, it was actually designed to give you a succulent bird.

Recommended roasting times vary widely: some people suggest nearly twice the time per 1 lb (450 g) than others. My experience is that the method below shortens the process, first because the turkey is not stuffed in the body cavity and, second, because of the effects of the steam. There does seem to be a rule that frozen turkeys need a bit longer than fresh ones, even if they have been thoroughly defrosted, and they must be. Whatever your choice of bird, try this method and you'll be rewarded with a succulent fowl plus delicious gravy and easy washing-up. What further recommendation could there be?

A few rules:

1 Defrost a frozen turkey for at least 48 hours.
2 Don't stuff the body cavity, only the breast end.
3 Consider a non-meat stuffing.
4 Keep the water topped up (see below).

PRE-HEAT THE OVEN TO GAS MARK 4, 350°F (180°C)

Place the turkey on a wire rack that will fit inside the roasting tin. Put $1\frac{1}{2}$ pints (900 ml) of water under the turkey and squeeze the juice of a lemon over the bird. Place the squeezed lemon halves in the body cavity. Season the bird highly, all over the skin, as well as in the body cavity, and cover (not wrap) with butter papers or buttered foil to make a tent. Roast the turkey for:

16 minutes per 1 lb (450 g) up to 12 lb (5.5 kg) in weight
14 minutes per 1 lb (450 g) up to 18 lb (8 kg) in weight
12 minutes per 1 lb (450 g) above 18 lb (8 kg) in weight
About 5 minutes longer per 1 lb (750 g) for frozen birds – but check. There are often instructions on the pack.

To make sure the turkey is cooked, pierce the thickest part of the thigh with a skewer. If the juice is clear, the turkey is done. If not, give it another 10–15 minutes. Leave to rest for at least 10 minutes while you dish up the vegetables, then pour off the liquid from the pan to use as a delicious gravy. You will, by the way, find it easier to carve if, before roasting, you remove the wishbone. You can then carve each half of the breast diagonally without having to fight your way along the side to produce ever-diminishing slices. Ask your butcher to remove the wishbone if you aren't too confident about doing it yourself, but a sharp pair of scissors and careful feeling for the ends of the wishbone make it a fairly easy process.

Orange and Cranberry Sauce

MAKES $1-1\frac{1}{4}$ LB (450–550 G)

1 lb (450 g) fresh or bottled cranberries

Juice and grated rind of 1 orange

6 oz (175 g) caster sugar

Put the cranberries and orange juice into a saucepan and bring to the boil. Cover the pan and simmer gently for 10 minutes (the cranberries will pop!). Add the sugar and the grated orange rind, and stir until the sugar is dissolved. Simmer for a further 10 minutes. Decant into jars and cool before serving.

ALTERNATIVES TO TURKEY

Turkey can be too big, or out of favour, or not acceptable. Fortunately there are some delicious alternatives. If you are a small family, roast pheasant is a smashing idea, and if you're a bit of a traditionalist, the roast goose. If you're vegetarian, the vegetarian Nut Wellington is ideal.

Roast Pheasant

Pheasant has lots of flavour and — provided it isn't too high — the texture isn't too greasy. It's easy to cook and, unlike duck, has lots of meat. A cock pheasant should serve four people, and a hen two or three. You can, of course, make delicious pheasant casseroles, but I think the festive season needs a festive roast. Make sure the bird has been properly hung (3–5 days) and do pre-heat the oven: speed is of the essence.

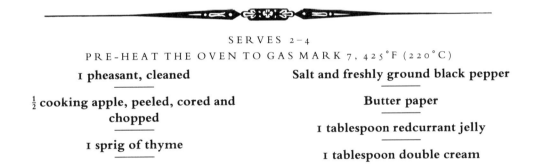

SERVES 2–4
PRE-HEAT THE OVEN TO GAS MARK 7, 425°F (220°C)

1 pheasant, cleaned	**Salt and freshly ground black pepper**
½ cooking apple, peeled, cored and chopped	**Butter paper**
1 sprig of thyme	**1 tablespoon redcurrant jelly**
	1 tablespoon double cream

Stuff the pheasant with the apple pieces and thyme. Season and place a wrap of butter paper over the top. Put in a baking tin and bake for 1 hour. (Remove the butter paper for the last 10 minutes of cooking.) Take the apple pieces out of the pheasant and put them into a saucepan with the juices from the baking tin. Add the redcurrant jelly and double cream. Carefully heat the sauce, stirring, until well blended, thick and creamy. (You may want to use a blender for smoothness.) Place the pheasant on a dish and carve. Carefully spoon the sauce around the pieces before serving. Or the sauce can be served in a gravy boat.

Goose

A goose was the top Christmas choice for centuries, and is now making a late-twentieth-century comeback. This is partly because of our considerable appetite for nostalgia, but also a sure sign of our rediscovered interest in more complex and mature flavours. Though the domestic goose isn't really game, its rich and strong savouriness is closer to that of wild game birds than to the blandness of our modern poultry.

Goose is not likely to be to most children's tastes – mine certainly prefer turkey – so save it for an adults-only Christmas lunch, or for a festive supper during the long holiday period that we enjoy these days. Fresh and frozen geese are now widely available. A bird weighing about 6–7 lb (2.75–3 kg) will feed six people only once.

Although goose isn't greasy when craftily cooked, it is rich. Sharp apple sauce goes especially well with it. So too does Red cabbage (see p. 144) and mashed or new potatoes.

SERVES 6

PRE-HEAT THE OVEN TO GAS MARK 5, 375°F (190°C)

6–7 lb (2.75–3 kg) goose, well thawed at room temperature if frozen

8 oz (225 g) Spanish onion, chopped

1 egg

1 tablespoon chopped fresh sage, or ½ tablespoon dried sage

4 oz (100 g) fresh breadcrumbs

Salt and freshly ground black pepper

1 lb (450 g) Bramley apples, peeled, cored and chopped

1 tablespoon water

1 oz (25 g) butter

Pinch of ground cloves

2 oz (50 g) sugar

Wash the goose carefully and then place it in a clean sink. Pour a kettle of boiling water over it, turning it half-way. Let it drain and then dry for 2 hours. This will help give a crisp skin and prevent greasiness. To make the stuffing, which is not essential but nice, mix the onion with the egg, sage and breadcrumbs. Season generously, then stuff the cavity. As with all stuffings, don't pack it in too tightly. Put the bird on a wire rack over a roasting tin and roast for 20 minutes per lb (450 g), plus 20 minutes more. Take the goose out of the oven and leave to stand for 15 minutes in a warm place. Keep the fat if you want to, but don't be tempted to try to turn it into gravy. Instead, make this sharp, spicy and very traditional sauce.

Gently cook the apples with 1 tablespoon water until soft. Add the butter, cloves and sugar, then simmer gently for 15 minutes until well blended; you can add more sugar when serving, but try it with a slice of the goose first.

To carve the goose remember it's easier and safer to carve the breast into 3 sections a side than to attempt delicate slices. The drumsticks, thighs and wings, much smaller than a turkey's, provide the remaining portions.

Don't forget to serve the stuffing – it will have taken on a delicious flavour.

Apricot and Pear Stuffing

An alternative stuffing for goose, this has many of the flavours of Middle Europe, with dried fruit counterbalancing the richness of the bird.

4 oz (100 g) dried apricots	**2 tablespoons chopped parsley**
4 oz (100 g) dried pears	**Pinch of fresh or dried sage**
6 oz (175 g) breadcrumbs	**2 eggs**
1 bunch spring onions, chopped	**Grated rind and juice of 1 lemon**

Soak the apricots and pears overnight. Drain, then chop well and mix with all the other ingredients. Stuff the bird. Weigh after stuffing to calculate the cooking time: 25 minutes per 1 lb (450 g).

Vegetarian Nut Wellington

I am indebted to Rose Elliot, the vegetarian cookery author, and to one of her ardent fans, for the idea behind this nut-cutlet with pretensions. The fan makes this on high days and holidays. It's quite scrumptious and grand enough for the poshest parties, although it fits a very modest pocket! I suggested it as a Christmas dish for vegetarians, and the response from them (and quite often from their non-vegetarian spouses) was tremendous. Vegetarian puff pastry, which contains no animal fats, is available from many supermarkets.

SERVES 4

PRE-HEAT THE OVEN TO GAS MARK 7, 425°F (220°C)

12 oz (350 g) vegetarian puff pastry	6 oz (175 g) chestnut purée
1 small onion, chopped	1 heaped teaspoon paprika
2 celery sticks, chopped	1 teaspoon dried oregano
2 garlic cloves, chopped	2 tablespoons lemon juice
Oil for frying	Salt and freshly ground black pepper
1 tablespoon oil	2 eggs
4 oz (100 g) walnuts	2 oz (50 g) button mushrooms, sliced
4 oz (100 g) cashew nuts	Beaten egg, to glaze

Roll out the pastry and line a 2 lb (1 kg) loaf tin, leaving enough overlapping on either side to cover the top. Fry the onion, celery and garlic in a little oil. Put in a bowl with the oil, walnuts, cashew nuts, chestnut purée, paprika, oregano, lemon juice and seasoning. Mix well and bind together with the eggs. Put the mushrooms into the bottom of the lined loaf tin, then fill the tin with the mixture, pressing it down firmly to fill the spaces in between the mushrooms. Brush the pastry edges with a little beaten egg to seal, and cover the pie with the overlapping pastry. Trim the edges. Put a baking sheet on top of the loaf tin and turn over. Carefully remove the loaf tin. Decorate with pastry leaves, make a few cuts in the pastry, and brush lightly with beaten egg. Cook for about 1 hour. Half-way through the cooking, reduce the temperature to gas mark 4, 350°F (180°C).

LEFT-OVERS

Here are two easy ideas for left-overs, one grand and one very simple. They presume turkey left-overs but can be used with the meat from a capon or goose.

Parson

*T*his traditional dish was inspired by the spices that started to arrive in Britain from India at the end of the eighteenth century. Its original, spicy flavour is a welcome antidote to the tedium of endless cold cuts. Serve with moulded rice and mango chutney.

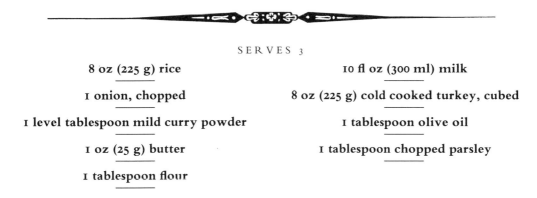

SERVES 3

8 oz (225 g) rice

1 onion, chopped

1 level tablespoon mild curry powder

1 oz (25 g) butter

1 tablespoon flour

10 fl oz (300 ml) milk

8 oz (225 g) cold cooked turkey, cubed

1 tablespoon olive oil

1 tablespoon chopped parsley

Boil the rice in plenty of water until cooked, then drain and keep hot. Meanwhile, fry the onion with the curry powder in the butter for 2 minutes. Stir in the flour and gradually add the milk. Whisk to a smooth sauce. Simmer gently for 5 minutes and then add the turkey. Heat through. Grease a ring mould with the olive oil. Sprinkle some chopped parsley on the bottom of the mould and then add the cooked rice. Press it down firmly and cover the mould with a plate. Turn it upside down, give the mould a sharp tap and turn the rice out on to a serving plate. Fill the centre with the turkey and serve imediately.

Turkey Roulade

Turkey left-overs are always a Christmas dilemma, though I find that turkey and cranberry sandwiches rarely seem to lose their charm with my family. If you fancy something a little more elegant, try this delicious and spectacular savoury Swiss roll, with left-over vegetables wrapped around spiced-up turkey chunks. Have courage – it's almost easier to do than read about. Garnish with lettuce, tomatoes and parsley.

SERVES 6
PRE-HEAT THE OVEN TO GAS MARK 6, 400°F (200°C)

2 oz (50 g) flour

10 fl oz (300 ml) milk

2 oz (50 g) butter

1 teaspoon grain mustard

3 oz (75 g) Cheddar cheese

3 eggs, separated

3 oz (75 g) left-over stuffing, crumbled

12 oz (350 g) cooked vegetables, chopped

Salt and freshly ground black pepper

1 tablespoon grated Parmesan cheese

For the filling:
8 oz (225 g) cooked turkey, diced

2 tablespoons mango chutney

3 tablespoons milk

Grease an 8 x 12 in (21 x 30 cm) Swiss roll tin, line it with greaseproof paper and grease again. Put the flour, milk and butter in a saucepan and bring to the boil, stirring continuously. Simmer for 1–2 minutes, stirring, until the sauce has thickened. Mix in the mustard and Cheddar and remove from the heat. Divide the sauce in half and put one half aside. Stir the egg yolks and stuffing into one half of the sauce, together with the vegetables. Season and mix thoroughly. Whisk the egg whites until stiff and gently fold into the sauce and vegetable mixture with a metal spoon. Pour the mixture into the prepared tin and smooth over the surface. Sprinkle with the Parmesan cheese. Bake for 20 minutes until the roulade is well risen and golden. Meanwhile, add the turkey, chutney and milk to the remaining sauce and heat through, stirring gently. Spread the turkey mixture on the roulade and roll up carefully along the long edge, like a Swiss roll. Two big spatulas help.

THE LOW-FAT CHRISTMAS TRIO

These are my favourite Christmas dishes. Although they taste wonderfully rich, they are remarkably light and, unlike the traditional versions, don't contain huge quantities of animal fat. However, they don't keep as long as the old-fashioned varieties do, so make the cake not more than 3–4 weeks before Christmas, and the pudding likewise. The mincemeat will keep in jars for up to 2 months.

Fruit and Nut Christmas Cake

This is a fabulous Christmas cake, so full of fruit and nuts there's hardly any room left for cake! It is so rich that it's best made in a ring mould which allows it to be thinly sliced. Not only does it taste good: the multicoloured glacé cherries give it a jewelled appearance.

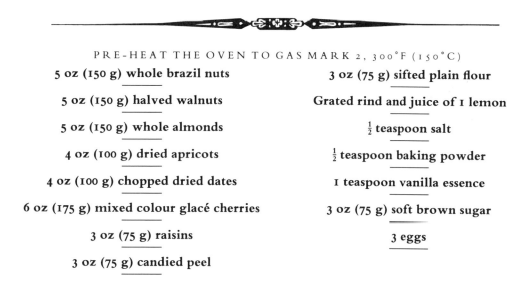

PRE-HEAT THE OVEN TO GAS MARK 2, 300°F (150°C)

5 oz (150 g) whole brazil nuts

5 oz (150 g) halved walnuts

5 oz (150 g) whole almonds

4 oz (100 g) dried apricots

4 oz (100 g) chopped dried dates

6 oz (175 g) mixed colour glacé cherries

3 oz (75 g) raisins

3 oz (75 g) candied peel

3 oz (75 g) sifted plain flour

Grated rind and juice of 1 lemon

$\frac{1}{2}$ teaspoon salt

$\frac{1}{2}$ teaspoon baking powder

1 teaspoon vanilla essence

3 oz (75 g) soft brown sugar

3 eggs

Mix all the fruit and nuts together. In a separate large bowl, whisk together all the other ingredients to make a smooth batter. Add the nuts and fruit to the batter and stir well until they are covered and bound together. Line and grease an 8 in (20 cm) cake tin or, best of all, a ring mould, and pour in the cake mixture. Bake for 2 hours. This cake can be made up to 3 days before Christmas and will keep for up to 1 month in an airtight cake tin.

Low-fat Christmas Pudding

The low-fat Christmas pudding plays an important part in the search for a yummy but healthy Christmas. Except for the oils inherent in ingredients like nuts and milk, this is a no-fat dish – no suet, butter or oil are added. It is deliciously dark and fruity with the authentic taste, but not the leaden weight, of the traditional pudding. It responds well to being flamed with rum or brandy and can be re-heated very successfully. What it doesn't take kindly to, is long storage. It is mature after a week and, unless kept in very dry, cool conditions can develop mould within 1 month. It is therefore best made in December, ideally 1–2 weeks before Christmas, and kept in an airtight container.

You can buy traditional moulds to give a spherical and truly Dickensian pudding.

SERVES 4–6

1 lb (450 g) wholemeal breadcrumbs	Juice and rind of 1 lemon
8 oz (225 g) currants	3 teaspoons mixed spice
8 oz (225 g) sultanas	1 oz (25 g) almonds, chopped
4 oz (100 g) apples, grated but not peeled	3 eggs
4 oz (100 g) bananas, chopped	10 fl oz (300 ml) milk
4 oz (100 g) brazil nuts, chopped	1 teaspoon salt
8 oz (225 g) soft brown sugar	

Mix together all the ingredients and stir well. Put the mixture into a greased pudding basin, and cover securely with greaseproof paper. The quantities given make enough for 1 x 4 pint (2.25 litre) basin or 2 x 2 pint (1.2 litre) basins. Steam for 3 hours then allow to cool. Store in a cool, dry place until Christmas Day. Steam for 1 hour, before serving in the traditional way. In a pressure cooker the first steaming takes 1 hour and the second one takes 25 minutes.

Low-fat Mince Pies

*T*he dietary problem with mince pies isn't the mincemeat: the recipe below, for instance, creates a wonderful, completely fat-free filling. The problem is the pastry. There is no fatless pastry – although Greek (or Turkish) filo pastry contains no fat, it's usually cooked with butter. Unfortunately, none of the substitutes for flaky pastry taste anything like the real thing. The only suggestion that seems to make sense is to make the pastry with half the quantity of fat you would normally use, and to roll it very thin. Top the pies with a dollop of meringue mixture rather than more pastry. This method doesn't altogether cut out the fat, but does reduce it dramatically. This recipe makes 7 lb (3 kg) of mincemeat that will keep in jars for up to 2 months in a cool, dark place.

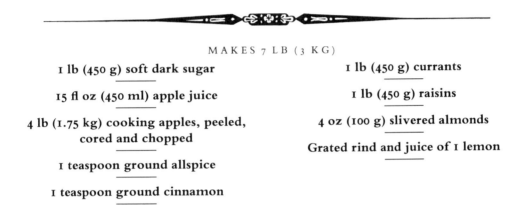

MAKES 7 LB (3 KG)

1 lb (450 g) soft dark sugar

15 fl oz (450 ml) apple juice

4 lb (1.75 kg) cooking apples, peeled, cored and chopped

1 teaspoon ground allspice

1 teaspoon ground cinnamon

1 lb (450 g) currants

1 lb (450 g) raisins

4 oz (100 g) slivered almonds

Grated rind and juice of 1 lemon

Melt the sugar in the apple juice over a lot heat. When the sugar is completely dissolved, add the apples and all the other ingredients. Bring to the boil and simmer gently, covered, for 30 minutes until they blend together in a soft mash. Put into sterilised jars while hot. Put greaseproof discs on top and tighten seals when the mincemeat is cool.

EXTRAS

Chocolate Truffles

*A*nd *now, after a really healthy Christmas, the moment of self-indulgence you crave.
Make these the week before Christmas and keep them hidden in the refrigerator –
if you don't they'll never last until the appointed day. They are better than anything
you can buy, cheap to make, and part of my wish for your Happy Christmas.*

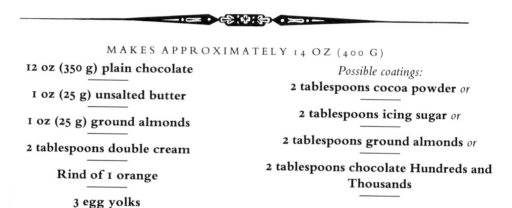

MAKES APPROXIMATELY 14 OZ (400 G)

12 oz (350 g) plain chocolate

1 oz (25 g) unsalted butter

1 oz (25 g) ground almonds

2 tablespoons double cream

Rind of 1 orange

3 egg yolks

Possible coatings:

2 tablespoons cocoa powder *or*

2 tablespoons icing sugar *or*

2 tablespoons ground almonds *or*

2 tablespoons chocolate Hundreds and
Thousands

Put all the truffle ingredients except the egg yolks in a saucepan and heat gently,
stirring until the mixture has blended into a smooth consistency. Remove from
the heat, beat in the egg yolks, and pour on to a plate. Place in the refrigerator
for 1 hour. Sprinkle the cocoa powder, icing sugar, ground almonds or chocolate
Hundreds and Thousands on to a Swiss roll tin. After 1 hour, remove the
chocolate mixture from the refrigerator, scoop a teaspoon out of the mixture
and roll it into a ball. Repeat until you've used up all the chocolate, then roll
each ball thoroughly in the coating. Place the chocolates in paper casings and
chill for at least 1 hour before eating. Best within 4–5 days.

Pompes de Nöel

*I*n *Provence, Christmas Day is celebrated with a feast, but without a set menu. Traditionally, the highlight will have taken place by Christmas Eve with a meal ending in* les treize desserts, *or Thirteen Desserts, which are eaten throughout the holiday. The number of desserts, and their nature, is hallowed through custom, but individual items vary between families. There is normally a centrepiece,* Pompes de Nöel, *or Provençal Christmas buns, and combinations of three fresh fruits, three dried fruits, three nuts and three sweets like nougat or almond truffles. All are enjoyed between as well as after meals. The* Pompes de Nöel *are named and made slightly differently in different parts of southern France. This recipe produces pretty, and delicious, buns.*

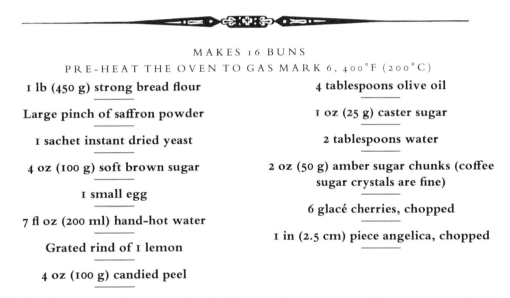

MAKES 16 BUNS
PRE-HEAT THE OVEN TO GAS MARK 6, 400°F (200°C)

1 lb (450 g) strong bread flour

Large pinch of saffron powder

1 sachet instant dried yeast

4 oz (100 g) soft brown sugar

1 small egg

7 fl oz (200 ml) hand-hot water

Grated rind of 1 lemon

4 oz (100 g) candied peel

4 tablespoons olive oil

1 oz (25 g) caster sugar

2 tablespoons water

2 oz (50 g) amber sugar chunks (coffee sugar crystals are fine)

6 glacé cherries, chopped

1 in (2.5 cm) piece angelica, chopped

Sift the flour into a large bowl and add the saffron, yeast and brown sugar. Leave in a warm place. Beat the egg in a measuring jug and top up with hand-hot water to the 8 fl oz (250 ml) mark. Beat again and add to the flour. Mix and knead for 2 minutes to form an elastic dough. Place in a lightly oiled bowl, cover with cling film and leave in a warm place for 1 hour. Then, knead the dough, adding the lemon rind, 3 oz (75 g) of the candied peel and the oil. Divide into 16 balls, flatten each one slightly on a baking sheet and leave uncovered to rise in a warm place for 45 minutes. When risen, bake for 15 minutes, then remove from the oven. Meanwhile, place the sugar in a small pan with the water. Dissolve the sugar over a low heat then boil for 2 minutes. Paint each bun with the syrup and scatter with a little of the remaining candied peel, some sugar chunks and a few pieces of cherry and angelica for a pretty jewelled effect.

Return to the oven for 5 minutes to crystallise the syrup.

THE CRAFTY COOK'S TOUR

One of the great privileges of working on *Food and Drink* is that I get to travel a lot – and when I travel I'm always on the receiving end of treats. People always want me to see the best of their land and taste their most delicious food, in the most beautiful and splendid locations. It sometimes seems too good to be true – that I see and do, for my job, what other people would give their eye teeth to be able to pay for. I only hope that I can pass on some of the pleasure and, occasionally, the knowledge I've gained on these trips.

Three favourite journeys were to very different parts of the world: the East Coast of the United States; Japan; and the Delhi area of India. I have recipes, and memories to go with them, from each of these places. American cooking, at first, is more accessible, but do try the Indian and, especially, the Japanese food which is comparatively new to Britain. It's a style of cooking that has influenced recent food developments in the West remarkably deeply, even though we don't always acknowledge it. Much of the inspiration for nouvelle cuisine came from Japan: two great French chefs who spent some time there were vastly impressed by what they saw and incorporated features of Japanese cuisine in their recipes. First though, West not East

THE UNITED STATES

Although my trip was to the East Coast, my admiration for American food stretches further afield than that. When I enthuse about it, most people greet my protestations with anything from polite amusement to blatant contempt. If only they knew how wrong they were! This commonly held view is partly the result of America's success in selling her cinema image: the brilliantly constructed 'adman's' dreams of teenagers in hot rods living on junk foods, often eaten without first removing the chewing gum, are pervasive and world-wide. But in many respects they are false, and even the worst excesses of American diet are relatively recent. The hamburger was first put in a bun only early this century, and it was in Los Angeles in the 1920s, when Hollywood was becoming the world's entertainment centre, that pickles, tomato, lettuce and 'mayo' were added to it.

Across America, but especially in the eastern seaboard states, from New England in the north to Louisiana in the south, there is a tradition of fine and robust cooking that goes back hundreds of years. It is a tradition that often recalls, better than in their present-day native lands, the original dishes of the settlers who made America their home. And the traditions could hardly be more varied. The French, and then the English, came into the old Spanish colony of Florida to add their influence, and all the time most of the cooking was being done by black slaves or servants brought from all over Africa, who added their own touches. The result is the justly famous Creole cuisine with its gumbos, fabulous fish dishes, and the meal it gave to the world: brunch – after jazz, New Orleans' most famous export.

Today, America's wealth, its wide range of climate and geography, plus its mastery of food production, mean that almost every foodstuff known to man, from pineapples to pink salmon, olive oil to oysters, is produced there. The raw materials are superb and, outside the confines of the fast-food emporia, they are used with imagination and conviction. Even the way in which American street foods and drinks have become the world's standard in fast food – burgers, fries and colas – demonstrates that at mass-market level they are universally appealing and accessible. Here, then, are some of the dishes I believe support my thesis that American food is fun to cook and great to eat.

Salt Beef Sandwiches
(Boston)

The most recent slice of American culture to have hit these shores has been American football. The gladiatorial rushes of its body-armoured teams of giants culminate each year in the Superbowl – 4 hours of nail-biting action that require frequent refuelling by its 60 million television spectators. Salt beef sandwiches are a popular choice, just beating hot dogs as instant energy food. Salt, or 'corned' beef (not to be confused with the tinned product enjoyed in this country) has been eaten in the north-east United States since the days of the settlers; the arrival of Irish immigrants in the last century gave it renewed popularity. It's good hot, sliced with cabbage, or re-heated as corned beef hash. For sandwiches, serve it in light rye or soft-grain white bread, with dill pickles (gherkins), American mustard, crinkle-cut crisps and Hot potato salad (see page 159).

Silverside or brisket, ready salted (available from supermarkets and butcher shops)

6 juniper berries

6 peppercorns

1 bay leaf

4 cloves

A few coriander seeds

Put everything in a pressure cooker or large saucepan. If using a pressure cooker, add 1 pint (600 ml) water and cook for 20 minutes per 1 lb (450 g). To cook in an ordinary saucepan, cover with water and cook for 1 hour per 1 lb (450 g). Remove from the pan, drain the water and slice the meat. Eat while hot in well-filled sandwiches, or on a plate with cabbage, mustard and potatoes.

Spaghetti and Meatballs
(New York)

The people who emigrated to America at the turn of the century were – in the famous words on Ellis Island – the tired and the poor. In their new country, they found a better life which gave them the wealth to transform their diets. However, they kept their taste for highly seasoned and robust flavours. This was especially true of the Italian immigrants who settled in New York and Boston.
Here is north-eastern America's answer to Bologna.

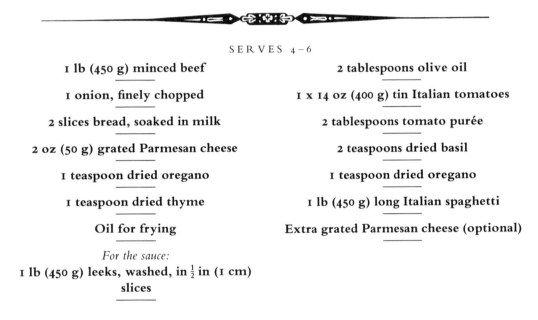

SERVES 4–6

1 lb (450 g) minced beef	2 tablespoons olive oil
1 onion, finely chopped	1 x 14 oz (400 g) tin Italian tomatoes
2 slices bread, soaked in milk	2 tablespoons tomato purée
2 oz (50 g) grated Parmesan cheese	2 teaspoons dried basil
1 teaspoon dried oregano	1 teaspoon dried oregano
1 teaspoon dried thyme	1 lb (450 g) long Italian spaghetti
Oil for frying	Extra grated Parmesan cheese (optional)

For the sauce:
1 lb (450 g) leeks, washed, in ½ in (1 cm) slices

Mix the meatball ingredients and knead until firm. Roll into 12 balls and fry gently in the oil until brown. To make the sauce, sauté the leeks in olive oil for 2 minutes. Add the other sauce ingredients, mash them together to blend and simmer for 20 minutes. Add the meatballs and simmer gently for another 10 minutes. Cook the spaghetti in a big pan of boiling salted water for 3 minutes, take it off the heat, cover and leave for 7 minutes.

Drain the spaghetti and pile into a big serving dish. Pour over the sauce and meatballs and serve. You can offer more Parmesan cheese to sprinkle over.

Southern Fried Chicken
(Maryland)

There are as many versions of this recipe as there are cooks who can claim to be Southern. My crafty version doesn't use breadcrumbs, but you can coat the chicken with them – brush a little egg on first – and still be authentic. Either way, you get moist, juicy chicken inside a really crisp coating. The secret is the lidded frying-pan! In the southern states this would be served with Corn fritters (see below), sautéed sliced bananas and plenty of mashed potato.

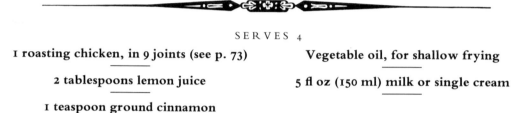

SERVES 4

1 roasting chicken, in 9 joints (see p. 73)	Vegetable oil, for shallow frying
2 tablespoons lemon juice	5 fl oz (150 ml) milk or single cream
1 teaspoon ground cinnamon	
4 tablespoons flour, seasoned with paprika and ground bay leaf	

Rub the chicken joints with the lemon juice and cinnamon, and dip in 3 tablespoons of the seasoned flour. Put $\frac{1}{4}$ in (5 mm) oil in a big frying-pan that has a lid. Heat the oil until it is just below smoking and put in the chicken. Brown on all sides, and turn the heat down. Cover the pan and cook for 20 minutes, turning once. Remove the chicken to a serving dish, pour off all the oil and add the remaining seasoned flour to the pan. Cook, stirring, until brown, then pour in the milk or cream. Stir again to make a smooth gravy.

Serve with the chicken.

Corn Fritters

MAKES 8 FRITTERS

6 oz (175 g) flour	Pinch of salt
2 oz (50 g) cornmeal	1 egg
1 tablespoon oil	4 oz (100 g) whole kernel sweetcorn

Mix the flour, cornmeal, oil and salt together, and add enough water to make the consistency of single cream – appoximately 5 fl oz (150 ml). Beat in the egg and add the sweetcorn kernels. Heat a pancake- or omelette- or frying-pan, smear it with a little oil, and put tablespoons of the mixture on to the pan at regular intervals, allowing the mixture to spread out. Cook over a medium heat until golden-brown on both sides, turning once. The fritters can be turned out in $1-1\frac{1}{2}$ minutes and kept warm while you use up all the mixture.

Key Lime Pie
(Florida)

*T*his is Florida's tropical answer to the trans-American favourite: lemon meringue
*pie. And because this is America, it is sometimes known as 'mile-high' Key lime
pie: a pie shell filled with a sweet and sharp fruit filling and topped with a cloud of
meringue up to 12 in (30 cm) high. You can make it with just a couple of inches of
meringue, and still cause quite a stir. Limes are widely available in Britain.
'Key' is the name for 100 or more islands that form a chain from Miami across the
Caribbean down to Key West, half-way to the Bahamas. A special kind of lime used
to grow on them, which is where the name comes from. You'll need an 8 in (20 cm) pie
shell of Shortcrust pastry (see p. 169), baked blind for 10–12 minutes.*

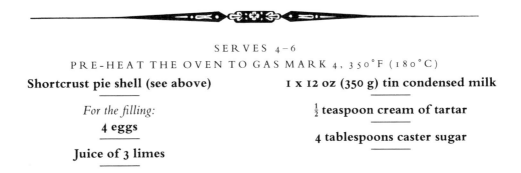

SERVES 4–6
PRE-HEAT THE OVEN TO GAS MARK 4, 350°F (180°C)

Shortcrust pie shell (see above)

For the filling:
4 eggs

Juice of 3 limes

1 x 12 oz (350 g) tin condensed milk

½ teaspoon cream of tartar

4 tablespoons caster sugar

Separate the eggs and whisk the yolks with the lime juice and condensed milk until thick. Add 1 stiffly beaten egg white and pour into the pie shell.

To make the meringue, whisk the rest of the egg whites with the cream of tartar until stiff. Whisk in all but 1 teaspoon of the sugar, a tablespoon at a time, until it's absorbed and the meringue is shiny.

Pile the meringue on to the filling and fork up into peaks. Sprinkle on the remaining sugar and bake for 30 minutes, or until the meringue starts to turn golden. Cool on a wire rack for at least 3 hours before serving.

NEW ENGLAND SPECIALITIES

I was based in Massachusetts on my visit to New England, but slipped over a border or two into Vermont and Rhode Island, and even out to sea to Nantucket of *Moby Dick* fame. I met some terrific people and had an amazing range of treats; I've selected one or two special ones to share with you.

Apple Butter

*I*n colonial days fruit was preserved for winter use in the form of fruit butters. They *contain no butter, but can be spread on bread like butter, or even on pastry to make a tart rather like the British jam tart. The method of making them is very simple and produces a quite delicious preserve, unlike anything on this side of the Atlantic.*

MAKES 3–4 LB (1.5–1.75 KG)

5 lb (2.25 kg) red apples, washed and cored, but not peeled

1 teaspoon whole allspice

1 teaspoon whole cloves

3 cinnamon sticks

2 lemons, cut up

3 pints (1.75 litres) apple juice

1 lb (450 g) sugar

Cut the apples into chunks and put them in a large, heavy preserving pan. Add the spices and the lemons and just cover with boiling water. Cook slowly, uncovered, until the apples are slushy. Take the cinnamon sticks out and put the apple mixture through a sieve, or purée in a food processor. Put the apple juice and sugar into the pan, bring it to the boil gently, and wait until the sugar dissolves. Add the apple purée and cook over a low, low heat, stirring gently, for about 1 hour. Don't scrape the bottom which may occasionally catch. To test for readiness spread the purée on a saucer that has been chilled in the refrigerator. If it sets immediately, it's done. If not, give it another 30 minutes.

Pour the apple butter into sterilised jars, seal and store for at least 1 month and up to 2 years.

Thanksgiving

One of the great American festivals, particularly in New England, is Thanksgiving, when the Pilgrim Fathers' first harvest after landing on what seemed the inhospitable shores of Massachusetts is commemorated. Today's Thanksgiving dinner is almost identical to our Christmas meal, much of which has come to us from across the Atlantic. The American version has one or two special dishes, as well as the basic roast turkey and mashed potatoes, which make it very much a New England special. Cranberries, of course, are at the heart of some of these dishes. Here is a relish and a super stuffing for the turkey.

Vermont Chestnut Turkey Stuffing

This has become my family's favourite stuffing at Christmas time. I use it only to stuff the crop of the turkey, leaving the body cavity empty to make sure that the bird cooks all the way through. But I cook a dish of the stuffing in the oven alongside the turkey, so there's plenty to go round.

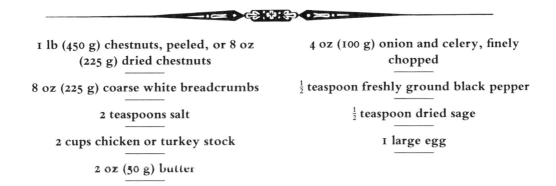

1 lb (450 g) chestnuts, peeled, or 8 oz (225 g) dried chestnuts

8 oz (225 g) coarse white breadcrumbs

2 teaspoons salt

2 cups chicken or turkey stock

2 oz (50 g) butter

4 oz (100 g) onion and celery, finely chopped

$\frac{1}{2}$ teaspoon freshly ground black pepper

$\frac{1}{2}$ teaspoon dried sage

1 large egg

If you're using fresh chestnuts, simmer them for 10 minutes in boiling water. If you're using dried ones, they need soaking overnight first, and probably 15–20 minutes boiling. Chop the chestnuts roughly when cooked and add the breadcrumbs and salt. Put the mixture in a large bowl and add the turkey or chicken stock. Sauté the onion and celery in the butter, add it to the bread mixture and season. Add the sage and stir in the egg. Mix together. Stuff the crop of the turkey loosely. Put the rest in a greased oven dish, and cook with the turkey for about 1 hour.

Cranberry Relish

This relish is made in moments in a blender or food processor.

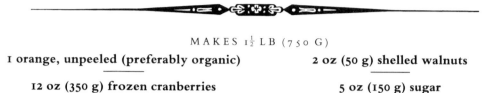

MAKES 1½ LB (750 G)

1 orange, unpeeled (preferably organic)

12 oz (350 g) frozen cranberries

2 oz (50 g) shelled walnuts

5 oz (150 g) sugar

Cut the orange into quarters and de-pip. Put the cranberries, walnuts and orange pieces into a blender and process until roughly chopped but not puréed. Tip half the mixture into a bowl and sprinkle on the sugar. Then add the remaining chopped cranberries and mix well. Leave for 2 hours to mature before serving.

The relish will keep in a refrigerator for 2 weeks.

Candied Sweet Potatoes

S weet potatoes were one of the foods the New England settlers found growing in their newly adopted country. This way of cooking them is said to come from much further south, down in Louisiana and Washington. However, in New England this dish is a key part of Thanksgiving Day.

SERVES 4
PRE-HEAT THE OVEN TO GAS MARK 7, 425°F (220°C)

1 lb (450 g) sweet potatoes, unpeeled

2 oz (50 g) butter

1 tablespoon soft brown sugar

1 teaspoon ground cinnamon

½ teaspoon salt

½ teaspoon freshly ground black pepper

Scrub the sweet potatoes and simmer whole in a pan of water for 20 minutes until boiled. To peel, rub them under cold water and the skins will fall off. Cut the potatoes into round slices ½ in (1 cm) thick and arrange in a buttered baking dish. Dot with the butter and sprinkle with the sugar, cinnamon and salt and pepper. Grill under a high heat for 3–4 minutes, or bake for 15 minutes until the sugar is bubbling and the potatoes soft.

INDIA

From the West to the East, and to the Indian subcontinent where food varies as much as Greek and Danish or Italian and Scottish food does. And, except where British influence still reigns supreme, it doesn't just consist of curries. Here are six varied regional dishes. They can be eaten together, or any two, with rice, will make a delicious meal for four people – vegetarian, fish- or meat-based.

Yoghurt with sliced cucumber, good chutney and some crisp poppadoms are ideal accompaniments.

Chana Dhal
(Madras)

A rich, hearty dish of solid pulses that is mild in flavour.

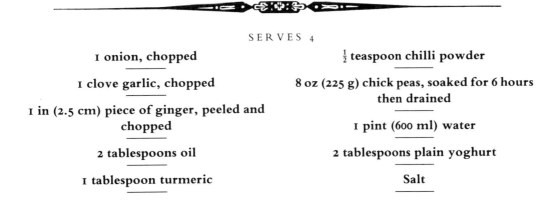

SERVES 4

1 onion, chopped	½ teaspoon chilli powder
1 clove garlic, chopped	8 oz (225 g) chick peas, soaked for 6 hours then drained
1 in (2.5 cm) piece of ginger, peeled and chopped	1 pint (600 ml) water
2 tablespoons oil	2 tablespoons plain yoghurt
1 tablespoon turmeric	Salt

Fry the onion, garlic and ginger in the oil over a high heat for 2 minutes. Add the turmeric, chilli powder and chick peas, and stir for 1 minute. Add the water, bring to the boil, and simmer for 1–1½ hours until the chick peas are tender. The water should be almost all absorbed: if not, boil briskly until dry. Stir in the yoghurt, season generously with salt, and serve.

Kheema and Peas
(Karachi)

In a country where the tenderness of the meat can leave a lot to be desired, and hanging – before refrigeration – was hardly an option, mince became the answer. This dish is easy, delicious and can, at a pinch, be made with a mild curry powder.

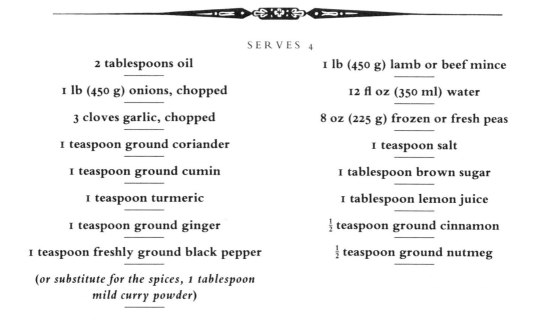

SERVES 4

2 tablespoons oil

1 lb (450 g) onions, chopped

3 cloves garlic, chopped

1 teaspoon ground coriander

1 teaspoon ground cumin

1 teaspoon turmeric

1 teaspoon ground ginger

1 teaspoon freshly ground black pepper

(*or substitute for the spices, 1 tablespoon mild curry powder*)

1 lb (450 g) lamb or beef mince

12 fl oz (350 ml) water

8 oz (225 g) frozen or fresh peas

1 teaspoon salt

1 tablespoon brown sugar

1 tablespoon lemon juice

$\frac{1}{2}$ teaspoon ground cinnamon

$\frac{1}{2}$ teaspoon ground nutmeg

Heat the oil in a saucepan and fry the onion and garlic over a medium heat until well browned. Add the coriander, cumin, turmeric, ginger and pepper, or the curry powder, and fry for a further 2 minutes. Put in the meat and fry, breaking up with a wooden spoon, until browned. Add the water and simmer, uncovered, for 15 minutes. Add the peas if fresh (if frozen, wait 10 minutes more) and simmer another 12 minutes. Add the remaining ingredients. Leave to stand 5 minutes and serve.

Bengali Fish
(Bangladesh)

Though hardly ever seen in Indian restaurants in Britain, fish is much eaten in India, which has thousands of miles of coast and some of the world's greatest rivers. This recipe is from Bengal where India's most famous fish, the hilsa, *is found.*

SERVES 4

2 tablespoons oil

8 oz (225 g) onions, sliced

1 clove garlic, chopped

1 teaspoon ground ginger

1 teaspoon ground cumin

1 teaspoon ground cinnamon

8 fl oz (250 ml) water

$\frac{1}{2}$ teaspoon chilli powder

$\frac{1}{2}$ teaspoon freshly ground black pepper

$\frac{1}{2}$ teaspoon salt

1 lb (450 g) white fish fillets (haddock, cod or coley), cut into 4 pieces

1 tablespoon brown sugar

1 tablespoon lemon juice

Heat the oil in a saucepan and fry the onions and garlic over a medium heat until well browned. Add the ginger, cumin and cinnamon and fry for a further 2 minutes. Add the water and simmer uncovered while you rub the chilli powder, pepper and salt on the fish. Put the fish in the saucepan and make sure it is covered by the sauce. Cook for 10–15 minutes until the fish is cooked through. Take out the fish pieces. Add the sugar and lemon to the sauce and boil for 2 minutes. Pour over the fish and serve.

Chicken Korma
(Delhi)

Light and creamy, this is one of the great dishes of India. Serve with rice.

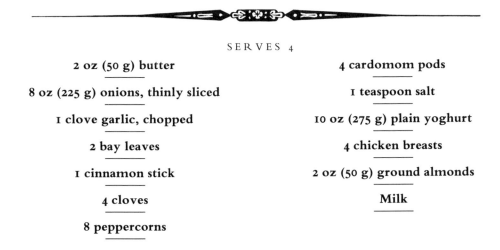

SERVES 4

2 oz (50 g) butter	4 cardomom pods
8 oz (225 g) onions, thinly sliced	1 teaspoon salt
1 clove garlic, chopped	10 oz (275 g) plain yoghurt
2 bay leaves	4 chicken breasts
1 cinnamon stick	2 oz (50 g) ground almonds
4 cloves	Milk
8 peppercorns	

Melt the butter in a saucepan or casserole and fry the onions and garlic gently for 15 minutes until light brown. Mix all the other ingredients except the chicken, almonds and milk, to make a marinade. Cut the chicken breasts in half crossways and marinate for 10 minutes. Add the chicken and yoghurt mixture to the onions, cover and cook gently for 40 minutes, stirring occasionally. Mix the almonds with a little milk and stir into the sauce. Bring to the boil and serve.

Egg and Potato Bhaji
(Punjab)

*N*o, *not a subcontinental fried egg and chips, but a bright and vivid-tasting casserole that traditionally uses duck eggs. Chickens' eggs also taste great.*

SERVES 4

2 tablespoons oil

8 oz (225 g) onions, thinly sliced

1 clove garlic, chopped

1 dessertspoon ground ginger

1 dessertspoon ground cumin

1 dessertspoon turmeric

1 teaspoon chilli powder (or less to taste)

1 x 8 oz (225 g) tin Italian tomatoes

6 hard-boiled eggs

6 egg-sized new potatoes, scrubbed and boiled for 5 minutes

Salt

Chopped coriander or parsley

Heat the oil in a saucepan and fry the onions and garlic over a medium heat for 10 minutes until browned. Add the ginger, cumin, turmeric and chilli powder and fry for 2 minutes more. Put in the tomatoes and their juice and mash with a fork until blended. Cover and simmer for 25 minutes. Halve the eggs and potatoes and place in the sauce. Simmer together, uncovered, for 10 minutes, then add salt to taste, and serve.

Chopped coriander or parsley sprinkled over the dish before serving looks pretty and tastes good.

Chicken Tikka
(North-West Frontier)

This is India's classic grilled-chicken dish. Now eaten throughout the subcontinent, it originated in the north-west near the Afghan border. Eat it with flat Indian bread and yoghurt chutney and serve with sliced lettuce, lemon quarters, caramelised onions and chutneys. To caramelise onions, simply slice them and then fry them in very hot shallow oil until crispy. Keep stirring or the onions will burn.

SERVES 4–6
PRE-HEAT THE OVEN TO GAS MARK 8, 450°F, (230°C)

6 skinned breasts of chicken, cut into smallish pieces

For the marinade:

5 oz (150 g) plain yoghurt

½ Spanish onion, sliced

Juice of ½ lemon

2–3 cloves garlic, chopped

2 teaspoons turmeric

2 teaspoons ground cumin

1 teaspoon ground ginger, or 1 heaped teaspoon fresh chopped ginger

1 teaspoon chilli powder

2 good teaspoons ground coriander

2 bay leaves

Salt

Mix the marinade ingredients together in a large bowl. Add the chicken pieces and leave in the refrigerator for 6 hours or longer. Lift the chicken out of the marinade, removing any large pieces of onion that might have stuck to it, and place on a raised wire rack over a baking tray. Sprinkle with a little salt and bake for 30–40 minutes until brown and crisp on the outside and soft in the middle.

Crafty Yoghurt Chutney

5 oz (150 g) plain yoghurt

2 in (5 cm) piece of cucumber, grated

2 teaspoons concentrated mint sauce

Mix all the ingredients and leave for 30 minutes before serving.

JAPAN

On my trip to Japan for *Food and Drink*, I was lucky enough to visit all sorts of eating places, from a Buddhist temple where the abbot was the chief chef and cooked food he had gathered from the surrounding woods, to noodle bars in the back streets of Tokyo. I ate, and began to learn to make, sushi in Tokyo's incredible fish market (the largest in the world). And I ate in the Ginza's most refined restaurants, and in ordinary hotels and homes in city after city linked by the incredible Shinkansen express trains. Japanese food I found extraordinary: extraordinarily pretty, extraordinarily delicious and extraordinarily healthy. It's really very different to food from anywhere else in the world, and its traditions are formed by a variety of influences.

The dominant one is, of course, Chinese, but China is not the only source of inspiration. In the sixteenth century, Portuguese missionaries brought with them deep-frying techniques and a taste for hot spices, and in recent years there has been the overwhelming effect of American culture. However, as so often happens, the Japanese have made foreign ideas their own. Whether in a back street café or expensive restaurant, food is always beautifully arranged, usually contains a high degree of raw ingredients, and is rice-based.

Apart from flavour and appearance, Japanese food has one other important aspect to recommend it: health. On average, the Japanese live years longer than us, and it seems that their diet is at the heart of their good health: very high levels of fish and seafood, lots of lightly cooked fresh vegetables and very little fat. Some aspects of Japanese food may seem alien to us, but its raw ingredients have a quality and freshness seldom seen here which makes them easy to enjoy.

I was overwhelmed by the care and dedication the Japanese give to their food. I have tried to pick a selection of dishes you can prepare in your own kitchen, with easy-to-find ingredients available in most supermarkets and health food shops. Do try the recipes, either individually or in combination, as an introduction to one of the healthiest, prettiest and most vivid cuisines in the world.

One-Pot Noodles

*L*ittle restaurants in side streets serve the most wonderful bowls of noodles, vegetables, fish, eggs and meat: Japanese fast, cheap food. Vary the toppings to suit yourself and what's easily available.

SERVES 4

12 oz (350 g) thick wheat noodles (or spaghetti)

4 carrots, peeled

6 spring onions

4 oz (100 g) button mushrooms

8 oz (225 g) spinach leaves in postcard-sized pieces

6 tablespoons shoyu sauce

4 fl oz (120 ml) water

8 oz (225 g) chicken breasts, sliced

$1\frac{3}{4}$ pints (1 litre) chicken stock

Salt

4 eggs

Rice vinegar

Cook the noodles in boiling salted water for 3 minutes, cover and leave for 5 minutes. Drain and rinse under cold water, then put aside, covered. Slice the carrots diagonally into thin slices, cut the spring onions into $\frac{1}{2}$ in (1 cm) slices, cut a star shape on the top of the mushrooms and trim the spinach. Blanch the vegetables in boiling water and drain. Mix 1 tablespoon of the shoyu sauce with the water and bring to the boil. Add the carrots and cook for 1 minute. Add the chicken and simmer for 2 minutes. Add the mushrooms and cook for 1 minute. Turn the heat off. In a large pan, put the chicken stock, the remaining shoyu sauce and pinch of salt. Bring to the boil. Put the noodles into 4 large soup bowls. Put a quarter of the carrot, chicken and mushroom mixture, and a quarter of the spinach, into each bowl. Pour the stock over and sprinkle with the spring onions. Poach the eggs in a separate saucepan in water to which a little rice vinegar has been added, and spoon one into each bowl.

Beef Teriyaki

*T*his is an easily accessible dish. In Japan, the meat is cooked on a charcoal barbecue *but it is easily done under a grill or in a ridged grill pan, designed to be used on top of the stove, that keeps the food out of the sauce.*

SERVES 4

6 oz (175 g) sirloin steak

6 fl oz (175 ml) teriyaki sauce

For a home-made sauce:
6 fl oz (175 ml) shoyu sauce

4 fl oz (120 ml) sake

4 fl oz (120 ml) mirin (Japanese sweet white wine) or 6 fl oz (175 ml) apple juice

Juice of $\frac{1}{2}$ lemon

2 tablespoons sugar

1 teaspoon salt

If making the sauce, boil all the ingredients until reduced by one-third. Cool. Marinate the steaks for 2–6 hours in the sauce. Set the grill to very hot or heat the frying-pan. Oil the frying-pan and fry the steaks, or grill them, for 2 minutes on one side. Re-dip in the marinade and cook the other side for 2 minutes. Dip again before serving. The coating should be glistening, coating the beef rather than running off it.

Sushi

A row of little rice balls topped or stuffed with fish or vegetables, and a bowl of soy sauce in which to dip them: this is sushi, one of the favourite Japanese ways of eating raw fish. Before you decide to skip past the recipe, I'm suggesting a way that involves only one kind of raw fish as a gentle introduction. Sushi can be kept in the refrigerator for about 30 minutes, but I don't recommend keeping it any longer. The basic ingredient of all sushi is Japanese rice, flavoured with vinegar and sugar after cooking. Serve with tea.

SERVES 4

4 oz (100 g) Japanese rice (see p. 249)

1 teaspoon sugar

$\frac{1}{2}$ teaspoon salt

2 tablespoons rice or cider vinegar

For the toppings:

3 in (7.5 cm) slice cucumber

4 large cooked Mediterranean prawns

4 oz (100 g) salmon fillet, skin and bones removed

1 teaspoon mixed mustard (wasabi, green Japanese mustard, if possible; if not, English)

To serve:

4 oz (100 g) long white radish (mooli or daikon), finely grated

2 oz (50 g) pickled ginger slices (optional)

4 oz (100 g) shoyu sauce

Cook the rice over a medium heat in twice its volume of water, uncovered, for 15 minutes until it looks dry. Meanwhile, dissolve the sugar and salt in the vinegar. When the rice is cooked, toss it with a fork and stir in the vinegar. Allow the rice to cool without a lid.

Wash and halve the cucumber, scoop out the seeds and slice lengthwise finely. Peel the prawns and slit them horizontally lengthwise. Cut the salmon along the grain into thin strips approximately $1\frac{1}{2}$ in (4 cm) long and $\frac{1}{2}$ in (1 cm) wide. Scoop up a tablespoon of rice and, in your hands, make it into an oval ball. Repeat until the rice is finished. Press 3 lengths of cucumber on to a rice ball. Make 4 cucumber sushis. Do the same with the salmon and prawn slices, spreading a little mustard on the rice before putting the fish on top. Set out prettily on boards or plates with the radish and ginger.

Each person picks up a piece of sushi and dips it into the shoyu sauce. The radish or ginger clean the palate between mouthfuls.

Sashimi

*T*he other great Japanese raw fish dish is sashimi, usually served near the beginning of a meal. This is a simple-to-make introduction, using readily available fish. Do try it – after all, we eat raw smoked salmon and oysters. It's very filling!

SERVES 4

Watercress or frisée lettuce

6 oz (175 g) salmon fillet, boned and skinned

2 scallops, or 2 oz (50 g) monkfish

1 lemon, thinly sliced

To serve:

4 tablespoons shoyu sauce

1 teaspoon wasabi (Japanese green mustard) or English mustard

Prepare individual serving plates by laying the watercress or lettuce leaves around the edges, leaving the centres empty. Slice both kinds of fish across the grain into paper-thin slices, approximately 2 in (5 cm) by 1 in (2.5 cm), and arrange the slices in a decorative pattern on each plate using colour and shape to achieve an effect like, for instance, a rose bud. Arrange the lemon slices on each plate then chill for no more than 40 minutes.

To serve, place a prepared plate in front of each diner, and pour the shoyu sauce into 4 small bowls. Stir a tiny dab of wasabi or English mustard into the shoyu sauce, and use as a dip for each piece of fish.

Tempura

This is Japan's answer to fish and chips.

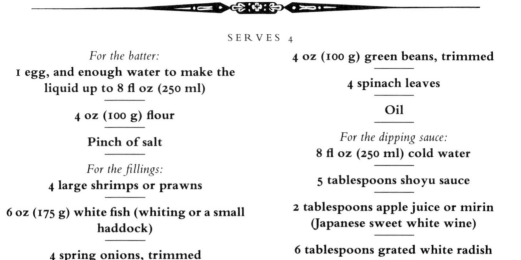

SERVES 4

For the batter:

1 egg, and enough water to make the liquid up to 8 fl oz (250 ml)

4 oz (100 g) flour

Pinch of salt

For the fillings:

4 large shrimps or prawns

6 oz (175 g) white fish (whiting or a small haddock)

4 spring onions, trimmed

2 large red or green peppers, de-seeded

8 button mushrooms, peeled

4 oz (100 g) green beans, trimmed

4 spinach leaves

Oil

For the dipping sauce:

8 fl oz (250 ml) cold water

5 tablespoons shoyu sauce

2 tablespoons apple juice or mirin (Japanese sweet white wine)

6 tablespoons grated white radish

1 dessertspoon grated fresh ginger

Juice of $\frac{1}{2}$ lemon

Mix the egg and water together, then stir in the flour and salt, whisking into a batter – don't worry if it has a few lumps.

Peel or clean the shrimps or prawns, and cut the fish into 2 in (5 cm) x $\frac{1}{2}$ in (1 cm) slices. Cut the spring onions into 4 in (10 cm) lengths, the peppers into $\frac{1}{4}$ in (5 mm) slices and the mushrooms into quarters. Leave the beans whole. Clean the spinach leaves and trim their stalks. Into a deep frying-pan or wok pour 2–3 in (5–7.5 cm) fresh frying oil. Heat until just below smoking point. Dip the prawns in the batter, holding by the tail, and fry. Do the same with the fish slices. Take out and keep warm on kitchen paper and repeat the process. Do the spring onions first, then the beans, followed by the peppers and mushrooms and, finally, the spinach. Do not crowd the pan. The food must cook crisply and quickly: nothing should take longer than $1\frac{1}{2}$ minutes.

Mix the sauce ingredients and dip the hot items into it before eating. Chop-sticks help, but fingers are OK.

Yakitori

For this Japanese kebab you need bamboo skewers about 9–12 in (23–30 cm) long. Serve with Japanese rice (249), Miso soup (see p. 250) and Pickles (see p. 251).

SERVES 4

12 oz (350 g) chicken breasts, in 1 in (2.5 cm) cubes

8 oz (225 g) chicken livers, in 1 in (2.5 cm) cubes

1 green pepper, de-seeded, in 1 in (2.5 cm) squares

4 spring onions, trimmed, in 1 in (2.5 cm) lengths

4 oz (100 g) button mushrooms, quartered

For the sauce:

1 tablespoon sugar

8 tablespoons soy sauce

4 tablespoons sweet sherry, apple juice or mirin (Japanese sweet white wine)

10 fl oz (300 ml) water

Boil the sauce ingredients then simmer until reduced by a third. Allow to cool a little, then pour into a tall glass. Prepare the skewers: one of peppers, onions and mushrooms, with a piece of chicken between each vegetable, one with mushrooms between each chicken piece; and one with chicken livers separated by the onions. Prepare a very hot grill, dip the skewers into the sauce and grill for 1 minute. Dip again, and grill for another minute. Repeat once more. Do not over-grill or allow to dry out.

Dip again and serve.

Japanese Rice

Japanese rice is not as long-grained as that available in Britain for savoury cooking. If you can't find it, buy a medium-grain rice from a health food shop. Allow 1½–2 oz (40–50 g) per person. It is usually served at the end of a meal, with soup and pickles.

Wash the rice in a sieve until the water runs clear. Place it in a measuring jug and note its volume. Put it in a saucepan and add 3 times the amount of cold water by volume to rice. Add 1 teaspoon salt. Bring to the boil, turn down to the lowest simmer, cover with a lid and cook for 15 minutes. Remove the lid: the rice should have absorbed all the water but still be slightly moist. Place a clean tea towel, folded into 4, across the saucepan and replace the lid. Steam very gently for another 10 minutes.

Miso Soup

This is the basic soup of Japan. Miso, now available in health food shops, is a thick paste made by fermenting grain and soya beans together. The taste varies depending on the region from which it comes. It can be mixed with vegetables or even used to top rice as a kind of relish. Buy mild miso made from rice and/or soya beans, if possible, and buy a little at a time. The soup can be very simple, or contain all kinds of goodies.

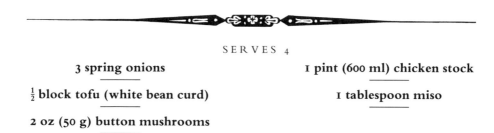

SERVES 4

3 spring onions

$\frac{1}{2}$ block tofu (white bean curd)

2 oz (50 g) button mushrooms

1 pint (600 ml) chicken stock

1 tablespoon miso

Trim the onions, leaving on as much green as possible, and cut into $\frac{1}{4}$ in (5 mm) lengths. Cut the tofu into $\frac{1}{4}$ in (5 mm) cubes. Thinly slice the mushrooms lengthwise. Bring the stock to the boil. Take a ladleful and mix it in a bowl with the miso until blended. Add the spring onions, tofu and mushrooms to the stock and cook for 1 minute, then take off the heat and add the miso. Stir quickly to blend. Heat the stock again, but don't let it boil once the miso has been added. The soup can be kept warm for up to 10 minutes, which allows the flavour to develop. Serve in bowls, each with a portion of tofu, onions and mushrooms.

Pickles

*I*t is possible to buy a wide variety of Japanese pickles, not only in specialist food stores but in most health food shops. If you would like to make your own, this is the authentic Japanese way – and pretty effortless. You serve 1 tablespoon per person, so one batch will last a long time.

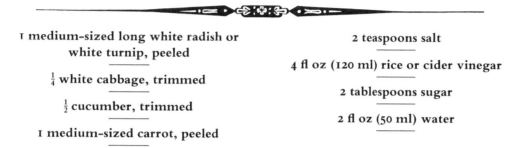

1 medium-sized long white radish or
white turnip, peeled

$\frac{1}{4}$ white cabbage, trimmed

$\frac{1}{2}$ cucumber, trimmed

1 medium-sized carrot, peeled

2 teaspoons salt

4 fl oz (120 ml) rice or cider vinegar

2 tablespoons sugar

2 fl oz (50 ml) water

Cut the vegetables into $\frac{1}{8}$ in (3 mm) slices. Put them into a large bowl, then thoroughly mix the salt, vinegar, sugar and water and pour over the vegetables. Put a plate or saucer inside the bowl and weight it with a tin or saucepan half-full of water. Leave for at least 12 hours and up to 24 hours.

You can if you wish, pickle the vegetables separately, in separate bowls.

The pickled vegetables will keep in the refrigerator unweighted for up to 5 days; in jars for slightly longer, but for no more than 14 days.

Japanese Green Tea

*A*lthough Japanese tea is called green, it comes in a variety of shades from light viridian to the more usual amber. In all cases, however, it differs from conventional tea drunk in Britain in its sharpness and flavour: the leaves are not fermented before drying. Served at the end of the meal, in smallish cups without milk and sugar, it is very refreshing. It contains plenty of caffeine, though. To brew it, treat it like English tea, using 1–2 teaspoons per pot for 4 people.

INDEX